# INDIA AND THE HINDOOS

# INDIA AND THE HINDOOS:

BEING

## A POPULAR VIEW

OF

THE GEOGRAPHY, HISTORY, GOVERNMENT, MANNERS, CUSTOMS, LITERATURE AND RELIGION OF THAT ANCIENT PEOPLE

F. DE. W. WARD

GYAN

*Published by*

GYAN

Gyan Publishing House
5, Ansari Road
Daryaganj, New Delhi-110002
Phone: 011-47034999, 9811692060
E-mail: books@gyanbooks.com

*Distribution Network*
gyanbooks.com
India, USA, Canada, UK, Australia



ISBN: 978-93-6920-367-3 (PB)

First Published, 1850

2nd Impression 2025

*Printed at:* Gyan Press, Delhi.



**INDIA AND THE HINDOOS**
Author: F. DE. W. WARD

F. Michelin, lith. 111 Nassau St.

PALANQUIN UNDERWAY

# INDIA AND THE HINDOOS:

BEING

## A POPULAR VIEW

OF

THE GEOGRAPHY, HISTORY, GOVERNMENT, MANNERS, CUSTOMS, LITERATURE AND RELIGION OF THAT ANCIENT PEOPLE;

WITH AN ACCOUNT OF

## CHRISTIAN MISSIONS AMONG THEM

BY

F. De W. WARD,

LATE MISSIONARY AT MADRAS, AND MEMBER OF THE "AMERICAN ORIENTAL SOCIETY."

NEW YORK:

CHARLES SCRIBNER,

1851.

TO

EDWARD ROBINSON, D.D.,

PRESIDENT;

WITH THE

OTHER OFFICERS AND MEMBERS

OF THE

AMERICAN ORIENTAL SOCIETY,

THIS VOLUME

IS RESPECTFULLY DEDICATED BY THEIR FELLOW LABORER IN THE

CAUSE OF EASTERN LEARNING,

THE AUTHOR.

## A FEW WORDS TO THE READER.

Of those who take this volume in hand, a few may recognize in the author an acquaintance and friend, while to others he is a stranger, whose name even they have never before heard. To this latter and more numerous class, a few introductory statements may not be inappropriate.

In the Fall of 1836 I sailed from Boston, a missionary to the natives of Southern India. My shipmates were the Rev. Messrs. Cherry, Cope, Crane, Muzzy, Tracy, Dr. Steele, and our wives. Two of these, Dr. Steele and Mrs. Muzzy, lie buried on the continent, and Mrs. Cherry at Jaffna, Ceylon. Our destination was the ancient and far-famed city of Madura,* where and in the neighboring villages Christian operations had been successfully commenced, under the direction of the Rev. Messrs. Todd, Eckard, Hall, Lawrence, Poor, and Dwight, the first and last three of whom were in the field when we arrived. After residing for about six years in that city, I removed to Madras, and was associated with Rev. Messrs. Winslow and Hutchings, and Mr. Hunt. Here I labored in preaching, superintending schools, and writing for the press, until the state of my health required a return to my native land, from which I had been absent ten years. During my residence in

* Pronounced Madjūrā.

India, I travelled much over the southern districts—went to Ceylon twice, and acquainted myself with the condition of that long-established and successful mission—journeyed southward and witnessed the wonderful effects of evangelizing efforts in Tinnevelly, with its whole villages of converts to Christianity —spent several days at Tanjore, under the roof of the aged and venerable Kohloff, a pupil and successor of the celebrated Swartz—travelled westward to Bangalore, where, during several months of ill health, I shared the hospitality of the Rev. Mr. Crisp, (whose necessary return to England cannot be too much regretted, so well qualified was he for the post he then held, of instructor to a large class of native young men, who were preparing for the ministry,)—passed on to Mysore, also the centre of interesting missions under the London and Wesleyan Societies. Hundreds of miles have I journeyed through native towns and villages, alone or accompanied by esteemed fellow-laborers, preaching the Gospel, superintending schools, circulating Bibles, distributing tracts, arguing with Brahmins, mingling with the thousands who were congregated at annual festivals, and warning them of their sin and danger—entreating the common people, who "heard us gladly," to behold the "Lamb of God," and using all means at our command to secure for our faith an interested attention from the multitude of idolaters. Hours were spent in exchanging thoughts with missionaries of all societies and denominations upon the condition of the Hindoos, and the most hopeful way of inducing them to embrace the better faith of Christ. While there, I took notes upon what I saw and heard; and since my return I have been permitted to plead for the Hindoos in most of the cities of New York, in many of the churches of Connecticut, in company with my worthy friend, the Rev. Mr. Cowles, and to a limited extent at the West. The reception I everywhere met with was of the most gratifying character, and I would express thus publicly my thanks to the many pastors who have allowed me to address their congregations upon this subject of deep and enduring interest—the wants of India, and the way to relieve them.

Providence at length indicated that I should assume a pastoral charge, which I have done, over an endeared people, but with no abatement of my interest in the cause of India missions.

During my journeyings over the country, it was often suggested to me, that when I had no further use for my manuscripts, in oral lectures and addresses, I should put them in a form for the press. Hence, this book, which is designed as a plain, colloquial statement of facts, the results of reading and conversation, confirmed and illustrated by personal observation and reflection. The aim of the work is to bring before the reader's mind *India as it was* and as it is, in a secular as well as a religious aspect.

Reader, allow me, in conclusion, to entreat you to think more about the Hindoos, especially in respect to their religious state and prospects. *Thinking* will lead to *feeling; feeling* to *prayer;* and *prayer* to *effort.* If this book awaken in any mind a deeper interest in the Hindoos, or lead in any instance to increased exertion for their social happiness or spiritual improvement, my aim will be secured and my prayer answered.

F. De W. WARD.

*Geneseo*, (*Livingston Co., N. Y.,*) *Sept.*, 1850.

# CONTENTS.

## CHAPTER I.

### GEOGRAPHICAL SURVEY.



## CHAPTER II.

### NATURAL PRODUCTIONS OF INDIA.

## CHAPTER VII.

### COURTEOUS CUSTOMS.



## CHAPTER VIII.

### A HINDOO AT HOME.



## CHAPTER IX.

### HINDOO WATER CRAFT AND SAILORS.



## CHAPTER X.

### HINDOO LAND CONVEYANCES.



## CHAPTER XI.

### HINDOO LITERATURE.

PAGE

## CHAPTER XV.

### MUSIC OF THE HINDOOS.



## CHAPTER XVI.

### PECULIAR CEREMONIES.



## CHAPTER XVII.

### WOMAN IN INDIA.

PAGE

## CHAPTER XVIII.

### HINDOO CASTE.



## CHAPTER XIX.

### RELIGION OF THE HINDOOS.



## CHAPTER XX.

### HINDOOISM IN PRACTICE.



## CHAPTER XXI.

### MEANS FOR ADVANCING CHRISTIANITY IN INDIA.

PAGE

## CHAPTER XXII.

### LIGHTS AND SHADES OF MISSIONS IN INDIA.



## CHAPTER XXIII.

### CHRISTIAN MISSIONS IN INDIA.



## CHAPTER XXIV.

### GLOSSARY;

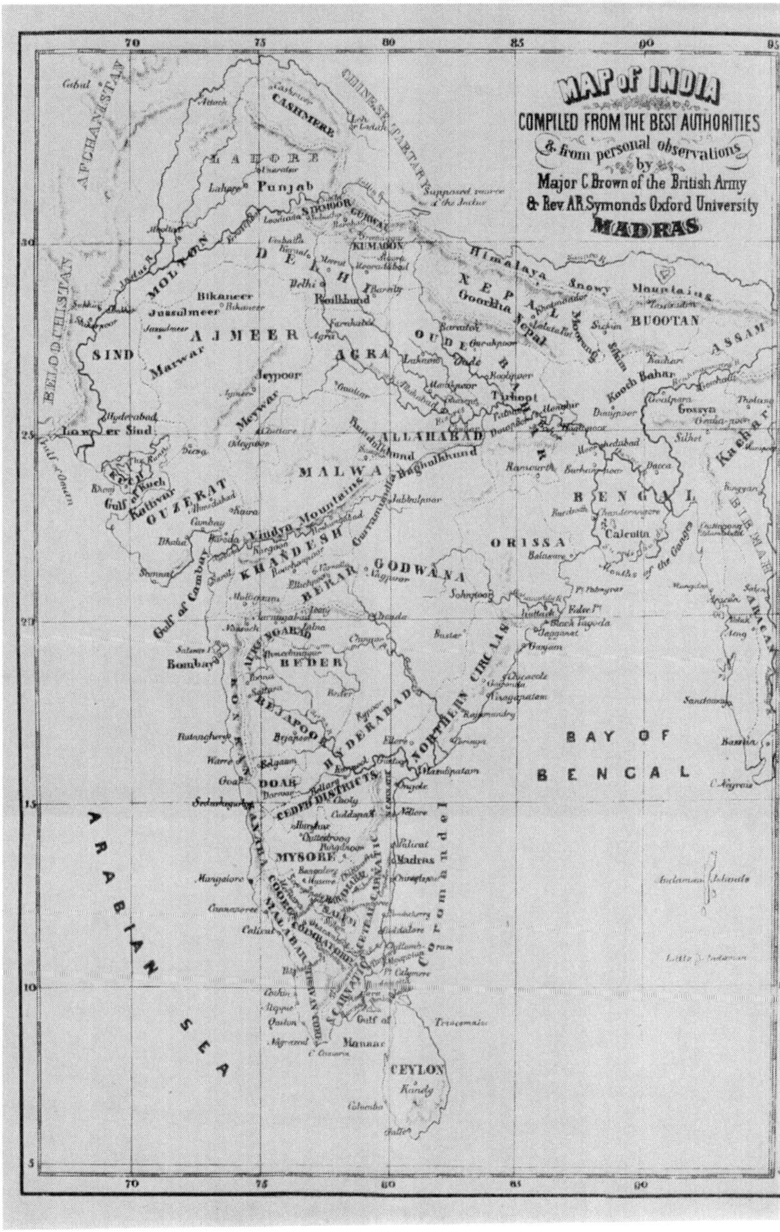
MAP of INDIA
COMPILED FROM THE BEST AUTHORITIES
& from personal observations
by
Major C. Brown of the British Army
& Rev. A.R. Symonds Oxford University
MADRAS
AFGHANISTAN
BELOOCHISTAN
CASHMERE
LAHORE
Punjab
SIND
AJMEER
Marwar
Jeypoor
Lower Sind
NEPAL
BUOTAN
ASSAM
Himalaya Snowy Mountains
OUDE
AGRA
ALLAHABAD
MALWA
GUZERAT
Vindya Mountains
KHANDESH
BERAR
GODWANA
ORISSA
BENGAL
Calcutta
Mouths of the Ganges
Gulf of Cambay
Bombay
BEDER
HYDERABAD
NORTHERN CIRCARS
BAY OF BENGAL
CEDED DISTRICTS
MYSORE
Madras
ARABIAN SEA
Gulf of Manaar
CEYLON
Kandy
Andaman Islands
70
75
80
85
90
95
30
25
20
15
10
5

# CHAPTER I.

## GEOGRAPHICAL SURVEY.

**Relative position—Boundaries—Geographical divisions—Names of opposite Sea Coasts—Mountains described—Droogs—Rivers—Tanks —Wells—Modes of drawing water—Cataracts—Courtallum—Nullahs—Hot Springs—Lakes—Salt Marshes—Face of the country —Seasons—Climate—Extremes of heat and cold—Means of avoiding the constant and oppressive warmth—Longevity—Diseases—Features of Constitution needful in a Foreigner who would live long in India—Rapidity of death's doings illustrated by facts—Comparative healthfulness of different seasons—Cities and large Towns named and described.**

THE vast continent of Asia terminates on the south in three peninsulas, the central and most important of which is India. Bounded on three sides by water, and on the fourth disjoined from the high table-land of Thibet by the lofty Himalayas, nineteen hundred miles in length and in breadth fifteen hundred, with its extreme points in 8° and 35′ North Latitude, and in 67° and 92′ East Longitude, this extensive country embraces within its ample limits forty districts, viz: in *Northern India*, Cashmere, Sirmoor, Gurwal, Kumaoon and Nepaul;—in *India Proper*,

Lahore or the Punjaub, Mooltan, Delhi, Oude, Sind, Ajneer or Rajpootana, Agra, Kuch, Guzerat, Malwa, Allahabad, Bahar and Bengal;—in the *Deccan*, Khandesh, Gondwana, Berar, Orissa, Aurungabad, Beder, Hyderabad, the Northern Circars, and Bejapoor; and in *Southern India*, Dooab, Ceded Districts, Northern Carnatic, Kanara, Mysore, Baramahal, Salem, Central Carnatic, Malabar, Koorg, Coimbatoor, Southern Carnatic and Travancore.

The Sea Coast on the west side from Bombay to Cape Comorin is called by Europeans the *Malabar*, and that on the East side the *Coromandel.*

The Mountains of the Peninsula are few in number, but lofty and majestic. The Himalayas (or "Seats of Snow") which form its northern boundary constitute one of the sublimest features in the structure of our globe, the highest peak as yet ascertained, rising 27,000 feet above the level of the sea, and lofty as the Green Mountains of Vermont if piled upon the Chimborazo of South America. This cloud-capped summit is esteemed the chosen residence of Siva, who, in retiring from Ceylon, threw up the Himalayahs as his place of retreat. Dewtas or spirits, are supposed to inhabit the most inaccessible glens, and by feigned sounds to lure the unfortunate traveller on to his ruin. In those lofty ranges the extremes of heat and cold are excessive, the former melting the snow and laying the mountains bare, while the latter is so intense as to split and detach huge masses of rock, which roll into the valleys and deep chasms below with loud and terrific reverberations. These mountains and elevated plains, rich in the precious metals, furnished, in the time of Herodotus and Ctesias, that quantity of native gold and auriferous sand, which gave rise to the fabled ants, industriously amassing stores of this precious ore, and fountains from which it bubbled up from a seemingly exhaustless depth. The inhabitants of the villages skirting the sides are poor, illiterate yet simple minded—the chiefs, however, being jealous of foreign visitors. This stupendous chain of hills is indented with "passes," through which travellers and, at times, armies journey to and from Nepaul on the south side and Thibet on the north, for commerce and on predatory excursions. Encircling the base is a plain about twenty miles broad (called "Tarryani") upon which the waters from above pour down with such profusion that the river beds, unable to contain the torrent, overflow and convert the ground into a species of swamp, which, acted upon by the rays of a tropical sun, throws up a rank vegetation, long grass and coarse shrubs, dense and almost impenetrable. In these gloomy regions the elephant, the tiger and rhinoceros, prowl unmolested, while the few human beings who can resist the pestilential vapors, present a meagre, dwarfish and sickly aspect. Waiving any special mention of the Kumaoon, Sewalick, and Vindhya Mountains, all of which lie north of the Dekkan, our attention may be directed to a double range of hills, lining the opposite coasts of the southern peninsula and called the Eastern and Western

*Ghats.* The latter commences near the river Tuptee, in 20° North Latitude, and extends to Cape Comorin, while the former, beginning near the river Kistna, in 16° North Latitude, stretches to the Cauvery River on the south. From the Gulf of Cambay to the Bay of Bengal is a tract of high country, which, with the two ranges before named, form a triangle enclosing a table land elevated three thousand and more feet above the level of the sea. The mountain scenery of this region, though destitute of those features which invest the Himalayas with so awful and sublime a character, is beautiful and picturesque. A traveller leaving Madras, after traversing a country of prairie smoothness for a distance of a hundred miles, finds himself at the foot of the Western Ghats, where a steep ascent of two thousand feet brings him upon the level surface when he moves forward with ease until he reach the base of the Neilgherries, to attain the summit of which he has six thousand feet more to rise. Here the air is clear, the climate cool and healthy, the fields fertile, well cultivated, and free from jungle, while, as a farther compensation for his labor, here he meets the violet, primrose, butter-cup, wild thyme, fern, dog-rose, woodbine, mosses and litchen, with various vegetables and fruits, which he has not before seen since leaving his fatherland. The native of that delightful region will tell you that he dwells in a favored spot—in a country whose origin was celestial. "The God Rama," he says, "being in pursuit of his enemy, Ravena, who had forcibly carried off the Divine

Goddess Sita, sped through the vaulted heavens, having his sword drawn, ready to deal the death-blow of revenge. In the forgetfulness of his direful wrath, lo! by an incautious wave of his mighty weapon, he struck the moon with the point thereof, and severed from the face of that beautiful orb a chain of verdant mountains, which immediately fell to the earth in the province of Coimbatoor and united the Eastern and Western Ghats. Hence the name Chandgherry, (or Mountains of the Moon,) which was subsequently changed by Rama to Neilgherri, (or Blue Mountains.) because he would not be reminded of his awkward mistake." In proof of his statement, the Coimbatori will point out the place on the lunar orb from which the hills fell off!

Ootacamund, a village about six thousand five hundred feet above the level of the sea, and two hundred miles S. West from Madras, is much resorted to by European invalids from all parts of the Peninsula, as also from the adjoining islands, because of its clear air and invigorating climate. Excepting these table lands and cloud-piercing heights, Southern India is very level, presenting immense areas of barren sand and dense jungle, with occasional rocks rising from the plain to the height of 100 to 200 feet, like icebergs in the northern seas. Upon the summit of these rocky acclivities the traveller often finds a fort, (called a Droog) which has done good service in years long past, when life and property were exposed to the invader's power. One of the most remarkable of these is the fortress of Dowlatabad, the Capital of Arungabad This fort is a mass of granite, standing more than a mile and a half from the hills, and rising to an elevation of five hundred feet. Another, and the most remarkable in India, is Sevendoorg, twenty miles northwest from Bangalore. This has a base of about eight miles in circumference and a height of about half a mile. In some cases a temple has been erected on the solitary summit which, with a pagoda at the base, secures a large share of reverential attention from Bramins and other devotees.

The largest RIVERS of India are the Indus, Sutlij, Jumna, Ganges, Brahmapootra, Nerbudda, Tuptee, Muhanuddee, Godavery, Toombudra, Pennar, Palar and Cavery—which run a united distance of about ten thousand miles:—most of them rising in the lofty Himalayas, and falling into the Bay of Bengal or Arabian sea. Of these the *Indus* is noted for its length and variety of appearance, flowing a distance of 1700 miles, and forming the boundary line between the Peninsula and Afghanistan. The *Ganges* is far famed for the spiritual efficacy of its waters, especially those parts of the stream which happen to run from South to North, contrary to the general direction. The *Brahmapootra* rises in Thibet, near the mouth of the Indus, sweeps through Assam with a curve westward, uniting with the Ganges just above Calcutta. The *Godavery* is sometimes called the Second Ganges, because of its sacred origin and purifying efficacy. The *Krishna*, from the resemblance in its color to that of Vishna in his ninth incarnation, is also an object of religious worship. The name of Punjaub (or land of streams) which the natives apply to a small portion of the Northern Hindostan is descriptive of at least one half of the peninsula. The valley of the Ganges is the most extensive and luxuriant on the face of the globe, forming a tract of 400,000 square miles, the greater part of which is susceptible of cultivation of some kind, and much is extremely fertile. In the southern district there are but few *perennial streams.* During a large part of the year the bed of the river presents the appearance of an extended plain of arid sand, with a mere brook running through its midst, but so soon as the rainy season sets in, the mountains pouring down the flood that has fallen upon them, the desert is converted into a stream, or more frequently a raging torrent, majestic to behold, refreshing to the neighboring vegetation but annoying to the traveller who must wait till it has subsided, ere he can safely attempt to cross. As these rivers are an uncertain reliance for agricultural purposes the country is supplied with *tanks* or large artificial lakes, measuring from two to twenty miles in circumference, encircled with an embankment of clay and clods, into which the water is allowed to flow during the rainy season, and is there retained for future use. Upon each side, gates are built, by the raising of which the neighboring fields are irrigated and made fruitful. One of these is essential to every extensive farm, as without it man and beast could not subsist, and the fields would lie barren and useless. There are, it is true, large *wells* to be frequently met with, but these would be quite insufficient to supply water for cattle, and field-irrigation. The mode of obtaining water from the wells or tanks (when a large quantity is needed) is by means of a sweep, or Pecotah. One man climbs an upright post and placing himself on a transverse beam, treads backward and forward, thus sinking and raising an iron bucket, which another standing below guides as it passes up and down and empties when full into the channel prepared for it. This labor is performed with great rapidity, and is accompanied by a pleasant song, almost the first sound the foreigner hears after landing, and the last he forgets.

In respect to *Waterfalls* India is unequalled. This might be expected from the loftiness and rugged character of the Himalayas and other mountain ranges. Two instances must suffice by way of illustration and proof. The river Shirawati or Carawooty rises in the western Ghats, and falls into the Arabian Sea not far from Bombay. The bed of the stream near the Cataract is one fourth of a mile in direct breadth, but the edge of the fall is elliptical, with a sweep of about half a mile. This body of water rushes, at first, for about three hundred feet at an angle of 45° in a sheet of white foam, and is then precipitated to the depth of eight hundred and fifty more into a black abyss, with a noise like thunder. It has, therefore, a depth of *eleven hundred and fifty feet, quadrupling Niagara* in the depth to which it sends its foaming waters. Another fall of less grandeur though greater utility is to be met with at Courtallum about 100 miles north from Cape Comorin. A horse-shoe indentation is made into the east side of the Ghats, near their southern extremity, about two miles in breadth and one in depth, within which the village is situated, with its native huts, foreign dwellings and consecrated temples. During the prevalence of the western monsoon the clouds are so driven as to cause almost hourly showers of light rain to fall within this enclosure, giving to the air a delightful and invigorating coolness, especially when contrasted with the heat which prevails but a few miles inland. Upon the summit of the mountain the water collects in large quantities and is precipitated over seven lofty ledges before it reaches the basin below. At this place Hindu superstition has erected several temples of large dimensions and great sanctity, and a native, who would not hesitate to take a false oath elsewhere, would tremble to do so on this sacred spot. This is a favorite resort for foreigners, who will bear patiently the greatest domestic inconvenience, if they can but inhale its refreshing air and bathe in its health-giving flood. So soon, however, as the western rains cease, a rank vegetation springs up, dangerous to the life of all but native inhabitants. I spent several weeks in this delightful Sanatarium and have full knowledge of its worth and beauties, as well as the society of the agreeable and good who are wont to assemble in that "happy valley."

The traveller through India is ever meeting with

small streams, from a few feet to several yards in breadth, called *nullahs*. These are either arms projecting from neighboring rivers, or streams from the adjacent hills, and, though not imposing in appearance, are useful in feeding tanks and watering the herds.

Hot Springs are very numerous in the mountains, and river beds being much frequented for medicinal purposes, and with religious reverence. An English officer speaks of one he met with near the source of the Jumna, the water of which was sufficiently warm to boil rice, and the deposition of which led him to suppose that it was occasioned by the decomposition of pyrites. In some of those Geysers the temperature is 170 and even 194° Fah., and at the elevation of ten thousand feet above the sea. Others have been found in the middle of the river Godavery, in the valley of the Nerbudda, in the Gondwana district, in Bundelcund, in a village near Pooree, in Setacuno on the Ganges, and in a village near the city of Delhi. In these springs the thermometer, plunged in, ranges from 100° to 140°, and a strong smell is diffused throughout the surrounding neighborhood.

Lakes are but few in number, and those of limited dimensions. Just north of the Bay of Cambay there is an immense region of marshy land called the "run," where the waters, accumulating during the monsoon, evaporate when the rain ceases to fall, leaving a saline incrustation, which the natives collect, cleanse, and use for culinary purposes. Another salt lake was found high in the Himalayas at an elevation of sixteen thousand feet.

As to the *face of the country* characterizing the four geographical divisions before named, *Northern* India is very mountainous, but the regions between the hills susceptible of high cultivation, India *Proper* is divided between the vast desert of Rajpootana, the extensive valleys of the Ganges and Indus, the salt marshes of Kutch, and the jungly regions about the mouth of the sacred stream, the *Dekkan* has the twofold features of level and sandy plains from the sea to the foot of the Ghats, and a table land upon their summit, while the same features belong to the Southern region, where it terminates in a dense jungle and remains without cultivation and well nigh uninhabited several miles north from the Cape.

Of SEASONS there are but two in India, the dry and rainy, produced by the periodical winds called *monsoons*. During the former, vegetation labors under a deadly languor, and the sunlight penetrates with difficulty the dense vapors with which the atmosphere is loaded. Then follow the rains, a fall of two or more weeks of which without interruption being not at all uncommon, during which inundations from the bursting of tanks and the overflowing of streams frequently level to the earth the mud hut of the distressed native, and drown his flocks beneath their swelling waves. In the year 1822, the Brahmapootra overflowed its banks, by which calamity thirty-seven thousand persons were drowned, besides sheep and cattle without number. If the rain come not at the ordinary time, or if not in sufficient quantities, disastrous effects follow during the entire year. In 1793 so great was the scarcity occasioned by the drought, that parents sold their children for a few pounds of rice. Distress of *such* severity is uncommon, but inconvenience, destitution and suffering from a like cause is far from unusual in those equatorial regions. To talk of an Indian *summer* would be to include the whole year; to speak of its *autumn* would be absurd, for its trees are never denuded of leaves; *spring* would be equally unmeaning, when vegetation blossoms in every month, and *winter* is there unknown.

The Climate of India, as distinguished from that of the western world, is characterized by warmth, continual, and often extreme. A few statistics will illustrate the point. During the month of January the mean temperature is—

| | | |
|---|---|---|
| in Calcutta . . . | 69° 5′ | Fah. |
| " Bombay . . . | 77° | " |
| " Madras . . . | 78° 15′ | " |

While in the State of New York it is 25°, making a difference during the coldest part of the year of 49°. Again during the month of May the mean temperature is—

| | | |
|---|---|---|
| in Calcutta . . . | 88° 6′ | Fah. |
| " Bombay . . . | 85° | " |
| " Madras . . . | 89° | " |

while in New York State it is 70 in July—making the difference in the warmest weather of 17°. The mean temperature throughout the year is 30° higher in India than in the State of New York. The average coldest month in India (the mountainous region excepted) is warmer by 6° than the average warmest month in this State. Over the largest part of the peninsula the thermometer never sinks below 60° while it often rises to 95 or 100°. In the Northern Circars it has stood at 100° at midnight and 110° at 8 o'clock A. M. On the 15th of May, 1849, the thermometer stood in the City of Madras as follows:

| | | |
|---|---|---|
| at 10 o'clock | . . . | 156° Fah. |
| " 12 " | . . . | 169 " |
| " 12 " | . . | 181 " |

This was, of course, under the direct action of the solar rays. In the shade, it was above 100°. Such is the intensity of the heat, that birds sometimes drop down dead in the streets and squares of Calcutta. Travellers who are compelled to pass the day in tents, often creep beneath the table or cot to shield themselves from the heat that strikes through the canvass. A modern author upon these equatorial regions, says, with much liveliness and truth: "It is all well for any one to sit by his fireside in Old England, and imagine and talk about the "sunny east" as superemimently splendid, and to be coveted; but if he ever have the opportunity of being conveyed in a palky, (palanquin) about 2, P. M., on any day in April, from Fort St. William to Government-house and back he will never after repine, though doomed forever to remain in that climate which Prince Cariciolli described to be in Britain, "where the sun is never seen; and where there is no ripe fruit, but roasted apples." The climate of India is little understood by Englishmen (Americans) "at home," and an instance of which appeared in a letter I read, in which the fair writer said "she could picture her correspondent reading under the shade of a palm-tree;" whereas the only endurable place was a room with all the blinds closed, and a punka waving over head. The reader may like to know what means are in use to shield the foreigner from the distressing effects of this constant and fatally-tending heat. Dwellings are located in places most open to the sea, are large and airy, with lofty ceilings, terraced roof for promenading, Venetian blinds, instead of window-sash and glass, bamboo mats for the floor, (carpets being too warm, and attractive to snakes, scorpions and smaller vermin,) and the whole painted white or green. Between the rising and setting of the sun, a foreigner should not leave his house without the shelter of a carriage, a palanquin, or a thick umbrella. Large fans, called *punkahs*, made of the fragrant Cuskus grass, are suspended from the ceiling, and kept in motion by a servant stationed on the verandah or in an adjoining room. Mats formed from the same material, are hung outside of the door and window, and kept saturated with water. These adjuncts relieve the heat of the parlor, the dining-room, office and church. Hand fans are often used at meals, by a native, standing behind the chair. Bathing once a day, is universally practiced, two or more rooms for this purpose being attached to each dwelling. It has become an admitted fact, after many and fatal trials, that spirituous liquors, and even wine and beer, so far from being needful to an Indian resident, are injurious and to be avoided. In the higher parts of the Peninsula, as at Delhi, in Lat. 28° the winter's cold is sometimes 3° or 4° below the freezing point, and the tanks are frozen over. The previous statements have respect to the country generally, those parts removed from the chilling influence of the snow-clad Himmalayahs.

With a due regard to these precautions, and a calm, contented disposition, a foreigner may live many years in that "land of the sun" while such is the liability to transgress in one or more of these important respects, that human life is held by a brittle thread. Extreme simplicity of diet, and great tranquility of mind, may procure for some of the native fakeers (or religious devotees) a lengthened life; but taken as an average, this is a climate in which the force of vitality receives a quick developement, and is subjected to speedy exhaustion. The oldest native I met in India, was a preacher in Tanjore—a pupil of Swartz, and ordained by that illustrious Missionary. He had passed his ninetieth year; was very decrepid, yet in preaching, his voice was clear, and sufficiently loud to be heard by a large audience, and his manner earnest and effective. But a few months after the occasion of my being at that interesting station, he, and the Rev. Mr. Kohloff, (pupils, both, of Swartz) ascended to the presence of that Saviour, whom for more than seventy years they had preached with boldness and success. India has been called "Scotland's church-yard," the tombs of those deceased islanders meeting the eye of the traveller at every stage of his journey.

The DISEASES most prevalent in India are cholera, fever, hepatic derangements, dysentery, and various forms of inflammation. Among the natives, scrofula, leprosy, elephantiasis, and opthalmia, are very common. Cholera had its origin in that land, and there remains the same mysterious and fell messenger now that it was forty years ago. Elephantiasis (where one leg or both assume the shape and almost the size of that of an elephant) and leprosy (where large white spots appear upon the face, hands, arms, and where the toes and fingers drop off in gradual succession) are very frequent with natives, and at times with Europeans.

Here I will repeat the remark of an eminent surgeon upon the features of constitution desirable in one who expects to live long and enjoy health in that land. "A vivid color, animated countenance, firm step and voice, clean tongue and inoffensive breath, with what is called the white of the eyes clear, or without the slightest yellow tinge, are in general very sufficient proofs of good digestion and well performed visceral secretions; and these, with the other requisites, may, with propriety entitle their possessor to a passport to the plains of India. On the other hand, young men who seem sluggish, sallow, with somewhat bloated countenances, whose movements are languid, and the white of whose eyes has a yellowish or suffused appearance, ought to meet with a decided rejection; for in them there certainly lurks the seed of future disease, which will not be slow to show itself if ever they are exposed to ardent heat in a tropical country."

If there be those of the human family to whom it may be with special appropriateness said, "Be ye ready, for at such an hour as ye think not the Son of man cometh"—it is to the foreigners resident in India.

> "This hour, perhaps, our friend is well,
> The next we hear his passing bell."

Let a few facts suffice by way of illustration:

A civilian of Bengal whose duty had led him to a remote district, was returning home on account of an attack of fever, having written to his wife, acquainting her of his intention. Resting, during the day, at the Bungalow of a village, he learned that a European had just breathed his last in an adjoining room. Anxious to secure decent interment for the body, he struggled with his illness, and attended the remains of his fellow sufferer to the grave, reading the burial service at the sepulture. Exhausted by this sad and painful duty, he got into his palanquin, but had not proceeded far before he was overtaken by the pangs of death; a paroxysm of fever seized him, and he died on the road. The bearers set down the palanquin and fled into the wood, leaving their deceased master alone, for nothing but the strongest attachment can induce a Hindoo to touch, or even to continue with the dead body of a person who belongs not to his caste. In the meantime, the wife of the deceased gentleman, alarmed by the tidings of his illness, had hastened to meet him, and was made acquainted with her loss by the frightful spectacle that met her eyes. She could gain no assistance from her own bearers, whose caste kept them aloof, and finding it impossible to induce them to touch the body, she sent them to a neighboring village to find those that would aid her, while she took upon herself the melancholy task of watching the fast decaying remains. She soon found that her utmost strength would be insufficient to repel the daring attacks of insects, ravenous birds, and savage animals, which were gathering around, waiting for an advantageous moment for attack, and, in the energy of despair, she tore away the earth with her hands and buried her dead husband! Such is the rapidity with which death does its work in that Eastern clime, such the heartlessness produced by the false system of religion there dominant, and such the trials to which females are subjected to in that strange land—trials under which they often sink beyond recovery, but sometimes display an energy and heroism which awaken in the beholders emotions of equal wonder and admiration.

When leaving Madras for a journey to the South, I parted with Mrs. Winslow, in the possession of usual health. Reaching Trichinopoly we found a letter informing us of her death on the day after we left. We had not long resided in Madura, when a letter from Ceylon brought the intelligence that Mr. and Mrs. Perry followed each other, at an interval of but two days, to their heavenly home. My colleague, the Rev. Mr. Dwight, attended divine service on Sabbath afternoon, and was a corpse next morning. Mrs. Cherry, and Mrs. North were called away during the same week. When Heber wrote those touching lines—

> "Death rides on every passing breeze,
> And lurks in every flower;
> Each season has its own disease,
> Its peril every hour,"

little did that amiable prelate imagine that he would himself illustrate their meaning, and confirm their truth. I have recited them when standing in the bath room at Trichinopoly, which he entered, in the possession of perfect health but to be brought out a lifeless corpse.

The comparative healthfulness of the different seasons is indicated by the following table, containing the observations made during seven years. Of 1000 deaths of Europeans, the proportions stood thus:

| | | | |
|---|---|---|---|
| 92⅓ | occurred in the | month of | January, |
| 67½ | " | " | February, |
| 65⅓ | " | " | March, |
| 69½ | " | " | April, |
| 63⅔ | " | " | May, |
| 54⅓ | " | " | June, |

| | | | |
|---|---|---|---|
| 70¾ | occurred in the | month of | July, |
| 90½ | " | " | August, |
| 98½ | " | " | September, |
| 104½ | " | " | October, |
| 116½ | " | " | November, |
| 106 | " | " | December. |

It may seem extraordinary that the cooler season of India is the most prejudicial to health. I give the reason in the language of another: "Accustomed to a constant and profuse determination of moisture to the skin, the cold season, causing a complete revulsion, occasions more unhealthiness than any other, and a dry, irritable state of the surface, which is indescribably unpleasant. To the old Indian it is peculiarly distressing." "I can bear the chilling blasts of Caledonia," said a Scotchman, "but *this cold, I know not what to do with it.*"

A descriptive view of the leading *cities* and *towns* of India, will conclude this geographical survey of the Peninsula.

## LOCALITY AND CHARACTERISTICS.

*Calcutta*, situated on the Hoogly, (a branch of the Ganges) one hundred miles from the Sea, in latitude 22° 30′ North, and little more than half a century ago a petty village of mud huts, is now the "city of palaces," the "metropolis of the East," the residence of the Governor-General, Metropolitan, with other high officials, civil, military and ecclesiastical, of the

East India Company, and contains an estimated population of 550,000.

*Madras*, a large and fortified town on the eastern coast in lat. 13° 5′ North, and the capital of the Southern provinces was obtained by purchase from the reigning prince in the year 1693, and now numbers about 450,000 inhabitants.

*Bombay*, the third principal English town in India, is situated on an island of the same name, at about 200 yards from the western coast, in lat. 18° 56′ North. Ceded by the Portuguese in 1661 it has become eminent for its excellent harbor, superior shipwrights, and extensive commerce, and comprises, of Hindoos, Parsees, Mohamedans, Portuguese, Jews, and Armenians not far from 200,000.

*Benares*, the "Jerusalem" of India, is located on the northern bank of the Ganges, in lat. 25° 30′, about 460 miles northeast from Calcutta. The Indian legends have it, that this place was originally constructed of gold, which, because of the wickedness of the people, has degenerated into mud and thatch! It is esteemed by religious Hindoos as "the most Holy City"—"the Lotus of the world, not founded on common earth, but on the point of Siva's trident, a place so sacred that even a *beaf-eater*, if he die there, (having been charitable to the Brahmins) is *sure of salvation*." The resort of pilgrims the country over, and a mart for very extensive commerce it contains a population of Hindoos, Mohammedans, Turks, Persians and Armenians to the number of 700,000.

*Delhi*, the ancient capital of the Mohammedan empire in India, lies upon the river Jumna, in lat. 28° 40′, and 900 miles N. E. from Calcutta. Ruins of splendid palaces, lofty gateways, and noble mansions, covering an area of twenty miles, attest its former grandeur. The Badshahi Mahal, built by the Emperor Shah Jehan, and still the residence of the royal family, retains its form and beauty—the boastful inscription surmounting the State presence-chamber, "*If there be a paradise on earth, it is this, it is this*," remaining legible as when first engraved. With a population, in the time of Aurungzebe, of not less than two millions, it has diminished, in these later years, to about 250,000

*Agra*, at one time the capital of the Môghul empire, and one of the most splendid cities of India, stands on the river Jumna, in lat. 27°, and about fifty miles south from Delhi. The Taj Mahal, an edifice erected by Shah Jehan, is considered the most perfect specimen of oriental architecture in existence. Its present importance is derived from its being the residence of the Lieut. Governor of the north-western provinces of the East India Company's dominions.

*Ahmenabad*, formerly a city of great opulence and commerce, lies on the river Subrmuttee, in lat. 23°, 321 miles north from Bombay, in the Guzerat district, and contains an estimated population of 100,000.

*Ahmednuggur*—one of the principal stations of the British government in the Deccan, is situated in lat.

19° 12′, with inhabitants to the number of about 200,000.

*Allahabad*, at the confluence of the Jumna and Ganges, in lat. 25° 27′, is maintained by the British government, as the chief military depôt of the upper provinces. Its position at the junction of two sacred streams gives to it unusual sanctity, and suicide at the spot where the rivers unite is a frequent practice. The travelling distance from Benares is about 75 miles eastward.

*Aurungabad*, the favorite residence of Aurungzebe when viceroy of the Deccan, is situated in lat. 19° 54′, and about 150 miles east from Bombay.

*Bangalore* is a large fortified town, upon the first summit of the Eastern Ghats, and about 200 miles fom Madras. The healthfulness of the climate causes it to be much resorted to by invalids from the low country.

*Bejapoor*, in lat. 17°, was, in former times, one of the largest cities in Asia, the fort measuring eight miles round the outside. The principal object of interest now remaining, is the Mausoleum of Mohammed Shah, a plain square building surmounted by a dome of 350 feet in circumference, and visible fourteen miles distant.

*Calicut*, on the Western coast, in lat. 11° 15′, is celebrated as being the landing place, and first settlement of the Portuguese in 1498.

*Cuddalore*, a town on the Eastern coast, 12 miles South from Pondicherry, derives historical importance from its being the locality of the third English factory established in the country.

*Dindigul* a populous village, about 40 miles north from the city of Madura, is the seat of one of the Missionary Stations under the direction of the American Board of Foreign Missions.

*Goa*, situated upon a small island on the Eastern coast, in lat. 15° 30′, and once the most splendid city in India, and for many years capital of the Portuguese dominions in the East, retains but a shadow of its former greatness. The city, with a territory of 40 miles in length and 20 in breadth, still belongs to the crown of Portugal.

*Hyderabad*, standing on the south side of the Moosan, in lat. 17° is the capital of a Mussulman government, the principal resort of the Mohammedan families of the Deccan, and contains a population of about 200,000.

*Juggernaut*, on the Bengal coast, in lat. 19° 49′, is one of the most celebrated places of Hindoo pilgrimage in India, and multitudes annually resort thither to be present at the bathing and car festivals.

*Kuttack* is a large, well-built town, in lat. 20° 27′, containing, of native inhabitants, not far from 40,000.

*Loodiana* and *Ferozepoor* are important stations of the British territories, on the north-western frontier, both in lat. 30, and the centre of Missionary establishments under the Presbyterian Church of America.

*Madura*, (pronounced Madjŭră) the former capital of a Hindoo kingdom is situated in lat. 9° 55′, on the south side of the river Vygaroo, and contains some of the most extraordinary specimens of Hindoo architecture now extant; among which is the temple of Tiroomul-Naik, measuring 312 feet in length, and covered with descriptive sculptures. Travelling distance south from Madras, 292 miles. It is known to the people of this country as the centre of a successful Missionary Station; having connected with it, Dindigul, Teramungulum, Tirapovanum, Sivagunga, and Maloor.

*Moorshedabad*, in lat. 24, was the capital of Bengal until superseded by Calcutta, and contains a present population of 160,000.

*Nellore*, a populous town, about 100 miles north from Madras, is the seat of the Am. Baptist Mission.

*Seringapatam*, memorable in the wars of Hyder and Tippoo, Cornwallis and Harris, is situated in lat. 12, and, from being one of great populousness and importance, has been almost abandoned, on account of its remarkable unhealthiness.

*Tinnevelly*, a region just north from Cape Comorin, is agreeably known as the centre of a most successful Missionary establishment of the English Episcopalians.

*Trichinopoly*, a large and populous town on the Cauvery River, was much noted in the wars between the English and the French, having in its centre a rock 300 feet high, on which are a pagoda and other buildings, and is at present one of the principal military

2

stations of the British government. Situated in lat. 10° 30′; it is 207 miles south from Madras.

*Tanjore*, near to Trichinopoly, was, at one time, the chief seat of learning in Southern India, and is still memorable as the residence of the Missionary Swartz.

*Tranquebar*, just east from Tanjore was settled by the Danes in the year 1616, and sold to the English about four years since.

*Pondicherry*, on the coast, about 90 miles south from Madras is a well-built city, belonging to the French, and was once the most splendid European settlement in India.

The reader will do the author injustice by supposing that the statements now made respecting the geography of India, have had for their object the imparting of information never before met with. The design has been the rather the bringing to his recollection partially forgotten truths, or effaced impressions, that thus the way may be prepared for a more interested perusal of the pages which are to follow. India has now been entered—its mountains, rivers, plains, and cities have been hastily surveyed—the way is thus cleared for a nearer view of its productions, history, and national manners and customs.

# CHAPTER II.

## NATURAL PRODUCTIONS OF INDIA.

**Introductory remarks—Elephants—Rajah of Mysore's State Carriage—Rhinoceros—Wild Boar—Camel—Dromedary—Bear (anecdote of an Indian Hunter and Mountain Bear)—Deer, various species—Goat—Sheep—Buffalo—Ox—Cow—Brahminee Bull—Ganjal—Arnee—Yak—Horse—Ass—Mule—Dziggetai—Monkey, various tribes (anecdote of a Monkey and flock of Crows)—Bat—Porcupine—Sloth—Armadillo—Mangoose—Loris—Squirrel—Chipmuck—Rats—Ratel—Rabbits Martin—Civet—Ichneumon—Tiger—Lion—Panther—Leopard—Cheetah (mode of use by hunters)—Cat—Jackal—Hyena—Lynx—Thibet Dog—Native Dog—Lizzard—Gecko—Scorpion—Centipede—Tarantula—Cobra-de-Capella—Tic Polonga—Mountain Snake—Crocodile—Anaconda—Tortoise—Frog—Insects (scene presented when entering a long-closed house)—White Ant (a choice dish)—Ant Hills as seen by Bp. Heber. Birds and Fishes, a large variety of each Class—Botany, including Vegetable, Fruit and Forest Trees, Flowers—Minerals, &c.**

India abounds with illustrations of zoological, botanical, and mineralogical science. Almost touching the equator on the south, and on the north, losing itself in snowy peaks of unmeasured height; presenting vast wastes of arid and barren sand intersected with large tracts of jungle and forest, where the foot of man has seldom trod; with a climate that passes from the extreme of tropical heat to arctic cold, the peninsula is an 'epitome of the world,' and its natural productions answer in variety and value to this diversity of climate and soil.

Beginning with *animated nature*, the *Elephant* first claims our attention. This large and noble animal abounds throughout the moist forests of Southern Bengal, a portion of the western Ghats and the base of the Himalaya Mountains. Vast droves tenant the forests of Ceylon, where they are captured for their massive trunks of valued ivory, and for transportation to the continent, there to become the auxiliary of armies, the pride of princes, and the servant of merchants. When at Bangalore, I counted seventy elephants of various sizes and age, attached to the palace of the Rajah, several of which were trained to draw the royal chariot. In the temples of the land, may be seen from one to ten of these animals, ready for use in imparting eclat to religious processions and marriage festivities. We are told that at Vizier Ali's wedding, in the year 1796, there was a grand procession of twelve hundred elephants; of which a hundred had howdahs, magnificently adorned with silver trappings; while that upon the animal which the Nabob rode was made of massive gold, richly set with precious stones. The elephant has been much used by Europeans and native princes, in hunting the tiger, but the sport is attended with great danger, and is repulsive to this naturally mild and timid animal, though in the contest it is usually the victor—receiving its enemy on its tusks, tossing it into the air, and standing ready to stamp its ponderous foot upon it so soon as it reaches the ground.

The *Rhinoceros* exceeds the elephant in clumsiness of figure, and is not much inferior in size and weight. The leading feature of interest in its physical structure, is the *horn upon its nose*, which projects, not unfrequently, thirty inches upward. So long as the animal is quiet, this appendage lies loose between the nostrils; but when excited, the muscular tension is so great that it becomes immovably fixed, and can be darted into a tree to the depth of several inches. From the earliest times, this horn has been regarded as an antidote against poison. Goblets made from it were much in use among the Hindoo princes, because, when poisonous liquids were poured into them, the noxious qualities were, it was thought, certain of betrayal, by a brisk effervescence. In some of the northern districts, attempts have been made to render this animal available for carrying travellers and burdens, but with little success. Bishop Heber mentions meeting with one which was so tame as to allow a howdah and driver upon its back. The rhinoceros lives in Bengal, and the lower ranges of the Himalayahs; feeding on coarse grass and other vegetable substances, especially those containing much succulent matter; seeking amidst mud and water protection from the scorching heat; disposed to be at peace with the tiger and its other neighbors, but when provoked, becoming a furious and deadly foe. A few, only, have been brought to the western continent, the expense of transportation being great, its appetite voracious, and hunger throws it into a paroxysm of rage.

The *Wild Boar* still roams the jungles of India, and to hunt it is one of the field sports to which foreigners are enthusiastically attached; though the ardor has somewhat abated during later years.

*Camels* are found in large droves throughout Guzerat, Patna, and Mooltan; and, like the elephant, are made serviceable to the merchant, the traveller, and the warrior. The East India Company maintain a corps of *Dromedaries*, mounted by two men each, and armed with musketoons and swivels.

Two species of *Bear* are common in India, of which the kind inhabiting the Ghats is hardly exceeded in ferocity of temper by the tiger or hyena; and the second, or Ursine, which makes its appearance in the forests of Oude, Orissa, the Carnatic and Coromandel, is far more mild and harmless. A northern traveller gives us an account of an escape from the fatal embrace of the former species, which indicates much forethought and ingenuity on the part of his native attendant. I present it in the words of the writer. "Upon gaining the summit of a hill which overhung a precipice, a *bear* started from a recess in a neighboring covert, and advanced, evidently with sinister intentions, towards us. I was about to fire when one of my guides motioned me to desist, giving me to understand that he would attack the enemy unarmed. Almost upon the extreme edge of the precipice, stood a tall tree with vertical branches, very tough and elastic. The hill-man approached the bear, and thus withdrew its attention from me, toward himself, when he adroitly sprang upon the tree, as nimbly followed by the exasperated beast. Having reached the upper branches, the man slipped a strong cord over the top of the limb upon which he stood, at the same time dropping the reverse end upon the ground. This was instantly seized by another native, who, pulling with all his strength, drew the point of the bough downward until the branch projected nearly in a horizontal line from the stem. This being done, the mountaineer crept cautiously as near the extremity as he safely could, followed as cautiously by the bear: but so soon as he saw his angry foe upon the bent bough he dexterously let himself down by a cord to the ground. The bear thus unexpectedly deprived of its victim made an effort to retrace its steps, when no sooner had it relaxed its grasp of the bough for this purpose, than the hill-man suddenly cut the cord, which had been securely tied to a tree, and the depressed branch instantly gained its original position with an irresistible momentum. The suddenness and vigor of the recoil shook the disappointed and angry creature from its hold, elancing it, like the fragment of a rock, into the empty air, from whence, uttering a stifled groan, it was hurled over the precipice, and falling with a dull crash upon the rocks below, became food for beasts and birds of prey." Bears of smaller size and milder temper are led about the country with trained monkeys and goats, soliciting attention by their absurd postures and antic movements, by which not a little gain comes to the owners from the amused and astonished multitude.

Of the *Deer tribe* India contains many species. The *Antelope*, which occupies the place of Capricorn in the Indian zodiac, and in size and form resembles the Arabian gazelle, the well-known emblem of maiden beauty, is spread over the entire peninsula, and is remarkable for elasticity of bound, symmetry of figure, and soft lustre of its full and hazle eye. The *Musk deer* is a nocturnal animal of a solitary disposition, dwelling among the elevated ranges of the Himalaya Mountains. The perfume for which it is hunted is contained in a bag beneath its belly, and is removed from the creature when alive, otherwise it is taken up by the absorbents, and thus lost to the hunter, and the flesh throughout rendered unfit for food. The *Ceylon deer* is the smallest of the cervine tribe, being about the size of a fox, and furnished with exquisitely-formed legs, scarcely larger than a lady's finger. The *Nepaul stag* nearly resembles the red deer of America. The *Rusa* or *Tamboo deer* is antlered, strong and brave, and roams free and fearless amid the jungles of Bengal and Ceylon. The *Spotted Axis* is similar to the fallow deer, and abounds in Bengal and on the banks of the Ganges. The *Hog deer* is found in the Rohilla country and Decca districts, roaming in heavy grass jungles, feeding at night, and sleeping during the day. It is easily irritated and ferocious in defence. The *common Roebuck* makes its home among the crags and ravines of the western frontier. The *White Oryx*, a species of the antelope, with a bulky body, slender legs and dark mane, is met with upon the banks of the Indus. The *Chira*, another species of the antelope, and an inhabitant of the Himalayas is the unicorn of traditionary existence. The *Chickara*, or four-horned antelope, which inhabits the forests and hilly districts of Bengal and Bahar is small in height, fleet in movement, and timid in disposition. The *Nyl-ghaw*, or blue cow, a dweller in the central provinces and base of the Himalayas, is large and strong, and considered in past times as royal game to be hunted only by princes. The *Giraffe* is occasionally met with in the north-western provinces.

Among the *Goat-tribe*, by far the most noted and valuable is the species spread throughout Thibet, and in the valley of Cashmere, from the wool of which are made the shawls of world-wide fame. The Empress Aurungzebe had one of so delicate texture that she could draw it through the ring of her finger. Goats of a more common kind are numerous throughout the country, being kept for their flesh, milk and skins. *Sheep* are numerous and their flesh much used as an articlo of food.

The *Indian Buffalo* is large and ungainly, with long, rough horns, lying back almost upon its shoulders, its dark skin, covered with hair short and wiry, its eyes dull and unmeaning, its gait slow and measured. But for all these disagreeable and repulsive features there is the compensation of great utility for the plow and heavy draught, while the female furnishes milk from which is made a butter much used in culinary preparations. The buffalo is well-nigh amphibious, delighting in the long, rank pasture which springs up in moist and undrained lands, and lying for hours submerged almost to the muzzle beneath the cooling waters.

The *Indian Ox* resembles the American in varieties of color and size, but with the exceptions of having a bunch above the shoulders, and a dewlap hanging half way to the ground. Those used in the artillery corps and by travellers are large and strong, moving at the rate of three to four miles per hour.

*Cows* yield much less milk, and that of an inferior quality in the eastern than western continent. Those of English breed are at times to be met with among Europeans, but seldom among the natives. The cow, as first created of all animals, is held in highest veneration by pious Hindoos, and to kill it is the last of pardonable offences. Several years ago, a king of Travancore, in order to atone for his cruelties, caused a *colossal golden cow* to be made, through the body of which he passed with profoundest reverence, and made it the era from which all his edicts were dated. The rock from beneath which the Ganges takes its rise is supposed to be a petrified cow, and the orifice is called the "*cow's mouth*."

The *Brahminee Bull* claims a special notice. These creatures are consecrated when calves to the divinity Siva, whose emblem is usually painted upon

F. Michelin lith. 111 Nassau St.

THE BRAMINEE BULL

their haunches and forehead. They are allowed full liberty to go where they please and feed upon what they like. One is always to be seen near the bazaar, where it unceremoniously appropriates to itself grain, grass, hay, or whatever takes its fancy; the owner bearing the depredation with religious patience, believing that to inflict upon it a blow would ensure the divine displeasure. They are the greatest pests with which the country is annoyed, and respect to national prejudices alone saves them from the fatal bullet of the vexed foreigner.

India presents many species of *Wild Oxen*, some of which have been domesticated and made useful to the agriculturist and traveller. Of these the *Ganjal* is most important, resembling in size and shape the English bull. A species called the *Arnee* inhabits the southern base of the Himalayah Mountains, and exceeds in size any of the cattle kind yet discovered. One shot near Sangree Island weighed 2,000 pounds, though pronounced by ship butchers but two years old. Some of the native princes keep them, under the name of fighting bullocks.

The *Yak* roams over the mountainous regions of Bootan and Thibet, and is domesticated throughout the central parts of the Peninsula. The *horse-tails*, as they are commonly called, used as standards by the Persians and Turks, are made of hair (dyed of a fine crimson) from the tail of this animal.

*Horses* are numerous throughout India, those of highest value being brought from Arabia, the Cape of

Good Hope and England. The native horse is small, ugly and slow, its use being confined almost wholly to the aborigines. *Ponies* imported from Pegu and Acheen are in very general use, the former resembling in shape, strength and temper the Canadian pony—the latter that of our western prairie. The value of a first class Arabian or Cape steed varies from two hundred dollars to four hundred, though one of sufficient excellence for family purposes may be purchased for one hundred and fifty. A civilian of rank, with a family, keeps from three to six horses, the climate requiring great care in their use. Each animal has a groom, who not only attends to it when stabled, but who runs by its side when the gentleman goes out for a ride, and is ready to receive the reins when he alights. Horses are not used for drawing conveyances except within the city or town limits, long journeys being performed in palanquins, or spring carts, drawn by oxen.

In the northern districts the traveller meets with the *Wild Ass*, where it frequents the salt marshes and open plains of Cutch and Guzerat.

*Mules* are common, the country over, and are serviceable in conveying burdens, especially salt and rice; —a useful but abused animal. Far in the north, the *Dziggetai* is met with in large droves. Quick and watchful, it takes alarm at the least appearance of danger, and, on the approach of the enemy, skims the desert, clears the hills, and bids defiance to pursuit.

Turning to the quadrumanous order of animals, the

*Monkey* claims our special consideration. With this creature India greatly abounds. In addition to a favorable climate and agreeable food, a reason for this abundance may be found in the fact that the monkey is held in religious esteem. Temples of magnificent structure and gorgeous decoration have been erected in its honor, one of which, when plundered by the Portugese on the island of Ceylon, contained the tooth of an ape, encased in pure gold. In such esteem was this relic held by the natives, that they offered 700,000 ducats for its ransom. At Ahmenabad, the Capital of Guzerat, there are three hospitals for monkeys, where the sick and lame are fed and nursed by salaried medical attendants. City, town, and village, throng with these mischievous, chattering, and amusing specimens of mock humanity When a resident of Madura, I saw them by hundreds, fearlessly scaling the lofty pagodas which grace that ancient city, perched upon the dwellings of the native inhabitants, engaged in earnest and noisy discussions, or committing depredations by tearing off the tiles, and grinning at the surprised and vexed inmates thus unceremoniously exposed to sun and rain; —all this, in part, to satisfy hunger, but the rather as it would seem, to gratify an instinctive desire for mischief and fun. The following scene was witnessed but a short time since, at Tillicherry, and is thus stated by the beholder himself. "A few yards from the house where I was stopping, a thick pole, at least thirty feet high, had been fixed into the earth, round which was an iron ring, and to this was attached a strong chain, of considerable length, fastened to a collar round the monkey's middle. The ring being loose, easily slid upon the pole when he ascended or descended. He was in the habit of taking his station upon the top, where he seemed perched, as if to enjoy the beauties of the prospect around. The crows, which in India are very abundant and audacious, taking advantage of his elevated position, had been in the daily habit of robbing him of his food, which was placed every morning and evening at the foot of the pole. To this, he had vainly expressed his dislike, by chattering and other indications of his displeasure equally ineffectual. Finding that he was perfectly unheeded, he adopted a plan of revenge equally ingenious and successful. One morning, when his tormentors had been particularly troublesome, he appeared as if seriously indisposed. No sooner were his ordinary rations placed at the foot of the bamboo, than the crows watching their opportunity, descended in great numbers, and began as usual to demolish his provisions. The monkey now began to slide down the pole by slow degrees, as if the effort were painful to him, and reaching the ground, rolled about for some time in apparently great agony, until he found himself close by the vessel containing his food, where he lay in a state of seeming insensibility, waiting a favorable opportunity of perfecting his scheme. With one eye but half closed, he sees a crow approaching; it nears him; it stretches out its neck, when, lo! it is seized by the wrathful avenger, who, after a few preliminary grimaces and chatterings, deliberately placed the captive between his knees, and began to pluck it, with the most humorous gravity. When he had completely stripped it, except the large feathers in the pinions and tail, he flung it into the air as high as his strength would permit, and, after flapping its wings for a few seconds, it fell on the ground with a stunning shock. The other crows, which had been fortunate enough to escape a similar castigation, now surrounded it and immediately picked the poor thing to death. The expression of joy on the monkey's countenance was altogether indescribable. Never again was he molested by those voracious intruders."

After what I have personally observed of this animal, I am prepared to attach full credence to this singular incident. My friend, the Rev. Mr Crane, of Dindigul, had a large black monkey with a face most tastefully decorated with whisker, mustache, and like genteel appendage, which, if placed in similar circumstances, would fully equal his Tillicherry brother. The species most common in India, are the *Gibbon*, or long-armed, the *Entellus*, or long-tailed, the *Wanderer*, and the *Togul*. A few specimens of the *Ourang Outang* have been met with in the central regions.

*Bats* of various sizes are numerous, and to the traveller, in his bungalow, exceedingly annoying. Some of them are furnished with wings, which, when outstretched, measure five feet from tip to tip, and are very destructive to fruit-trees in Guzerat and on the Coromandel Coast.

*Porcupines* extensively inhabit the mountainous ranges, and the long quills with which they are furnished, and which they annually shed, are gathered by the natives, and used for beautifying boxes and dresses, in the same way as by our American Indians, but more perfectly wrought.

On different occasions I purchased a *Sloth* and an *Armadillo*, both of which I kept for several weeks, observing their habits, which were curious and instructive. In Bengal, and along the eastern shore, is found the *Two-toed Sloth ;* and in Bahar there is a variety which has a considerable resemblance to the bear, and lives on ants.

The *Mangoose* is about the size of a weasel, and is the only creature that dare attack the cobra de capella. If bitten, it runs into the neighboring wood, feeds, it is thought, upon some antidote, and returns to the combat. The animal is domesticated, and trained to guard the sleeping infant from snakes and vermin, while the mother is at work in the field.

The *Bengal loris*, or slow lemur, is about the size of a small cat, of a pale brown color, and, during most of the day, sleeps, or lies without motion, like the sloth, of which some consider it but another species.

Among various kinds of *Squirrel*, the Malabar holds a first rank. It measures from fourteen to twenty inches in length, and is furnished with a fine bushy tail, and moves with much ease and gracefulness.

*Chipmucks* are abundant, as also various species of *Rats* and *Mice*. Among the former of which, is the *Ratel*, which is very troublesome in disinterring and feeding upon the buried dead.

*Hares*, *Rabbits*, and *Martins*, find a home in the northern districts, while *Civets*, *Badgers*, *Racoons*, and *Ichneumons* hunt the rats, bats, and larger serpents.

Among the *Carnivorous Quadrupeds* of India, the *Tiger* holds a distinguished place. This most agile and daring of beasts, which forms a prominent feature in the zoology of that land, makes its home amid the jungles of Bengal, and the mountain ranges of the northern and central districts, where it roams free and fearless, finding no enemy daring to measure strength with it, except, occasionally, the elephant and rhinoceros. In the the province of Khandesh one thousand and thirty-two of these fierce creatures were killed between the years 1825 and 1829, as given in official reports. To hunt the tiger, mounted upon the lofty elephant, was once a favorite sport with native princes and foreign residents ; but its extreme danger has led to its general abandonment. The bound of the tiger, when springing upon its prey, is tremendous, extending, as it is said, to the distance of one hundred or more feet. It is from this spring that the animal gets his name. He, as it were, "shoots himself at his prey ;" and *tiger*, in the Arminian language, signifies the *arrow*—the name also given to the

River *Tigris*, on account of its velocity. In many of the Indian languages, the name of tiger is *tippoo.*

*Lions* exist in vast numbers throughout the provinces of Saharampoor and Loodianah, some of them equalling in size those at the Cape. A maneless species is so numerous in Guzerat, that an English officer killed eleven in one month. The Bengal lion has the mane magnificently developed, attains a very large stature, and displays equal courage with that of its African relative.

*Panthers* and *Leopards* tenant the jungly and hilly districts of the peninsula, and are hunted for their beautiful skins, which are used by religious mendicants and Government officers. A species of leopard called the *Cheetah*, with limbs long and slender, is trained to aid the hunter in his field and jungle sports. One of them, after being blinded and chained, is placed upon a cart and carried far out into the field, and when the hunter sees an antelope or deer, turning the head of the Cheetah in that direction, he removes the blinds and chains, allowing it to move, as its instinct suggests, slowly and stealthily towards its victim. When approaching sufficiently near, it makes a few astounding springs, seizes its prey by the neck, and will not relax its hold till the owner entice it away by pieces of meat and a draught of fresh blood.

Other of the feline genus, as the *Domestic Cat* and the *Nepaul tiger cat*, make their habitation in the Peninsula, though to a limited extent.

Of the Canine tribes inhabiting India, a prominent

place belongs to the *Jackal.* The foreigner has not to journey far into the interior before becoming acquainted with its nocturnal cries, (resembling the scream of a woman in deepest distress) arousing him from his slumbers by its unwonted sounds. So soon as night falls they commence their predatory excursions to the villages, seizing upon fowls and other domestic animals, carrying away lifeless carcasses and offal, thus uniting the evil habit of the thief with the good offices of a scavenger. In some parts of the country the custom prevails of bathing the hands in the blood of a slain jackal, whenever one kills or witnesses the death of a wild beast. The origin of this strange habit has not come to my knowledge.

The *Striped Hyena* resides in the caverns of the mountains and clefts of rocks or in dens, from which it comes forth with more strength and daring than the wolf, following the flocks, breaking open sheepcotes at night, and committing ravages with an insatiable voracity. In some instances the hyena has become tame and domestic like the dog.

The *Lynx* lives in the northern provinces, and the *Caracal* makes his appearance in Bengal. The *Ounce* is found in all the central part of the Deccan, and in Guzerat. The most remarkable of the canine animals of India is the *Thibet dog*, a gigantic kind of mastiff, which inhabits the table-lands of the Himalayas. It is used as a watch dog, for which it is well adapted by its size, strength and ferocity of temper. Another of the canine species frequenting jungly and hilly regions, and resembling in many features the jackal, hunt in packs, and even will rush upon the tiger, tearing him in pieces ere he can strike more than two or three down with his fatal paw.

The domestic or *Pariar dog* is mean in appearance and destitute of all those noble traits which belong to his western relative, and, as a consequence, receives rough usage from native and foreigner.

In our view of the animated nature of India, the next class to be noticed is that of Reptiles, including various species, from the *Crocodile* to the harmless *Lizard*;—with which last-named creature our illustrations will begin. "Shaped like unto a crocodile, of a sad, green color, and but a little creature, the fear of whom presents itself mostly to the eye, for they are in no wise hurtful," is a description of the lizard, which, though quaint, is correct and graphic. Measuring from three to six inches in length, having feet so shaped as to allow of creeping safely and rapidly upon the sides and ceiling of the smoothest wall, it feeds upon flies and insects, which it approaches with a slow and cautious tread, and transfixes with a sudden thrust of its sharp and forked tongue. To look upward and see a half dozen of these reptiles creeping upon the polished ceiling is not at all agreeable to a new comer, while to have one fall upon the hand when writing or reading sends a chill through the frame not to be coveted. But the alarm is not all on one side, for the animal makes such a descent solely by a mistake, and were it possible would certainly apologize for this intrusion, as he rectifies his error in the very practical manner of making himself off with the greatest possible speed. A few of these harmless creatures find their home upon every wall, remaining concealed behind a mirror or other suspended frame during the day, and coming forth at night to seize upon their tiny prey. In some parts of the country there is a large green lizard called the *Gecko*, named from its favorite and habitual sound, and in distinction from the last mentioned, containing a bag filled with poison, with which it can suffuse its victim and produce death, unless the part be removed.

India abounds with *Scorpions* of various sizes and color, from one which may be covered with a dollar coin to that which equals a full-sized hand, the former usually of a light cast, and the latter dark or jet black. An elongated body terminates in a slender tail, formed of several joints, the last of which ends in a small, conical bag containing the poisonous fluid, to which is attached a tubular sting, through which it is thrown into the object it seeks to harm. This tail is carried above the body, when the animal is walking, and is projected beyond the front of the head when put to harmful use. The wound is painful though seldom destructive, ammonia being the most successful curative. The cautious Hindoo will not put his hand into or under a jar or box before he assures himself that he will not encounter this noxious reptile. It is currently believed that if encircled with fire it will sting itself to death. A celebrated naturalist speaks of putting a female scorpion with her young into a glass case. She soon destroyed all but one, which took refuge upon the back of its parent, and avenged the death of its brethren by killing the old one in its turn. It is a timid creature, flying rapidly from impending danger, and never using its sting except as a means of defence, or to secure food.

*Centipedes* are found in similar localities with the scorpion, and are at times more than a foot long and thick as a man's finger, having two sharp teeth with which they inflict wounds painful and dangerous.

*Tarantulas*, the largest of the spider kind, are occasionally met with in unfrequented places, or long unopened rooms. I killed one, the body of which was nearly the size of the palm of my hand, of an olive brown color, and covered with a soft down. The bite is painful, though not fatal.

Dr. Russel, an eminent scholar in zoology, has described *forty-three* distinct species of *Snakes* common in India. Among the seven which are poisonous, there is one—the *Cobra-de-Capella*—that is dreaded beyond any object with which our earth is cursed. In length from three to six feet, in circumference about two inches, its head is small, and covered on the forepart with large smooth scales, just below which is a dilatation of the skin which is capable of being raised or depressed at the pleasure of the animal. When irritated the skin is expanded and elevated like a hood; hence the name of "hooded snake." The animal never bites so long as this outer skin is folded, but its erection, with an accompanying hiss, is a signal of aggression and peril—*peril*, for let the minutest globule of the concentrated poison find its way into the system and death must ensue. Lunar caustic, though efficacious as remedial to the bite of the viper, is found of little or no avail as a counteraction to the venom of the cobra. Jugglers carry them about the country for exhibition and reward, keeping them in subjection by the power of music. Though very numerous there are but few instances on record of death from their attacks, such precautions are used to avoid the places where they dwell. By the natives they are regarded with religious reverence, and the title of "good snake" is that by which they are usually designated.

On the Island of Ceylon a venomous snake called the *Tic Polonga* is occasionally met with. Such is the strength of its poison that the first bite will kill a fowl in less than a minute. It is naturally indolent, and will not attack unless it is irritated.

The *Whip Snake* conceals itself among the foliage of trees, darts at cattle grazing below, causing the largest ox to die of agony within an hour's time.

*Mountain Snakes*, from four to eight feet in length, and quite harmless, are carried about the country by indigent, low-bred natives for exhibition, with trained monkeys and bears.

The *Crocodile of the Ganges* is distinguished from the Nilotic species by its projecting eyes, and narrow, elongated muzzle. Its teeth are many, and disposition carnivorous. The habit of throwing infants and small children to these monsters of the sacred stream, has long formed a leading feature in the superstitious observances of that idolatrous land. *Alligators* are common in the rivers of the north, especially the Ganges, upon the shores of which they are ever seen basking in the rays of the sun.

*Anacondas*, twenty to thirty feet in length, infest the Delta of the Ganges, concealing themselves in large trees standing upon the water's edge, and by a terrible fling of their massive and powerful bodies encircling and crushing whatever comes within their fatal reach.

We have an account of a *Boa Constrictor*, killed upon the banks of the Ganges but a few years since which was found to measure sixty-two feet and some inches in length.

*Tortoises* measuring four and a half feet from the tip of the nose to the tail, and fourteen inches high, are to be met with at times in the northern regions.

*Frogs* are abundant. Bishop Heber speaks of seeing one which was large as a gosling, and very beautiful, being green, speckled with black, and almost transparent.

India swarms with INSECTS, arising chiefly from the warmth of the climate, there being no portion of the year throughout the largest districts, when the cold is sufficient to destroy the minutest animal life. Let a house remain closed for a few weeks, and upon opening the door and windows, the reader, were he here, would observe several things which would startle, if not terrify him. Turning his eye upward he would see two, three, or more lizards (before referred to) seemingly ready to make a descent upon him. Looking downward he would observe the mat covered with innumerable tiny, black *ants* moving in all directions with business-like order and speed. If there be a table in the room he would notice the upright post provided with an encircling brass cup, into which water or oil may be poured, and thus the food be guarded from the attacks of these intruders, and a like precaution with the bedsteads, bureaus, and safes. He would observe tho book-case standing at a little remove from the wall, to protect it from the ravages of the *white ant*, that marvel in natural history. Though small and apparently harmless, they are the most destructive creatures with which we are acquainted. Nothing but stone or mortar can resist their power of devastation. Moving just beneath the surface, mole-like, they enter by myriads a table, box of books, chest of clothes, or whatever be left exposed to their intrusion, and cease not their work of destruction until nothing is left but the bare shell. Boxes must be placed upon a stone or some metallic substance three to four inches in height—books must be bound in Russia leather, or often removed and brushed—beams of dwellings must be saturated with tar; and all to guard against one of the tiniest, most insignificant-looking, and yet most formidable of the animate creation. Let the visitor beware how he lift up the corner of the mat lest the sting of a concealed *scorpion* make him repent the incautious act, or a *snake* erect its threatening crest. Let him wait till evening draws on, and a light is brought into the room, and if it be at the right season of the year, a cloud of *winged ants* will make their entrance, encircling the lamp in a countless swarm, some just burning their feet upon the glass shade, others more boldly flying right into the crater, there to meet their death. In an hour or so they begin to disappear, leaving their wings on the table, and adopting the more humble mode of *creeping* like their less aspiring brethren. Let him go out the next morning, and the native lad will be seen, bag in hand, gathering from their hiding places these wingless visitors, from which is made a *curry* more delicious than turtle soup to an alderman! If he retire to rest without the shelter of a muslin hanging surrounding his couch the music and fang of the *mosquito* will forbid repose. If upon rising he take not the precaution of looking into his shoes his foot may come in contact with a scorpion, or small snake. Casting his eye around during the day he would see the common fly without number. Opening a drawer a company of *roaches* will manifest their terror by a sudden and rapid withdrawal from notice. The *wasp* will be seen passing up and down the Venetian blind in search of food, and the *locust* will pierce the ear with its sharp, shrill notes. These statements may give to the reader a no very pleasant impression of a residence in that Eastern clime. I state but the facts in the case, admitting, however, that there is such a thing as becoming so accustomed to these sights that they may be seen and heard with but slight effect upon the weakest nerves. Constant precautions are needful in protecting person and property from their painful and destructive visits, but the eye becomes so habituated to seeing them in all places and times, that no special emotions are awakened *so long as they keep at a respectful distance.* At night *fire-flies* glitter among the boughs of the Banyan tree, or dance around the spreading tamarind, producing a singular but beautiful effect. *Bees* abound in hilly districts, building their nests in hollow trees and rocky caverns, and yielding a honey of but inferior excellence. The *silkworm* produces materials for a fabric greatly used in years past, but confined at present to Brahmins, Mohammedans, and the more wealthy of the natives. The *Termes* form a substance which yields a beautiful vermillion, and was much used before the discovery of cochineal. Within another insect is an article called *lac*, which is much used in fabricating brads, rings, and other ornaments of female dress. *Ant-hills*, seven and more feet in circumference, and five and six feet high, are often met with upon the plains, especially in jungly districts, which seem so much beyond the power of a tiny insect to construct as to lead to an ancient opinion that " in India there are monstrous ants, as large as foxes." Bishop Heber remarks, that " the pyramids, when the comparative bulk of those who reared them is taken into the estimate, are as nothing compared to the works of these *termites.* The counterpart of one of these hills is as if a nation should set to work to build up an artificial Snowdon and bore it full of halls and galleries."

The BIRDS of India, though less *splendid* on the whole than those of South America, are, in many cases remarkable for *splendor* of plumage, symmetry of form, and sweetness of tone. We have the *Condor*, occasionally met with in the extreme northern regions measuring fifteen feet between the tips of its outspread pinions; the *Pondicherry Vulture*, equalling in size a large goose; the *Bengal Vulture*, which is often seen preying upon the human corpses that float down the sacred Ganges to the sea; the *Lammergeyer* or bearded vulture, a rare and unsocial bird, whose home is among the Himmalaya ranges; the *Pondicherry Eagle*, esteemed sacred on the Malabar coast; the *Finch-Falcon* of Bengal; the *Fork-tailed Shrike*, also a native of Bengal, and named "king of the crows," because of its incessant assaults upon that tamer and weaker race; the *Calao* of Malabar; the *Malabar Shrike*, with its head surmounted by a tufted plume; the *Rhinoceros Horn Bill;* the *Jocose Shrike*, named from its lively disposition and amusing manners, and known in the writings of Hafiz as the Bulbul or Persian nightingale; the *Mina* or *Grakle*, most noted linguist of the feathered tribes; the *Paradise Grakle*, remarkable for its destruction of locusts and which, when kept near the farmyard, spontaneously acquires the various cries of ducks, dogs, geese, sheep, pigs, and poultry; the *Pagoda Thrush*, so called from its frequent occurrence among the pagodas of Malabar and Coramandel; the *King Fisher*, inhabiting the hottest parts of the continent; the *Wood-pecker* ranging the whole country from the southern Cape to the sombre forests of the Himalayas; *Parrots* of various kinds and abundant in number; the *Peacock* which roams in a wild state throughout the forests of the Peninsula; the *Jungle cock*, whose locality is among the Ghats; the *Crow*, which in multitudes throng the yard of every dwelling, allowing no fragment of food to escape their vigilant eye and ravenous appetite; the *Impeyan Pheasant*, whose home is in the northern mountains; the *Horned Pheasant*, common in the Nepaul district; the *Quail and Patridge* of various species, and general distribution; the *Passarage Bustard* highly esteemed on account of the delicacy and fine flavor of its flesh and consequently bearing a high price in the India market; the *Golden Plover;* the *Coromandel Courier;* the *Promeprop;* the *Gigantic Stork* or *Adjutant*, a voracious creature, devouring at one meal what would satisfy four men, very useful as a scavenger in clearing the streets of offal, and regarded with superstitious reverence because supposed to be possessed of the souls of Brahmins; the *Pondicherry and Coromandel Heron*, which last is also common on the banks of the Ganges and other Indian rivers; the *Bengal Snipe;* the *Horned Turkey of Bengal*, with a fleshy, blue, callous substance behind each eye giving it the full effect of a horned animal; the *Pearly-plumaged Gull;* the

*Black-backed Goose ;* with many species of the *Duck kind*, and *Poultry* such as are found in the farmyards of the western continent.

Our limits allow little else than the naming of these various tribes, leaving the reader to consult elaborate treatises on ornithology for a more extended acquaintance with their pecularities of structure and habit.

India being almost surrounded by water, is supplied with a variety of excellent FISH, among which may be named the *Pomfret*, of a flavor more delicate than the turbot ; the *Robal*, the *Scir Fish*, the *Bumbalo*, which, when dried, forms a principal article of food among the Lascars, or Hindoo sailors ; the pale brown *Eel*, *King of the herrings*, more than eight feet in length ; the *Russelian Gymnetris*, the *Remora*, which is employed by the natives in capturing the tortoise ; the *Dolphin*, distinguished by the splendor of its varying hues ; the insidious *Dory*, inhabiting the rivers and other fresh waters, which, when perceiving a flying insect hovering over the water, shoots out a jet of water from its tubular mouth so suddenly, and with such unerring aim, as to tumble the insect in a stupified state upon the surface of the stream ; the *Unicorn Acantharus* ; the *Climbing Sparus*, which moves at pleasure up the trunks of trees growing by the water side, remaining hours out of water ; the *Soher*, with pre-eminent flavor and beauty ; the *Whrahl*, inhabiting the lakes, and much esteemed as a nutritious and healthful food for invalids ; the *Leopard*

*Mackerel*, the *Flying Gurnard*, which swim in shoals, ever and anon darting into the air, and making its way to a considerable distance; the *Carp;* and the *Mangoe Fish*, called by the natives *Tupsy Muchee*, and regarded by Europeans as the most delicate food brought into market, and is, therefore, dried and salted for sale; with several lesser species not worthy of special notice. India does not excel in the character of its *Shell-fish*, though the number is great. *Oysters* and *Lobsters* are abundant, but of an inferior flavor. *Crabs* are large, palatable, and often dressed for the table of the European. Tanks swarm with small *Land Crabs*, which are eaten only by the more indigent natives. The *Pearl Oyster* inhabits the straits of Manaar, between the Continent and Ceylon, and is obtained by diving. These beds are less abundant and valuable than in former years, yet still yielding a revenue to government and wealth to individuals. The *shells* to be found upon the shores of India, are world-renowned, and need no particular mention. A valve of the *Tridacna Gigas*, the largest shell known, presented to Francis I. of France, is used as a baptismal font, in the church of St. Sulpice, in Paris.

Thus far of *zoology*, or animated nature, as it appears in India. A few facts must suffice upon its Botany. The vegetable productions of a country so extensive, and with such varieties of temperature and soil as those in Hindostan, must be very numerous and diverse. The herbarium in the museum of the East India Company, contains about nine thousand species, which would be greatly multiplied were the whole country to be searched with the diligence and zeal that portions have already been. The vales of Cashmere, Delhi, and Serinagur, abound with varieties of the *rose* and the flowering *jessamine.* In addition to these, we find in different parts of the country the elegant *atimuca*; the *tchambaga*, much used for adorning the hair and perfuming the clothes; the *missænda*, with its white leaves and blood-red flowers; the *ixora*, which, from boughs six feet in height, exhibits its scarlet and yellow tufts of bloom, enlivening the foliage of the wood; the *sindrimal*, opening at four in the evening and closing at four in the morning; the *nyctanthes sambac*, with which the Hindoos perfume their hair before retiring to rest; the *nagatalli*, which creeps along the wall, covering them with its foliage, together with various species of the *violet*, *primrose*, *buttercup*, *lily*, &c., which are chiefly found on the mountain sides or deep valleys.

The chief food of the frugal Hindoo is RICE, in which all the provinces abound. Wheat, barley, maze, and millet, are also grown, especially wheat, which is the prevailing crop throughout the northern districts. To these may be added peas, beans, and several vegetable species, unknown in this western world, are met with in the uplands, as also potatoes and many kinds of berries. Commerce is indebted to India for indigo, opium, flax, hemp, tobacco, sarsaparilla, jalap, cotton, anise, betel, saffron, sesamum, many dyes, besides various reeds and canes. These are cultivated with different degrees of success throughout the peninsula.

Among the forest TREES of India, the first place in utility, and far from the last in majestic beauty, belongs to the *Teak*, a hard and almost incorruptible timber, fitted to supply the place of the oak in ship-building, and is, in this respect, its superior; that it will not corrode iron, nails, and bolts. For universal application, rapid growth and durability, the *Bamboo* occupies the next place. It shoots up to the height of sixty feet in a single season, acquires a diameter of more than six inches at the base, is tough, strong, firm and light, and may be made to answer a variety of most needful purposes. Thick jungles of bamboo cover large portions of the peninsula, and by preventing circulation of air make the regions around very unwholesome. Various species of *Palm trees* give a character to the scenery of India and furnish the inhabitants with many valuable products. Of this large tribe the *Cocoanut tree* holds the first place. Our limits forbid an enumeration of the various uses to which this tree is appropriated, and it must suffice to say that not a portion is allowed to remain unused. The *great fan palm* furnishes roofs for the native cottages. The *smaller fan palm* and *palmyra* yield toddy, an intoxicating liquor much used among the lower class of Hindoos, and leaves upon which letters &c., are written with the iron style; and the *Sago* and *Arca* palm. The *Babul tree* is one of the most beautiful and ornamental in India, its flowers emitting a delightful fragrance, and its timber much esteemed where lightness and strength are required. To these may be added the *Sandal wood tree*, which grows in the south-west part of Mysore, and is exported to Arabia and China, and to close the list the *Indian fig* or *Banyan*, which stretches its immense branches and holy shade not only over the pagodas and choultries, but over serpents and other venomous creatures—an emblem of benevolent nature which sustains and blesses the evil and the good. This tree is regarded with religious homage by the Hindoos, believing, as they do, that the birth-place of their god, Vishnoo, was beneath its overspreading branches: temples are erected near it and images placed under its shade. On the banks of the river Nerbudda stands a tree of this venerated species which measures two thousand feet around the principal stems, the larger trunks of which amount to three hundred and fifty, and the smaller ones exceed three thousand. This tree is called *Cubbeer-burr* by the Hindoos, in memory of a favorite saint, who took it under his special patronage and care, and it has been known to shelter *seven thousand men* beneath its shade. This species, though thus honored and useful, is doing more to demolish the splendid edifices of India than any other cause, the seeds falling into the crevices of the wall, vegetating, spreading apart the long-cemented piles of stone and brick, causing temples and palaces and pagodas to become heaps of shapeless ruin. The *Saul tree*, producing a resin much used for naval purposes, and as incense in the temples. This tree is used in detecting witchcraft, an account of which the reader will find in the last chapter of the volume; the *Cadukah* of Telinga, bearing a gall producing a very permanent *yellow;* the *Jack tree*, with its pumpkin shape fruit hanging from its loftiest branches.

Our fruit trees, as the apple, pear, plum, apricot, peach, walnut, almond, &c., thrive in the northern provinces, while the southern districts abound in mangoes, guavas, plantains, custard apple,·limes, lemons, but not oranges, (these being confined to the northern regions and Ceylon,) pine apple and shaddock. In the Himalaya Mountains trees are sometimes of enormous size, measuring twenty feet in girth, more than a hundred and fifty in height, and exhibiting a sheer branchless trunk of sixty feet, surmounted by a vast crest which waves above like a gigantic canopy. In those regions all kinds of European trees and plants flourish in abundance.

Among the smaller trees and shrubs common to India are the *Daphne Cannabina*, from which is manufactured common, but useful, papor; the *Rice-paper plant* which grows luxuriously in Bengal; and the *Acacia*, well-known for its airy and elegant foliage, besides yielding the gum-arabic of commerce.

In respect to *Mineral wealth* India is one of the richest of known countries. Grains of gold are to be found in the bed of many of the northern rivers, while rich mines of the same precious ore and of *silver* occur in the Carnatic, Assam and Bengal. There are *copper mines* in the mountains of Kumaoon, and in the provinces of Agra and Ajmere. *Iron* is common throughout the peninsula. Assam and the Kumaoon Mountains furnish large quantities of *Lead.* Some mines of *Tin* are worked in the district of Ajmere. *Zinc* is exported in large quantities from India to England. *Quicksilver* and *Antimony* are found in a few places. This, too, is the land of the *Diamond*, *Ruby*, *Sapphire*, *Amethyst*, *Onyx* and other precious stones. And in this country are quarries of *Marble* and *Alabaster*, of *Sulphur*, *Coal* and *Naptha*, of common *Salt* and *Saltpetre.* Tradition has hardly exaggerated in the accounts it has transmitted to us respecting the minerals and metals—the precious stones and gems of heaven-favored Ind.

Such is a rapid view of nature, animate and inanimate, as presented in that eastern clime. We but enter the field of inquiry and research before we are compelled to leave it, the proportionate limits allowed to this branch of the subject being more than reached, and yet much remaining to be said. But what we have seen suffices to convince us that the Hindoos have ample acquaintance with the Most High as made known by His works, so that they are "without excuse" if they render not to Him the homage of gratitude and praise.

## CHAPTER III.

### HISTORICAL SURVEY.

What is known of Ancient India—Invasions by Sesostris, Semiramis, Darius and Alexander—Invasion by Mahmoud of Guznee—Somnaut Captured—Its venerated Idol and Temple Gate—Successors of Mahmoud—Invasions by the Portuguese—Dutch—East India Company—Black Hole of Calcutta—Governors-General—Relation of India to England—Remark of Dr. Duff—Measures pursued by the English—Opinions and Feelings of the Hindoos—An Historic Law respecting India—Characteristics of the several Periods of Hindoo History—An Eloquent Extract.

"Whoever attempts to trace the operations of men in remote times, and to mark the various steps of their progress in any line of exertion, will soon have the mortification to find that the period of authentic history is very limited. Beyond the era of written annals lies the region of uncertainty and conjecture."

Respecting no country does the student of antiquity find this to be more true than of India. The Hindoos having no historical records that deserve the name, and such accounts as they do possess are mixed up with so many improbable and monstrous fictions, that we are left in total ignorance as to well-determined facts. From the "Vedas," which were written about the time of King David, and the "Institutes of Menu," we learn that the country anciently composed several separate kingdoms, varying in extent, and at constant warfare among themselves. Two families, in a special manner, bore rule, distinguished as the *sun* and *moon*, probably on account of their comparative power and splendor. Other accounts tell us that in the early days there were ten kingdoms in India, speaking different languages, five of which occupied the southern, and five the northern districts. It is a well-ascertained fact that neither the present race of Hindoos or their immediate ancestors are the aborigines of the soil—but who the original possessors of the country were, and whence they came, are questions which have called into requisition the learning and research of England and the Continent, though with ill success. The Rev. Dr. Ward, of Serampore, closes a labored examination of Hindoo manuscripts in this decisive manner : "Such is Hindoo history as given by themselves, or rather an imperfect gleaning from a great and confused mass of materials, which have been thrown together in the Puranas, to arrange and settle which, so as to chose what is true and reject what is false, requires a mind more than human. A real and accurate history of this country, from its commencement to the present time, with the dates of events attached to them, is *out of the question*." Sir Wm. Jones says, "The dawn of true Indian history appears only three or four centuries before the Christian era, the preceding ages being clouded by allegory and fable." Major Milford, an eminent

Orientalist, adds his testimony, that "with regard to history the Hindoos have really nothing but romances, from which but occasional truths may be extracted." After saying that India was one of the earliest inhabited portions of our earth, the sober historian is compelled to admit that a veil of obscurity hangs above its rise and early progress, which has thus far baffled all attempts at removal. But few can hope for victory where Robertson and Jones and Milford have met with signal and admitted defeat.

Leaving ancient India concealed beneath the mist of antiquity and fable we will view the country when shone upon by the rays of historical truth.

Sesostris, Semiramis, Darius and Alexander were the earliest to bring that peninsula before the modern world. Respecting the first of these heroes there is much difference of opinion. Some contending that he came against India in the year 970 before Christ and made large conquests, and exported much booty, while Robertson and others are in doubt as to the extent and even the fact of these invasions. It is thought "that some light may be thrown upon this subject by the researches now in progress for the interpretation of Egyptian hieroglyphics." The expedition undertaken by *Semiramis* rests upon more reliable testimony and commands our more intelligent belief. From the pages of Diodorus we learn that this illustrious queen having extended her dominion over western Asia to Bactria, and having been informed that India was the most populous, wealthy, and beautiful of kingdoms, determined upon its conquest. After three years spent in preparation, she landed an army of half a million horse and foot upon the eastern bank of the Indus, crossing upon a bridge of boats built under the direction of architects from Phœnicia, Cyprus, and other maratime provinces. Here she was met by Strabrobates, a Hindoo general, who had collected a force even greater than that of Semiramis, supported by a numerous band of elephants trained for warfare. The contest was long, sanguinary and doubtful, but at length the proud and ambitious invader was obliged to sound a retreat to the boats, amid the wild confusion of which it is thought that she herself perished. Next following the Egyptian king and Phœnician queen, we read of Darius, the Persian monarch, as undertaking to explore and conquer that country. Having learned through a general whom he sent thither, the populousness, fertility and high cultivation of the country lying east of the Indus, he crossed that stream with an invading army in the beginning of the fifth century before Christ; subdued the provinces of Mooltan, Lahore, and possibly Guzerat, drawing from these conquered princes a large tribute in gold and other valuable commodities. This dominion of the Persians continued for less than two hundred years, but during the latter part of that period it was merely nominal.

In the year 327 before Christ, Alexander the Great having conquered the Persian empire, crossed the Indus with the professed design of compelling these tributary states to pay their dues to him as the successor of Darius. Commencing his march for the far-famed Ganges he was met by Porus at the head of a numerous army of native soldiery. This resistance, added to a mutiny in his ranks upon the banks of the Sutledge, compelled him with much reluctance to retrace his steps without gratifying his ambitious designs and long-cherished hopes. Determining, however, not to return in disgrace, he performed the extraordinary and hitherto unattempted project of sailing down the Indus, exultingly beholding the Arabian Sea, and thence, after incredible toil and danger, returning to his capital. When Alexander withdrew, the natives set about corrupting the troops left behind, by encouraging them in every manner of excess, which resulted in the final extinction of all foreign supremacy among them. Seleucus, and after him several generals, ending with Antiochus, undertook excursions to regain those distant possessions, but their success was limited in extent and duration.

After these repeated inroads of the Persian and Greek armies, the Hindoos enjoyed a quiet of several centuries, during which an enemy was preparing, whose impression upon the country was to be extensive, lamentable and lasting.

About the middle of the sixth century of the Christian era the eagle eye of Mohammedan ambition and rapacity was directed towards India, and this ill-fated land was destined to become the prey of conquerors surpassing in cruelty all who had as yet crossed its borders. After several attempts at a permanent dominion, but repulsion by the Hindoo princes, the time was at hand when resistance would no longer avail for their protection and freedom. In the year 998 Mahmoud ascended the throne of Ghuznee, one of the most important principalities of Afghanistan, and speedily commenced preparations for adding India to his dominions. In the year 1001 he made his first appearance on the east of the Indus, penetrating so far into the Punjaub as totally to defeat the King of Lahore and Mooltan, returning with fame and booty to his mountain fastnesses. During the following twenty-four years he made twelve expeditions into the country, in the course of which he overran most of the western provinces, plundering Delhi and other eminent cities, carrying away vast stores of gold and silver, diamonds and precious stones, which he displayed to the admiring gaze of the Ghuznee mountaineers, thus arousing their ambition and eager desire for more extensive inroads upon a land so teeming with wealth and luxury. In the last of these incursions Mahmoud entered the province of Guzerat, upon the southern boundary of which was located the village of Somnaut, renowned as the abode of a shrine of extraordinary sanctity. Attached to this far-famed temple were two thousand Brahmins, five hundred dancing girls, three hundred musicians, and other attendants in great numbers. After a long and desperate contest Mahmoud succeeded in capturing this venerated town, and upon beholding the gigantic and far-famed idol, with wrathful zeal struck off its nose, giving orders for its entire and instant demolition. As the attendant Brahmins saw the threatened downfall of this object of their profoundest veneration, they fell on their knees and proffered an immense sum for its preservation;—but the king indignantly replied, "*I am a breaker, not a buyer of Idols.*" The work of demolition proceeded; and on its reaching the interior of the image, there was disclosed a treasure in *pearls*, *rubies*, and *diamonds*, almost beyond conception, and far surpassing the immense sum tendered for its redemption." These were carried to the metropolis, and conspired, with other events, to render Ghuznee for the time one of the most eminent cities of the east. With the treasures of Somnaut, Mahmoud carried the *gates* of that town wherewith to grace his mountain home—which latter trophy has obtained no little modern notoriety from the attempt of a late governor-general to reconvey them to their former abode—an attempt which brought upon his lordship the reproof of Christendom, the rebuke of his employers, and which conspired with other acts of like folly to lose him his viceregal crown. In the year 1291 Mohammed (successor of Mahmoud) succeeded in establishing himself at Delhi, and thus commenced the first Afghan or Patan dynasty, the second commencing in the year 1291, and continuing until near the close of the fifteenth century. Then followed the Mogul dynasty begun by Baber, a descendant of Tamerlane, in the year 1525, when Mohammedanism reached its height in India, extending from Allahabad on the North to Ahmednuggur, (40 miles East from Bombay) on the South. One of the most eminent of these Mogul emperors was Akber Khan, who flourished between the years 1556 and 1695, and who ruled with so much excellence of wisdom and righteousness that the native historian tells us that "*his memory still floats upon the tears of all India.*" By his daring and judicious management the central provinces were preserved in complete tranquillity, and Guzerat, Bengal, and a part of the Deccan were added to his already extensive empire. During the reign of his son Jehoughier (1605 to 1628) the English first established themselves on the western coasts of the Peninsula. Then followed Aurungzebe, great-grandson of Akber, who ruled from 1658 to 1707. From his great-grandson Feroksere the East India Company obtained the grant of a large township in Bengal, through the personal influence of Dr. Hamilton who had succeeded in relieving the Emperor of a painful malady. The Persians, under the celebrated Nadir Shah, obtained a short-lived notoriety over parts of this down-trodden land. Our limits forbid a detailed narrative of the events that signalized the rule of Mahmoud and his successors during their rule over India. "Nothing in modern times has equalled the ferocity and desperation of these Moslem conquerors. Urged on by a mad enthusiasm; intoxicated with the hope of rich booty, and inspired with the promise of beatitude if they died fighting with the infidels, they sprang like tigers on their prey. A fertile country was left desolate ; flourishing cities, heaps of ruins; palaces were burnt, temples pillaged, and rivers sacred to their fathers flowed with human blood."

During the reign of *Tamerlane*, surnamed the "*destroying prince*," an hundred thousand natives were massacred in a single hour. *Timur* the "*fire-brand of the universe*" and greatest wholesale butcher of our species ever known, plundered and massacred without distinction of religion or sex; "his track was followed by blood, desolation, famine and pestilence." The Mogul *Aurungzebe* and Mahrattee *Sevagee*, were scarcely less ruthless destroyers of the Hindoo race, wherever obstacles were presented to their mad and plundering ambition. *Nadir Shah* entered India, slaughtered the inhabitants of Delhi, without regard to age or sex—captured Oude—seized upon the imperial treasures and conveying thence $15,000,000 in specie—$5,000,000 in plate, $75,000,000 in jewels, —the renowned Peacock throne valued at $5,000,000 and other valuables to the amount of $60,000,000, besides elephants, horses and camp equipage of the deposed Emperor. From the ill-fated days of Nadir Shah, the Moghul Empire in India began to decline—the various provinces became independent principalities, some under Mohammedan governors, and others under Mahrattas, until the city of Delhi, with a small district around, formed all that remained to the house of Timur.

"The cessation of the Mohammedan power in India

can never be regretted by one to whom are familiar the records of that beautiful but ill-fated country." Providence was so arranging events that these ruthless spoilers of that fair land were to yield their dominion to a people of another faith and higher impulse. No more do we read of twenty, seventy, or an hundred thousand slaughtered in one day without compunction of conscience, or the assigning of any plausible excuse, the inhabitants of whole provinces hunted like wild beasts for royal amusement, women devouring their own children in excess of agony. That dark volume finds a close, and the day has dawned, dim and faint at first, but the light of which will ever increase till that land become enlightened and Christian.

In the year of our Lord 1498, Vasco de Gama, a Portuguese navigator, having performed the unwonted feat of doubling the Cape of Good Hope, landed at Calicut, a place of great trade upon the western coast of the peninsula. The period was very favorable to the interests he sought to promote, and which were ere long to be realized. After fewer delays and less opposition than might have been anticipated, the Portuguese established a commercial empire which lasted a century, and to which, whether we consider its extent, its opulence, or the slender power by which it was formed, or the splendor by which the government of it was conducted, there had been nothing comparable in the history of nations. When de Gama landed for the first time on the shores of India, he endeavored, by the numbers of his retinue, their splendid attire, and orderly movements to make a favorable and deep impression. But the historian has recorded a *mistake* made by these foreigners, which detracts somewhat from the dignity of the occasion. Some of the sailors, seeing a pagoda and concluding from the beads worn by the Brahmins and the sandal wood incense, that it was a Christian temple, at once entered, and noticing a variety of pictures upon the wall, prostrated themselves before them, as before the Madonna and Saints. But one of the worshippers, as by chance he looked up and observed the strange and uncouth aspect of these imaginary apostles, some of whom brandished four and five arms, and had enormous teeth projecting out of their mouths, judged it advisable to guard himself by the exclamation, "*If these be devils it is God whom I worship.*"

In the year 1596, *Houtman*, a Dutch navigator, sailed for India in charge of four ships laden with merchandize, and well equipped for an encounter with enemies on sea or land. Traffic was commenced with the islands of Sumatra and Java—was extended in 1605 to Ceylon, and thence to India. Omitting historical detail, let it suffice to say that "so bold, assiduous and enterprising were the Dutch, that in less than eighty years from the time that Houtman first sailed from Rotterdam they possessed all the ports and places at which the Portuguese had been established, with the exception of Goa and a few subordinate towns, and had, besides, formed settlements on the Coromandel coast."

But the golden prize, the land of gold and gems, was destined a third time to change possessors. An English armament, coursing the Southern and Eastern seas, captured, on different occasions, Portuguese and Dutch Indiamen, laden with spices, calicoes, pearls, porcelain. ebony, and other rich productions of this teeming land. A display of these, in London and other cities of Great Britain, inflamed the desire of the English to be engaged in so lucrative a trade and accordingly application was made to Elizabeth, the reigning queen, for the necessary charter of protection and privilege. In the year 1599, her Majesty complied with the request, and "granted an exclusive charter to a company of London merchants, to trade with all the countries between the Cape of Good Hope and the Straits of Magellan," under a name similar to that which is still retained to their successors of the present day. One feature of the Charter was that *nò gentleman* should be connected with the company—a dubious privilege in our modern estimation. The first factories or trading houses of this company were established at Surat, Ahmenabad and Gogo, on the Gulf of Cambay ;—then followed the acquisition in 1639 of Madras, in 1664 of Bombay, in 1696 of Caloutta, and in succeeding years, of Benares, Seringapatam, Ceylon, Guzerat, Sinde, and, lastly, the Punjaub. In many of these instances of annexation, resistance was made by the native residents, in some cases aided by the French and other European Colonists. but under Clive, Hastings, Wellesley, Cornwallis, Harris, Col. Wellesley (now Duke of Wellington,) and other eminent English Generals, Hindoos and Mohammedans, rulers and people have been compelled to cower before the English lion.

The history of that vast and powerful monopoly, "The East India Company," is deeply interesting as illustrating the trite adage of "great effects from little causes." The charter which was granted in December of 1600, received modifications and renewals in 1609 '36 '57 '61 '67 '83 '86 '98 and in 1702 '8, and throughout the reigns of the Georges, to the year 1812—while the company itself has been extending its limits, increasing its power, until its terminus has become the limit of the Peninsula itself. Events of thrilling and often most painful interest arrest the reader's attention when perusing the history of British ascendency in India. Let one suffice. For fifty or more years after the occupancy of Calcutta as a trading town, an event occurred, which, for condensed suffering and terrible results, scarcely has an equal in the annals of human barbarity and war. The reigning Prince (Suraja Dowlah) had become suspicious of the foreigners and manifested a determination to visit them with displeasure. Unable, from the condition of their fort and fewness of their numbers, to resist an invasion were it made, they determined to desert their insecure abode, and embark on the ships which lay in the river. But when the hour of embarkation arrived, the crew of the vessels, anxious for their own safety, moved down the stream and could not be induced by the most earnest appeals addressed to their humanity and patriotism, to return for the rescue of their endangered countrymen. Night was at hand, and with it a command from the Nabob, to keep the foreigners in custody for examination on the coming day. In looking for a place of confinement, the guard found a room in the Fort which had been employed to confine refractory soldiers, and here were they destined to pass that memorable and to many of them a last night.

"The place selected was but eighteen feet square, with only two small windows barred with iron, opening into a close verandah, and scarcely admitting a breath of air. Into this narrow receptacle the whole of the officers and troops, *one hundred and sixteen* in number, were compelled to enter, and on their venturing to remonstrate, the commander ordered every one who should remonstrate to be instantly cut down. Thus were they forcibly thrust into this fearful dungeon, into which the whole number could with difficulty be squeezed, and the door was then fast barred from without. Their first impression upon finding themselves thus immured, was the utter impossibility of surviving one night, and the necessity of extricating themselves at whatever cost. The Jemadars (or Indian Guards) were walking before the window and Mr. Holwell seeing one who bore upon his face a more than usual expression of humanity, adjured him to procure for them room in which they could breath, assuring him of a reward next morning of a thousand rupees. The man went away, but returned, saying it was impossible. The prisoners thinking the offer too low, tendered two thousand. The man again went and returned saying that the Nabob was asleep and no one durst wake him. The lives of *a hundred and forty-six men* were nothing in comparison with disturbing for a moment the slumbers of a tyrant! Every moment added to their distress. All attempts to obtain relief by a change of posture, from the painful pressure to which it gave rise, only aggravated their suffering. The air soon became pestilential, producing at every respiration a feeling of suffocation. The perspiration flowed in streams and they were tormented with the most burning thirst. Loud cries being made for "water," the humane Jemadar pushed through the bars several skins filled with that fluid, but this produced only an increase of calamity, through the violent efforts made to obtain it. About eleven o'clock the prisoners began to die fast—six of Mr. Holwell's best friends expiring at his feet and being trampled upon by the survivors. Of those still alive, a great proportion were raving or delirious; some uttered incoherent prayers, others the most fearful blasphemies. They endeavored by most furious invectives to induce the guards to fire into the prison and end their miseries—but without effect. When day dawned the few who had not expired, were most of them either raving or insensible, and of the one hundred and forty-six who had been enclosed, there breathed only *twenty-three!*" The reader after perusing this narrative, will no longer wonder that the "*black hole of Calcutta*" is proverbial, the world over.

The news of this disaster reaching Madras, Col. (afterwards Lord) Clive was at once despatched to Calcutta with a considerable force by land and sea, to avenge the death of their countrymen. Success attended the enterprise—the author of the black-hole tragedy fell by an assassin's hand—and the commencement of British rule in Bengal may be dated from that hour. The reins of government first held by Lord Clive, passed, in 1772, to Warren Hastings, and successively to Lords Cornwallis—Teignmouth—Wellesley—Minto—Marquis Hastings—Bentinck—Auckland—Ellenborough—Hardinge and Dalhousie—whose differences of character gained for them the titles of the "unscrupulous," "prudent," "ambitious," "good," "foolish," "brave," &c., but whose administrations without exception, though in different ways, tended to produce the result we now behold—that of *British Sovereignty from the Himalayas to Cape Comorin, and from the Bay of Bengal to the Arabian Sea.* Within these limits there are, it is true, small territories under the jurisdiction of other European powers. The French, the Portuguese, and the Danes have small colonies on the Eastern and Western Coasts at Pondicherry, Goa, &c. These they are allowed to retain by courtesy and because attempts at their expulsion might involve the home governments in war. Serampore, near Calcutta, once held by the Danes, has been purchased by the East

India Company as also Tranquebar, south from Madras, and the like transfer will be made ere long of the other territories. There are also several provinces, the native rulers of which are allowed to retain an appearance of independent possession and rule. Such are Hyderabad, Nagpore, Oude, Guzerat, Mysore, and Travancore. These territories differ but in name from other parts of the country. They are directly subservient to the East India Company, and let them act as if independent they would soon wake from their delusion. An English gentleman, called "Resident," is placed near the capital of these tributary provinces and a military force officered by Englishmen is paid from the treasury of the Rajah. Let this Prince, with all his parade of royalty and independence adopt a course opposed to the will of this Resident, he is at first warned, and if that do not suffice the semblance of power is taken from him and he incarcerated (perhaps in his own palace) with a large pension, but still a State prisoner.

This topic may be closed with the following remarks from the eloquent pen of Rev. Dr. Duff: "A region of Asia, equal in extent to the whole of Europe (exclusive of Russia) with a population of more than a hundred and forty millions,—all of them aliens in blood, language, and religion; and many consisting of warlike tribes, so gallant and brave as to have again and again repelled the combined hosts of the Moslem conquerors, with a heroism not unworthy of the best sons of Greece:—this vast region, situate, by the ordinary route, at a distance exceeding half the globe's circumference, has, to its uttermost borders, been subjected to the uncontrolled dominion of British sway. So absolute and undisputed is the supremacy of the British sceptre—so regular and perfect the organization of the British power,—that an English subject, under the designation of Governor-General—who may never have trodden on the Indian soil,—may embark on board a vessel in the Thames—traverse fifteen thousand miles of ocean—proceed up the mighty Ganges as far as Dover is from Gibraltar—perch himself on one of the peaks of the Himalayas—and there, by a single sentence from his lips, or a stroke of his pen, as by the waving wand of a mighty enchanter, set all the teeming millions of India in motion!" This language though strong and eulogistic of national prowess, is strictly correct. The Seiks were the last power to resist foreign invasion, but they have been compelled to succumb to the hitherto unconquered arms of the English in the East. All India is now in truth, what it has long been in name, "*British India.*"

"Have the measures employed to secure this result been, in all cases, accordant with justice, integrity and mercy?" Far from it. The public will not bear such a portraiture of Clive and Hastings as will present them free from blemishes dark and forbidding. In proof of this, the reader is commended to the narratives of those earliest Governors of India from the powerful pen of Macaulay. Without wishing to class these officers with Teignmouth and Metcalf and "honest William Bentinck," yet history compels us to the opinion that, with great differences in the characters of the Governors, the same general features have characterized every administration from Clive to Dalhousie, and that when force has not been practicable, recourse has been had to intrigue and other sinister measures.

"How do the Hindoos bear the yoke of their foreign conquerors?" They know that they are an enslaved people, and that for ages past they have been as dust under the rolling wheel of the war-chariot and attempts have been made to reassert their independence. One of the latest of these efforts occurred in the year 1806, at Vellore, when there perished of the four European companies encamped in the Fort, one hundred and sixty-four soldiers, besides many British officers. A later effort of the kind was made at Bangalore in the year 1834, which (had it not have been discovered) would have resulted in the death of the whole cantonment of a thousand or more persons. These instances are few in number and limited in results. The system of caste among the Hindoos is preventive of that unity of action essential to the success of such an enterprise, while the Mohammedans are too few in number (though not destitute of desire and zeal) for such an enterprize.

Much conversation with intelligent Hindoos and Mohammedans upon this subject, has led me to the advised conclusion, that however iniquitous may have been many of the measures by which India has become subjected to British control, and however painful and galling is the present state of servitude and debasement, the country is, on the whole, better governed than for centuries before the arrival of the first English vessel, and the mass of the people would be far from desiring a transfer of the reins of government to native rulers, or to any other European power. We may be assured that the wish is strongly reciprocated. The pages of history indicate this fact, that "*whatever city or nation has, in the lapse of past ages, held in its hand the keys of the Indian commerce and influence, that city or place has, for the time, stood forth in the van of the civilized world, as the richest and most flourishing.*" So long as *Arabia* enjoyed the full benefit of Indian commerce, it was far-famed as "Araby the blest." "Indian commerce found *Palmyra* composed of brick, and left it more precious than marble." Monopoly of the Indian trade enabled *Tyre*, single-handed, to resist, so long, the mightiest assaults of the Macedonian conqueror. Direct trade with India and the East, speedily raised *Alexandria* into such pre-eminence, as to eclipse all surrounding cities. Through Moslem victories *Bagdad* started up at once the Rome, the Alexandria, the Athens of the East; and *Ghuznee* was long famed as the "Celestial Bride." During the century of Portuguese dominion, Lisbon outpeered all her rivals.

England knows full well that she owes not a little of her present greatness to the fact that among her many colonies *India is one*, and loth will she be to part with that extensive and antique land. Australia—Singapore—the Cape—Helena—New Zealand—Canada. She would part with *all* before losing *India*. It is a crown jewel. But I must pause at this point.

The several periods brought to notice in this chapter may be thus characterized. When under the Native Rajahs, India seems to have excelled in wealth, magnificence, and literature;—under the Mohammedan conquerors, the land was cursed with oppression and cruelty, the only road to preferment being conversion to Islamism; while under the English rulers it is enjoying general quietude, peace and prosperity; the people gradually rising to the attainment of that character which will make them happy in this life, and blessed in the life to come.

I cannot better close this chapter than by presenting to the reader the following truthful and eloquent passages from a well-known writer upon the East. "It must have been to accomplish some very important *moral change* in the Eastern world, that so vast an empire as is comprised in British India, containing nearly an hundred and fifty millions of people, should have been placed under the dominion of one of the smallest portions of the civilized world, and that at the other extremity of the globe. Is it not manifest that in the mental and moral improvement of this vast empire, Great Britain has a work of benevolence before her, which, in national glory, will eclipse all her other achievements, as much as the meridian sun exceeds in splendor the morning star. Know, then, the country of the Howards and the Wilberforces, thy high destiny! Never were such miseries to be removed—never was such a mighty good put into the power of one nation—the raising of so many spirits from the darkness of error and the wretchedness of sin, to the light of truth, and the blessedness of heaven."

# CHAPTER IV.

## INHABITANTS OF INDIA CLASSIFIED.

Population—Native Hindoos—Mohamedans (Annual Festivities)—East Indians—European Residents, of several grades—Arabs—Parsees—Chinese and Jews.

India, within the limits before named, contains an estimated population of *one hundred and fifty millions.* This vast assemblage is divided into numerous tribes, differing widely from each other in origin, appearance, habits, interests, and religion. They may be arranged with sufficient accuracy, into four classes, of which the *first* are *Native Hindoos,* to the number of about one hundred and thirty-eight millions. These, though widely diverse in language and manners, adhere to a similar system of religious belief, and are thus united in the strong bond of sympathy and interest. Of this aboriginal population, the remaining pages of the volume will speak in detail, and, therefore, no further mention need be made in this place.

The *second* class comprises the *Mohamedans,* who number about *ten millions.* These are the descendants of the early invaders of the soil, and they are not ignorant or forgetful of the fact that their fathers once conquered and ruled the land. The Mohamedan is in *manner*, cold and repulsive, his countenance seldom wearing a smile, and his bearing lofty and austere; in *religion*, most bigotedly attached to his own modes of faith and worship, and, in heart, at deep enmity with his European conquerors—being ever ready to take an active and resolute part in their expulsion. Insurrections and mutinies have, with few exceptions, been traced to Mussulman craftiness and hate. Mosques, with their towering minarets, where the Koran is read, and prayers recited, are to be met with in all the leading cities and towns of the country. Wherever a Mohamedan be, or however engaged, he performs his devotions with the most scrupulous exactness, fearlessly confessing his attachment to the Prophet and his creed. Many of them are employed as seamen on the small craft that navigate the eastern seas, especially along the opposite coasts and to the neighboring islands of Ceylon and Singapore. I have often observed, and never without deep emotion, the following act of religious homage and conscious dependence, in these ever imperiled sons of the deep. Before weighing anchor, the captain stations himself near the mast, and commences, in a loud tone, the recitation of a prayer to the Prophet. At brief intervals the whole crew respond in unison, "*Allah*," and at the close of the supplication, they thrice repeat the sacred name. On one of their days of annual festivity, each Moorman masques himself in the most perfect manner possible, by painting his body with colors of various hue, decorating himself with most fantastic attire, and then "en masse" perambulating the streets with drums beating, horns blowing, banners flying, presenting a scene alike unique, grotesque, ludicrous, senseless and pitiable. On another day each follower of the Prophet hires or loans a horse or pony, and in military array, parades the streets, much to the amazement of the gazing multitude and the amusement of the foreign beholder. A Mohamedan's dress is more European than that of the Hindoo, being a pair of loose trowsers of silk, a flowing gown of cotton, with turban and shoes. Their language is Hindostanee, though they readily acquire the tongue of the people among whom they may chance to dwell. Their employments are as clerks and accountants, local and travelling tradesmen, soldiers, seamen, tailors, washermen and instructors of Europeans, (their's being the language of the army.) They are industrious, and less addicted to gross and open immorality than are their heathen neighbors, upon whom they look down with deepest contempt, despising them for their general character and conduct, and especially their worship of idols. But few accessions have been made to Christianity from among the followers of the Prophet, and but few of their youth are allowed to attend upon Missionary instruction.

A *third* division includes a large and increasing

number, to whom are given the names of Indo-Britains, East-Indians, country-born, or more euphoniously, and, to the persons concerned, more acceptably, Eurasians. The offspring of temporary unions, which gave them European fathers and native mothers, they are in general but lightly esteemed by those above and below them. The conduct of the European residents towards this class of citizens has, it cannot be denied, been in too many cases illiberal and highly wrong, especially as they, and two or more generations, in most instances, are wholly without crime in respect to their birth. There is no excuse for this wholesale dislike, especially while among them are many persons, than whom community can desire no better members. A policy more enlightened, liberal, and Christian, has begun to prevail, and the East-Indian will ere long occupy the place to which he appropriately belongs and be judged of, not according to his parentage, but by his real and personal merits. The great fault committed by this class is their wasteful expenditure in personal decorations, their mistake of the florid and bombastical, for the simple and appropriate in language and attire. This appears in the names they give to their children. "I believe a friend was adhering to truth, who, after observing, that if you meet with one Mary, Elizabeth, or Anne, you at least encounter five Floras, Theodosias, Calinas, and Clarissas. "Not long since," says a writer, "I was in a room where five Anglo-Indian ladies assembled, whose names were Amelia Wilhelmina Rose, Christiana Aurora Comfort, Jemima Clement, Amelia Theodosia Clarissa, and Augusta Diana Noel Babington. These improprieties are both the cause and effect of their so long and entire exclusion from European circles. The East-Indians are scattered over the Peninsula to the number of *four hundred thousand*, most of whom are content with the humble stations and small incomes of clerks and writers in government and commercial establishments, shopkeepers and musicians, while a few are enterprising, wealthy, and every way worthy of confidence and respect. The names of Messrs. Van S., C. and D. are familiar to all who have resided in the city of Madras; —philanthropy and religion having no more benevolent advocates than these Anglo-Indian gentlemen.

A *fourth* class is formed of foreign residents, to the number of about *fifty thousand.* Of these the large proportion are salaried agents of the British government, the rest being commission merchants or shopkeepers, lawyers, artizans, and Christian teachers. Of these, none but Missionaries contemplate a permanent residence in the country. The Governor-General remains so long as the Ministry with which he is connected is in power, except ill health or misdeeds require his return. Officers, civil and military, may revisit their father-land on furlough at the expiration of ten years, an additional ten allowing them to remain at home upon the pension of their rank. Judges and other high officials often reside in the country from thirty to forty years—their income being ample—their health but slightly impaired,—and their habits so Indianized as to render a return to European customs undesirable and repulsive. Common soldiers at the close of twenty years' service may return to their western home, though some among them form matrimonial alliances with the daughters of their countrymen or East Indians, constituting a community of their own, and subsisting on their annual stipend, with the addition of small sums they may in various ways secure. Among them are a few respectable and worthy persons, while the majority become enslaved to intemperance and lie down in a dishonored and unlamented grave. In the ranks of the India soldiery may at times be found men of high families, classical education, brilliant genius, and accomplished manners. Family feuds, disappointed attachments and vicious acts, caused them in haste or from seeming necessity to enlist, and here they are leading a life of toil and wretchedness—a sad, but self-inflicted punishment for error and sin. Parents and friends at times trace their relatives to India, and the Prodigal willingly accepts from those he left in disgust and rage, the *twenty pounds* required for his redemption from debasing and toilsome service. I am acquainted with editors, bank accountants, teachers, musicians, and artists, who went to India as common soldiers, and, through the benevolence of others, or borrowed money, obtained their release from military servitude.

The time has been when to be connected with a house of agency at Calcutta, Madras, or Bombay was a certain passport to a princely fortune. But those palmy days have long gone by. Property is, it is true, still accumulated, but with greater toil and less speed. The trade between India and the west furnishes, of course, much business to the houses of commission; but there are rival claimants for patronage, and years must elapse ere a sufficient amount be realized to allow the senior partner to retire, and yield his place to a junior colleague. Besides commission merchants, there are to be met with in the most important cities of India, auctioneers, artizans and shopkeepers, who are toiling for wealth in that misnomered land of gold and gems. The children of foreign residents are sent home at the early period of five to ten years; regard to health, habits and mental culture rendering the change absolutely necessary. The instances in which childhood and adult years have been passed in India with no prejudice to body, mind, or morals, are " few and far between."

In addition to the four general classes now named, the traveller through India meets with *Arabs*, the horse-jockies of the country, shrewd, daring and unscrupulous; with *Parsees*, or fire worshipping Ghebers, descended from the original inhabitants of Persia, who devote themselves to merchandise on a small scale; with *Chinese* adventurers, especially on the west and eastern frontiers, who import the fancy articles of their ingenious country, and manufacture shoes and other wearing apparel; and, at the southern extremity of the Peninsula, with *Jews* who for centuries have remained isolated and distinguished from the heathen and Mohamedans around, not "bowing down to idols" but worshipping God, after the manner indicated in the books of Moses and the Prophets.

These last are divided into ancient, or *Black*, and modern, or *White Jews*, whose origin and history has awakened just, and very deep interest, throughout the Christian world. The reader who would further acquaint himself with the descendants of an ancient and honored ancestry, as also with the *Syrian Christians*, who inhabit the same southern region, is commended to the writings of Dr. Buchanan, who visited those communities in the early part of the present century, and has left on record the results of his investigation, in his deeply interesting "*Researches in Asia.*"

## CHAPTER V.

### GOVERNMENT OF INDIA.

**The three Presidencies—Governor-General—Metropolitan Bishop—Officers, &c. in the four Departments, Revenue, Judicial, Military, and Ecclesiastical—General Remarks.**

INDIA has been divided by her British rulers, into the three *Presidencies* of Bengal, Madras, and Bombay, which are located in the north and north-east, south, and west and north-west parts of the Peninsula. These large sections are sub-divided into districts, Zillahs, villages and hamlets. Each presidency is under the guidance and control of a Governor, assisted by three members of council, all of whom receive their appointments from the Court of Directors in London—the governors of Madras and Bombay being inferior in rank and authority to the one residing at Calcutta, who is honored with the title of Governor-General. This officer supports a state dignity scarcely inferior to that of an independent sovereign. The office is sought for by the highest dignitaries of the realm, as, in addition to honor and emolument, the occupant is a Privy councillor, and entitled to vice-regal privileges and respect. The names of Clive, Hastings, Wellesley and Ellenborough occupy a leading place on the pages of English political history. In respect to rank, the officer next succeeding the Governor-General, is the Metropolitan, whose home is also at Calcutta. This post has been held by the learned Middleton, the amiable and lamented Heber, and the thoroughly protestant and boldly practical Wilson.

The British residents of a rank inferior to that of those named, may be arranged into four general classes:—the *revenue*—the *judicial*—the *military*—and the *ecclesiastical.*

The Revenue department includes those officers who are devoted to the general supervision of the people, with special reference to the collection of the rents. One of these resides in each district, under the title of Collector, with an Assistant. His power is great, respecting all, European or Native, within his limits; nothing of a public nature being allowed to occur without his knowledge and permission. His responsibilities are weighty, his duties arduous, and his better feelings often being put to a severe test. The British government is virtually a rack renting landlord:—the *Ryotwarre system*, as it is called, which prevails throughout most of the country being compared to a "cider screw, while each district is like the squeezed apple, the collectors applying the extent of their power and then transferring the handle to their successors." The assessment is variable, being annually made, according to an actual survey of every acre of the ground and its measure of productiveness. The whole extent of the Province is divided into three classes; the *dry field*, the *irrigated field*, and the *irrigated garden land:* these being again distinguished by a subordinate classification of twenty varieties in each division. When the peasant's crop fails or is defective, remissions of tax are made; when it is unusually abundant there is an increased assessment. When the crop of one inhabitant of a village fails, his neighbors are required to make good the deficiency; and when the crops of a whole village fail or are defective, the neighboring ones are required to make up the difference to the State. The estimated proportion of the gross produce of the soil, taken as tax by the government, under this system is *forty-five parts in a hundred.* But this is not all; for in every village there are several officers to each of whom a proportion must be allotted. There is the *Brahmin*, or public priest, the *Astrologer*, who lets the people know when the stars and seasons are in proper humor for favoring the labors and enterprizes of the village; the *Potail*, or Mayor, the *Clerk*, or register of events and transactions, the *Guardsman*, the *Schoolmaster*, the *Barber*, *Doctor*, *Musician*, *&c.*, each claiming his share, which the owner withholds at the peril of serious loss in the future. The respect in which the oppression is greatest, is, that the government is so unwilling or unable to lose the revenue, and the consequent effort made by the Zemindar or lessee to obtain the required amount from the people under his charge, be their harvest what it may. Here is demanded on the part of the revenue officer, constant and most watchful vigilance; the effort being ever made by the Zemindar and Rygots to convince him that payment of the full amount is quite impossible, and thus induce him to petition government for a reduction of assessment. If he be a person of natural kindness of heart, the appeal is hard to resist, while over against this Sylla stands the Charybdis of Governmental displeasure. The fact is notorious to those much versed in Indian affairs, that the "reputation and prospects of a collector depend, to a large extent, upon his realizing a full revenue and that a recommendation for reduction in the amount of assessment is considered in the light of a register of his own inefficiency.

> "But let their income fail them to a pound,
> 'Ware, 'ware, my friend, for this is tender ground.
> Lo! what a hubbub rises o'er his head;
> What sundry sharp and cutting things are said
> Of *mere incompetence* and *sheer neglect*,
> And what, if it recurs, he must expect."

These circumstances render the position of a Collector of Revenue onerous, responsible and trying. A contest is ever going on between the wishes of those between whom he stands as umpire and his own better feelings—his regard to mercy, truth, and faithfulness, and his self interest. But the office is one of great honor, and much emolument, (the salary averaging $15,000 per annum) and is, therefore, notwithstanding its toil and anxiety, eagerly sought and highly prized.

The *Judicial department* comprises the several officers who have in charge the administration of justice. Calcutta, Madras, and Bombay, are each the residence of a Chief Justice and Puisne Judge—persons eminent for their attainments in the legal profession, and placed, by the amount of their salaries, above all temptation of unfaithfulness to the truth. While Sir Wm. Jones was making deep research into Hindoo literature and science he was presiding with great ability over the Metropolitan Court. Of inferior rank to these are the *Session Judges*, which answer to the Justices of the State of New York, who examine into the merits, and adjudicate cases, which come before them through the Collector of the district, their decisions going to the Presidency Court for review. Each village has its police, with power to dispose of minor offences, reporting the same to the Collector. There is still another court, intermediate between the Sessions and the village, the judges of which are natives, or East-Indians, and conducted in the language of the country. In the chief cities there is a court of high grade, called the Foujde a dawlit, and answering to our Court of Appeals. Natives can be tried at any of these courts, Europeans only before the Judges of their own country. In the Supreme Courts, *juries* have the decision of cases, but in the Sessions this is left to the Judges, from whom appeals can be made to Calcutta, and thence to the "Queen in council." Every court of importance has attached to it natives, well versed in the different languages of the country, and in Hindoo and Mohamedan Law. The *Sherishtadar*, the Collector's assistant, is a native of rank and high salary. Integrity and truthfulness are essential requisites in one holding this appointment, but confidence is too often sadly misplaced. The *Tahsildar*, who presides over several villages, is entrusted with important duties, and maintains considerable state. *Peons*, or native constables, are ever to be met with, bearing their badge of office, in the form of a belt over the right, and under the left shoulder, and staff in hand ready to quell disturbance and afford relief.

The *Military department* is by far the largest of the four, though inferior in rank to those named. India was conquered by the sword, and force is still required to keep it in subjection. The Indian army is composed of two general classes;—the *European*, which forms part of the standing army of England, but who are sent to the East for a term of years, and at the expense of the E. India Company, the whole number of which, cavalry, artillery, infantry, sappers, miners, and engineers, varying not far from *forty thousand* rank and file; and the native *Seapoys*, of whom there are about two hundred regiments of a thousand each. These corps are officered by Englishmen, with native subordinates called *Subhadars*, *Jemadars*, *Harildars*, *Naiks*, &c. That these few thousand soldiery should be able to keep the millions of India in complete subjection, carrying their arms into rebellious territories, and neighboring provinces, and with uninterrupted success, is a fact which finds not its like in the history of any nation, present or past. It would appear, in looking at the subject from a distance, that a conquering state could not rely upon the fidelity of soldiers obtained from the nations conquered. Yet the native troops of India have shown that such confidence may be placed without harm. On repeated occasions have the faithfulness and heroism of the Seapoy been put to the severest test, but never has hope been disappointed. The disaffections that occurred at Vellore, Hyderabad, and Bangalore were occasioned by too great and needless encroachment upon national usages, and urged on by men of aspiring character and ancient family who aimed at a regaining of ancestral dignity and renown. The British Colonies in Burmah, China, Singapore, and Aden, are all defended by native troops from India. After a term of service, the Seapoy is pensioned by the government, which furnishes an additional motive to fidelity. Not less than half a million of natives are dependent upon the national treasury.

India has been territorially assigned to the Church of England and Scotland, and a revenue secured by land rental, goes to the support of the *Ecclesiastical department.* The Archbishop resides at Calcutta, and subordinate bishops at Madras and Bombay, and invested with such official importance that the *Lord Padre Sahib* is second only in rank to the governors.

*Chaplains* have been settled in some seventy or eighty places, among whom the names of Henry Martyn—Brown—Thomason—Buchanan—Corrie, and Hough, are not alone worthy of honorable mention for fidelity in ministerial duty.

By means of the four departments now named, revenues are secured for the advantage of the holders of the East India Company stock—the rights of justice are made to be respected by the community at large—rebellions are quelled, and quiet sustained—while the spiritual wants of the residents are supplied from teachers of their heaven-descended faith.

"The protection of private property is now generally effected by a British administration, though cases of personal hardship occur; bodily suffering and barbarian punishments are restrained; means for an equitable administration of justice have been provided; superior courts of appeal have been established; native chiefs and tributary princes have been compelled to submit to law, and observe something like equity in their proceedings; a vigilant police for the suppression of crime and trial by jury have been either established or restored; the most perfect toleration of religious differences exists, and protection is afforded to each person in the observance of the rites of his chosen religion; peace reigns in districts formerly distracted and torn by the contentions of despots; industry is protected from robbery and private wrong, while the enterprising and successful may amass capital without alarm and enjoy it in security; colonization by European citizens, and the increased liberty of the native and country-born population, the freedom of the press, and rapid intercourse with Britain is opening channels of instruction and giving an impetus to knowledge and enquiry, unprecedented in the past history of India."

Another writer, himself too, an Englishman, expresses himself very differently. A few lines from his poem will suffice to illustrate his view of the conduct of his countrymen towards that conquered people:

> "We're always taking, and we never give;
> We care not if they die or if they live;
> Hard task-masters! beyond a Pharoah's law,
> We first withhold, and then we take the straw,
> Yet look to see the tale of bricks the same,
> If not, 't is them, and not ourselves to blame:
> For joy or wretchedness, for weal or woe,
> We've one sole sentence, "*Pay us what you owe.*"

With no desire to act the part of an apologist for all of England's wrongs, past or present, towards India, I am yet of the opinion that the satirist has allowed himself a latitude of opinion, and severity of statement, better accordant with poetic license, and perhaps wounded ambition, than sober truth. While there is much of duty left undone, I do not believe that England is as faithless to her trust as this writer would fain have us believe. There is, however, ample room for improvement.

# CHAPTER VI.

## PERSONAL APPEARANCE AND DRESS OF THE HINDOOS.

Figure and Physiognomy—Bodily Structure and Strength—Pedestrian Agility and Endurance—Emblematical Marks upon the Forehead, Neck, &c.,—Dress of the Men, of the Women, of the Children—Ornaments; their Kind, Value, and Dangers.

WITH differences of figure and aspect, arising from varieties of climate and occupation, there is a family likeness among the native Hindoos, which sufficiently marks them as one people. Their complexion is of various shades, from a light brown to a deep jet—the face oval, with a forehead neither high nor commanding—eyes soft and dull—eyebrows generally well-formed—nose and mouth of European cast—hair black, long, wiry, and not at all inclined to curl—with a general expression soft and retiring, though accompanied with a dash of cunning, which puts you on your guard against that unfortunate hypocrisy which seldom has its concealed abode under a perfectly innocent exterior. Without the high cheek-bone of the North American Indian, or the thick lips and curly locks of the African, or the fiery eye of the Malay, or the impassioned look of the Arabian, the national features bear a close resemblance to those of the Caucasian race, of which they are commonly considered a branch, and from which they differ chiefly in the size and projection of their ears, and in general dignity of carriage and address, caused, to a large extent, by their condition as a conquered, enslaved, and, of course, obsequious people.

Women of the higher classes are characterized by forms delicate and graceful—hair fine and long—eyes dark and languishing—with skins polished and soft. No country furnishes a style of female beauty superior to that which is found among the higher circles of Hindoo society. Whatever of attractiveness the lower classes may possess during the early years of life, is effaced by uncontrolled tempers, menial pursuits, rough usage, and want of mental cultivation.

In *bodily form and structure* the Hindoos are, as a nation, of a much lighter frame than the inhabitants of higher and invigorating regions. Still, in this respect, a diversity exists, even in that country—the mountaineers of the North being strong and muscular, while the southerners are of a more slender and delicate form. The traveller is struck with the difference between the appearance of a company of India seapoys and British grenadiers, though the army contains some of the finest forms the country can supply.

Free use of ghee, and other oleaginous articles of food, often produces corpulency, (there deemed a great beauty,) but not a giant frame. Palanquin bearers,

Cavardy and other Coolies, by a practice which begins in childhood, become able to bear heavy burdens, but as a general rule, their physical organization is incompatible with great bodily strength.

In *pedestrian agility, and power of long endurance*, many Hindoos are scarcely behind the natives of North America. A set of bearers will carry a palanquin, heavily laden, forty miles between the setting and rising of the sun, returning with the same the following night. The groom always accompanies the horse, and is seldom far behind when the rider reaches the end of his course. The Coolies, employed in unlading ships, will carry bags of salt and rice, to and from the shore and store-house, scarcely inferior in weight, to those borne by London porters. Mail carriers move at a regular speed of six miles to the hour, be the contents of the leather bags upon their head ponderous or light. The mass of community, however, do not excel in strength of body and limb, but are far superior to Europeans in speed of foot.

A custom, universal among the native inhabitants of India, and one which attracts a foreigner's early attention, is that of *inscribing various marks upon the forehead, neck, and arms*, with a paste, made of sandal wood, and cow's manure, moistened by water, and rubbed upon a stone. Of these, the simplest is a small circle about an inch in diameter impressed on the middle of the forehead. Another mode is that of drawing horizontal lines across the forehead, neck, &c., or perpendicular ones from the top of the forehead to the nose. The origin of this singular custom is veiled in obscurity, but its present intent is twofold; it distinguishes the wearer as a disciple of Brahminism, while it indicates to which of the two great sects he belongs. The *Vishnuvites* make the lines *perpendicular*, and the *Sivites*, *horizontal*. A part of the religious observances of each morning is to imprint this emblematical sign, (a box or bag of the material being kept prepared in every dwelling,) and to be seen abroad without it, subjects the delinquent to the reproof and persecution of his neighbors and townsmen. One of the first and most absolute requirements of a Christian convert is to remove his "*sacred ashes*," and to appear in public with the least portion of this mark of the beast upon forehead, neck or arms, brings upon the transgressor the censure of his religious teacher, and, if it be repeated, exclusion from church communion and privileges. It is understood by all to be a declaration of attachment to Paganism in preference to any other creed. Females put but a small quantity upon the forehead, while the fakeers, or devotees, besmear their whole visible person with this whitened dust.

The *dress* of respectable Hindoos is simple, decorous, suited to the climate, and, when well adjusted, produces a very graceful effect. The garments worn by the *men* consist of a loose piece of white cotton cloth, in which there are neither strings, buttons or pins, wound close about the waist, and falling below the knees, with a second, of finer material, though similar color, thrown across the shoulder, like a Roman toga, and, except the head, arms, and feet, covering the entire body. A native, when he saw a picture of his majesty, George the Third, in a Roman habit, was heard to ask, "why he wore garments like the Hindoos, and not like the English?" The hair is usually cut or shaved close to the scalp, except a small lock in the rear of the head, the removal of which is an act of great turpitude. The majority of the people leave the head uncovered, unless the heat or cold constrain the person to draw his upper garment over it like a hood; (in this respect, also, imitating the custom of ancient Rome.) The more respectable classes, especially they who associate with foreigners, cover the head with the *turban*;—an article which consists of a strip of cotton cloth, narrow and long, wound, when damp, upon a block of a required size and shape, and, when dry, removed and worn as a hat. It can be unwound, washed, and re-made when need be—its color, shape, &c., suiting the taste of the wearer. Before a Hindoo puts on a new garment, he plucks a few threads out of it, which he offers to different divinities, that they may be propitious, and that it may wear well. The *feet* are protected from sharp stones, by means of the *sandal*, or leather sole, with a strap above the instep, and another across the large toe, or are encased in *shoes* made with velvet "uppers," covered with gold and silver thread, open at the heel, and turned up at the toe in true oriental style. Stockings are seldom worn, never, indeed, over two thirds of the Peninsula. Besides the expense, which could illy be incurred, and the great heat, this article of dress would stand much in the way of a free and unrestrained use of those serviceable parts of the human body—the *toes*. We, in this western world, place a high estimate upon these extremities of the frame—indispensable as they are deemed in walking. But to appreciate their exceeding utility, it is needful to go to the East. They are called by the Hindoos the "feet fingers." In addition to the use made in keeping the shoe on the foot, the tailor, if he does not thread his needle, twists his thread by them, the cook is aided by them in cutting his meat; the joiner in holding the board while he planes it; the driver wrenches the tail of the ox to make it move more quickly; the pedestrian picks up whatever may have fallen, by the same means. To confine the toes within the narrow limits of stockings or socks, were to deprive the Hindoo of a medium of effort he can illy dispense with. Natives who are much in the society of Europeans, wear a long, loose gown, beneath the toga, which completely covers the upper part of the body, and the arms. The ornaments worn by Hindoo gentlemen, are confined to rings upon the fingers, ear-drops, a band about the arm, and, after marriage, a small band around the toe. The more abundant, showy, and expensive decorations are left to their "better halves."

The *females* of India have fewer articles of dress than their sons and brothers, but these are large, and very graceful. The *Chalice* consists of a long piece of cotton, muslin or silk, wrapped round the middle, and falling in ample and elegant folds below the knees. One end is gathered into a bunch in front, while the other crosses the breast, and is thrown over the shoulder. Its length is from seven to ten yards, and as to color, texture, and value, may vary from one of plain white cotton, costing but a dollar, to one of muslin or silk, valued at ten times that amount. To this garment is at present very generally added a *jacket*, with half sleeves, which closely fits the form, and covers, though not conceals, the bust. This simple attire is in wide contrast with that which prevailed in this country less than twenty years ago, when two bushel sleeves, and a head dress broad as the umbrella of a native prince, gave the belles of America, an outline, which, if filled up with sinew and bone, would have made them, of all created beings, the most unmeaning in shape, either for use or beauty. I remarked that the ladies of India appropriated to themselves the larger share of decorative ornaments. Upon each wrist are bracelets of silver, konk-shell, or glass, called *bangles*, numbering from five to twenty. Pendants of gold, or less valuable material, are suspended from the ear to the shoulder, and hooks, through the nose, reach to the chin. Bands of silver, of much weight, encircle the arms and ancles. On two or more of the toes is a silver ring, one of which emits a tinkling sound when the wearer is walking Around the neck are hung strings of large beads, of coral, or glass, with collars set with small gems and precious stones. Married ladies wear about the neck, the *tarlé*, which is either a band of gold richly chased, or a silk net-work entwined with silver cord. This is put on at the bridal ceremony, and is not removed till the husband's death. The long black hair, neatly combed and made glossy with oil, is rolled up in a tasteful manner, and placed a little in the rear of the left ear. The face is daily covered with a solution of saffron in water, which produces the effect (of course *not designedly*) of concealing the lady's age. The eye-lashes are extended by means of a little paint, and the teeth reddened by a masticatory common in the country. An India lady's jewels are called her "joys," (suntōshŭms) and large sums are annually expended by husbands and fathers in their purchase.

*Children* wear but the slightest clothing until they reach the fifth or sixth year—though ofttimes decorated with ornaments, profuse and valuable.

The value of these ornaments tempt the cupidity of robbers, who mutilate the bodies of the sleeping females and children to gain possession of these coveted appendages.

# CHAPTER VII.

## COURTEOUS CUSTOMS.

Hindoos a polite people—Visit from a native—Salaam—Nămăskārŭm—Săshtămgăm—Modes of addressing Superiors—Epistles—Materials of writing—Different styles of address, to an inferior, an equal, and a superior—Remark by Abbé Du Bois.

In their forms of address and behavior in company, the Hindoos may be considered a polite nation. While it cannot be denied that many of their courteous phrases and lowly prostrations, are given as the requirement of custom, rather than the language of the heart, yet to the eye and ear there is much that is agreeable and prepossessing in their conversation and deportment, especially before strangers and superiors. An illustration of some of these customs will place the subject clearly before the mind of the reader.

I am at my table, writing, when a native visitor is announced. Permission being given him to come in —he slips off his sandals, leaving them on the verandah—removes his toga from his shoulders, binding it around his waist—and entering the room, approaches me, with his body slightly bent forward, his arms outstretched in front, and upon the upturned palms of his joined hands, presents me two or more limes, as a peace offering. These I graciously receive, with my *right* hand, and place them upon the table, while he makes his *salaam*, either by raising his right hand to his forehead, and letting it fall to its former position at the side, or bowing and touching my feet and his forehead in three rapid successions, or in bending still lower, grasping my feet and placing his hand on the crown of his head. This over, I ask him to take a seat, which he does, "*pedibus intortis*," on the *floor!* I do not request him to move his hat, for that is not required by the rules of Hindoo etiquette. In reply to the usual interrogatory, '*Are you well?*' he says: '*By your favor, sir, I am well*,' or, if he be of a serious disposition, '*By God's grace and your favor, sir, I am well.*' To avoid all unfortunate improprieties I ask no questions about his *wife*, but inquire, in general terms, if the *family are well*, to which a similar reply is returned. As various topics come up, it is noticeable that he dissents from nothing I advance—expresses a strong desire always to have my favor—enters into no argument, lest he seem to intimate an equality with me in mind and knowledge—in a word, he makes the greatest effort to increase my self-esteem, while he forgets not to put in a good word for himself and friends, and the opposite for his enemies. If at any time he does not quite hear me, he leans forward, *putting his hand upon his mouth*, that his breath may not incommode me. If a superior in rank, European or native, enter, he rises, makes his salaam, and resumes his lowly posture. After the interview has been continued for a sufficient time, I have a very convenient, and not at all ungenteel mode of dispensing with his society, in telling him, simply—*to go*. If he be of a highly respectable class, and one whose acquaintance I desire to continue —I say, slightly rising from my seat, and with a salaam-like movement of my hand, "*Going, come again*," and he at once returns my salutation, and departs. So far from being offended at the request, he has been waiting, it may be, to receive it, for *without such permission, he cannot with propriety close the interview*. It is not at all impossible that the reader may suggest the propriety of importing this custom into our more civilized country, it being very convenient, at times, to say to a visitor, *you have staid long enough for once, just go home and come at another time*.

So much for his appearance within doors; let us now observe him *without*. He has replaced his sandals, thrown his garment across his shoulder, and is passing from the yard on his way home. We will take our umbrella and follow at such a distance in the rear that he cannot understand our motive, while we may observe his movements. He pays no attention to any female, not even a wife and mother, except to ask a question or give a command. Did you see that movement? He put the palms of his hands together and raised them far above his head, letting them fall again to his side: that is called *Nămăskărŭm*, and was addressed to a Brahmin. Had we been near enough, we should have observed the priest stretch out his hands towards this passer by, palms upward, as if bestowing a blessing. Now, mark, he is passing a temple;—(observe his movements)—he stops—removes his sandals—gazes a moment at the shrine—prostrates himself at full length, so that toes, knees, hands, forehead, nose, and chin touch the ground, (an act of reverence called *Sāshtāmgăm*)—rises—crosses himself—mutters a few prayers—replaces his shoes—and pursues his way. You observe the great care he takes not to allow his dress to touch a passer by, as defilement would follow the unholy contact. A carriage is coming towards him, conveying a wealthy and honored townsman. (Mark his movements.) He stops at the roadside, slips off his sandals, adjusts his attire, and as the carriage moves by, he bends to the earth, carrying his hands rapidly from his head to the ground, and recovering his former position, goes onward as before. At no time do you hear him talk and laugh in a boisterous manner—this is beneath his dignity, and foreign to all rules of Hindoo propriety. He pays high regard to all whom he deems superior in rank, and whose favor it is his interest to seek or retain, slightly noticing his equals, and looking down with supercilious contempt upon all females and pariars. He has reached his dwelling, and there we lose sight of him, for into the domestic sanctuary a stranger may not intrude.

It may not be amiss, before closing my remarks upon Hindoo politeness, to mention a few of their phrases when addressing superiors, and benefactors. When a native of India enters the presence of his spiritual guide, he prostrates himself, and laying hold of his feet, looks up into his face and says, "*You are my Saviour;*"—to a benefactor, "*You are my father and mother;*"—to one whom he wishes to praise, "*You are religion incarnate,*" or, "*You are a sea of excellent qualities,*" or, "*You are the father and mother of brahmins and cows.*" The like complimentary expressions are employed in directing letters. Thus a letter to a *King* would be directed, "To the great, the excellent, the prosperous, the illustrious King K——, the nourisher of multitudes, the fragrance of whose fame has spread throughout the world, before whose glory the sun obscures its beams, whose fame is as pure as the queen of night," &c. To a *Father*, thus, "To the excellent person my father, the author of my existence, whose mind drinks the honey on the water-lily feet of the Deity," &c. To a *Mother*, thus, "To my excellent and dignified mother, who feeding, nourishing and comforting me, raised me to manhood, at thy feet I supplicate, which are the water-lilies on the reservoir of my heart," &c.

The missionary, little known in his own country, beyond a limited circle of relatives and neighbors, when in India, receives letters addressed to "*The great and powerful and illustrious Rajah*"—or "To the beneficent and glorious deity (*Swamy*.")

In external appearance, and construction of expressions, a Hindoo letter has noticeable features. The material is the palm leaf, the folds being about eighteen inches long, and an inch in breadth. The writing is executed with an iron stile, four to six inches long, and sharp pointed at the end. In writing neither chair or table is wanted, the leaf being supported on the middle finger of the left hand, and kept steady by being kept between the thumb and the forefinger. The right hand does not, as with us, move along the surface, but after finishing a few words, the writer fixes the point of the iron pen in the last letter, and pushes the leaf from the right hand toward the left, so as to enable him to finish his line. This becomes so habitual and easy that one often sees a Hindoo writing as he walks the street. As this species of penmanship is but a kind of faint engraving, the strokes of which are indistinct, and almost invisible, they besmear the leaf with an ink-like fluid, to make the characters clearly legible. In respect to an epistle, it is often put upon a single leaf, which, when finished, they envelope in an outer leaf, upon which they write the address. When there is occasion to communicate the decease of a relative, the custom is to *singe the point of the leaf* upon which the afflicting news is written. This has a like import as the black seal used by us. When a superior writes to an inferior, he puts his own name before that of the person to whom he writes, and the reverse when he writes to a superior. That the reader may have a view of the different modes of epistolary composition common in the country, I have extracted three letters from the volume by the Abbé Du Bois.

## I.

### LETTER TO AN INFERIOR.

They, the Brahmin Soubaya, to him, Lakshmana, who has all good qualities, who is true to his word, who is ever rendering service to his relations and friends.

Year of Kilaka, the fourth day of the month Phalguna. I am at Banavara, in good health. Send me news of thine. As soon as this letter shall have reached thee, thou shalt go to the most excellent Brahmin Anantaya, and prostrating thyself at all thy length at his feet, thou wilt offer him my most humble respects, and then, without delay, thou shalt present thyself before the Shelta (the merchant) Rangapa, and declare to him that if he shall now put into thy hands the three thousand Rupees which he owes me, with interest, at twenty-five per centum, I will forget all that is past, and the matter shall then be at an end. But if on the contrary, he makes shifts, and continues to defer the payment of the money, tell him that I am acquainted with a method of teaching him that no person shall safely break his word with a

Brahmin, such as I am. This is all I have to say to thee. *Aseervatham.*

## II.

### LETTER TO AN EQUAL.

To them, the Lord, to the Lord Ramaya, who possesses all the good qualities which can render a man esteemed, who is worthy to obtain all the favors which the gods can bestow; who is the beloved of beautiful women, who is the particular favorite of Lakshmi; who is great as the Mount Meru, and who has a perfect knowledge of the Yajur Veda: the Brahmin Sabaya; *Nămăskārŭm*, (respectful greeting).

The year Durmati, the sixteenth of the month Phalguna. I am at Balore, where I and all the members of my family enjoy good health. I shall learn with great gladness that it is the same with you; and I trust you will inform me particularly of all the subjects of satisfaction and contentment which you experience.

On the twenty-second of the month above mentioned, being a day in which all good omens unite, we have chosen that the marriage of my daughter Vijaya Lakshu shall be celebrated. I beg you will honor the ceremony with your presence, and be here before that day with all the persons of your household, without excepting any. I expect you will put yourself at the head of the ceremony, and that you will be pleased to conduct it; and if there is anything in which I can be of service to you, have the goodness to let me know it: This is all I have to apprise you of. *Nămăskăram.*

## III.

### LETTER TO A SUPERIOR.

To them, the Lord, to the Lord Brahmin to the great Brahmin Anantaya, who are endowed with every virtue and all good qualities; who are great as Mount Meru; who possess a perfect knowledge of the four Vedas; who, by the splendor of their good works, shine like the sun; whose renown pervades the fourteen worlds. I, Kisheraya, their humble servant, and slave, keeping my distance, with both hands joined, my mouth closed, mine eyes cast down, wait in this humble posture, until they shall vouchsafe to cast their eyes on him who is nothing in their presence, after obtaining their leave, approaching them with fear and trembling, and prostrating myself at my full length before the flowers of Nenryhar, on the ground where they stand; and thus submissive, with respectful kisses, will I address their feet with this humble supplication.

The year Vikari, the twentieth of the month Paushya, I, humble servant and slave, whom your excellence has deigned to regard as something, having received with both hands the letter which you humbled yourself by writing to me, after kissing it and putting it on my head, I afterwards read with the profoundest attention, and I will execute the orders it contains without departing from them the breadth of a grain of Sesamum. The affair on which your excellence vouchsafed to command me, is in good progress, and I hope that by the efficacy of your benediction, it will soon terminate to your entire satisfaction. As soon as that happens, I, your humble servant and slave, shall not fail to present myself (agreeably to the order of your excellence) at the flowers of Niluphar of your holy feet. I now entreat your excellence to impart to me the commands and instructions necessary to enable me so to demean myself as to be agreeable to their will, and that you will clearly point out to me in what manner I may render myself most acceptable to your blessed feet. For this, it will suffice, if I receive from your bounty a leaf of betel, indented with your nail, in care of some confidential person, who can verbally explain the orders of your excellency.

Such is my humble prayer.

The Abbé observes that the " style of these letters strikes us as extraordinary—being so remote from that in use among us. But if we attentively consider the epistolary forms that still prevail in the west, and analyze the letters which Europeans often write to their equals, generally concluding as an *honor* to be favored with admission in the number of their *most humble and most obedient servants*, it will not be easy to determine which style of the two is the more ridicu lous and puerile. The principal difference, perhaps is, that in the Hindoo letters, the fulsome compli ments are inserted at the *beginning*, and in ours, at the *end*."

# CHAPTER VIII.

## A HINDOO AT HOME.

**Native dwelling described—Furniture—Its apartments, especially the Room of Anger—The Hindoo returning home—Preparations for a meal—Rice and curry—Mode of eating—Sleeping-room—Different modes pertaining to different classes—Price of dwelling—Evil Eye, and other superstitious fears—Flower gardens—Market—Times of eating—Topics of conversation.**

THE wealth, taste, and rank of the owner or occupant have, of course, to do with the size, material, and elegance of the Hindoo house, though not as much as with us. I will select, for illustration, the home of a native belonging to the medium rank of society. His house is made of mud, hardened by the solar heat, or of unburnt brick, about thirty feet square, one story in height, covered with tiles placed upon rafters of bamboos or palmyra trees, split to the necessary size. Along the entire front of the building is a verandah about four feet deep, sheltered by the projecting roof, while in the wall are triangular indentations where lamps are placed when the street or building is to be illuminated. Entering the low door, which occupies a central position, we see on either side a small verandah or alcove, formed of baked clay; where the inmate receives visitors, or waits the preparation of the meal. Passing on, we remark that the centre of the house is an open court—unprotected from the sun and rain by any roof—upon the sides of which are rooms, small, and lighted by grated windows, which serve little purpose but to make "darkness more visible." One of these apartments is appropriated to the idol—(the Roman "Penates,") and the rest to the various members of the household. The articles of furniture are a few stools—a low wooden bedstead—a loose mat—and a box for clothing, books, and ornaments. In the kitchen may be seen several earthen vessels (called in southern India *chatties*) some for cooking, and others for holding the food when made ready—a few small brass drinking dishes—an earthen barrel to contain the unhulled rice, with a stone mortar and heavy pounder to prepare it for use—a brass pedestal to which is attached a lamp of eastern style, and sometimes a table of limited size and height—all of the most simple kind. Some of the nabobs of Calcutta and Madras, "*a la mode Anglais*," keep large pier glasses, chairs, couches, pictures, and the like, but these pertain not to a purely Hindoo dwelling, and often contrast most amusingly with surrounding objects. One apartment in the house of the rich Hindoo is appropriated to a purpose rather singular, and which, if rightly used, might be admired, though, as employed by them, of questionable utility. It is called the *room of anger, or the angry.* When a wife is much displeased she runs to this room and shuts herself up, there remaining till her husband comes, to learn the cause of her displeasure, and if possible, remove it. But her chagrin most frequently arises from her not having the luxuries of eating, dress, and equipage, which her more favored neighbor enjoys, and until that is provided for her, he must expect to be debarred the society of his amiable spouse. If it were not for fearing to impute to the husbands of our western continent less pliancy than their uncivilized brethren of the East manifest, the writer would be disposed to express a fear, that many wives of America would be allowed to remain in their self-imprisonment, with their demands ungratified, until hunger and thoughtfulness had appeased their irritation. But this by the way.

We have seen the Hindoo at the residence of a foreigner, our eye has been upon him when walking the street—though not allowed to enter his dwelling, we may, through the eyes of others, view him at home. The labors of the day are over, and he has returned to partake of the evening meal and enjoy a night's repose. His wife, during his absence, has been preparing his food, which, to a large extent, consists of a dish familiarly called "*rice and curry*," and may be thus briefly described: In an earthen vessel a quantity of rice is boiled, while in another, of smaller dimensions, is cooked in ghee a chicken, fish, or piece of mutton, to which are added from two to four or five spoonfuls of a powder composed of these among other ingredients: ginger, saffron, cummin, coriander, anniseed, red pepper, tamarind, tumeric, garlic, made liquid in cocoa-nut milk, the amount of these ingredients depending upon the palate and custom of the person. The meal being prepared, a small quantity is placed before the idol to propitiate his favor. The wife then puts upon the floor of an interior room a brass plate, or what is more usual, a large leaf (two or more sewed together, if one be not of sufficient size) upon which a goodly quantity of the boiled rice is then piled, and above it the before-named fragrant and delicious curry. Having brought a dish for her lord to lave his hands, he takes his lowly seat for the enjoyment of his repast. Then follows a brief prayer—which foreigners insinuate it would be well for Americans to follow. As there were wanting *table*, *chair*, *plate*, or *cloth*, what need of *knife*, *fork*, or *spoon?* The Hindoo has what is far more natural and convenient—his *fingers!* With these upon his *right* hand, he mixes the ingredients of his savory dish, and rolling a small quantity into a ball, *tosses it dexterously into his mouth*, great care being taken lest any portion fall back into the plate, since that mishap would defile the remaining mass. The reason of this extreme fastidiousness is the notion that the saliva is a very impure secretion. A Hindoo who is regardful of religious propriety never expectorates within doors (a custom to be imported also) nor, if a rigid adherent of the rules of caste, will he touch a letter which has been sealed by a wafer moistened by the tongue.

If no stranger be present, the women wait on the

men, but a Hindoo woman never sits down to eat with her husband—she and her daughters sit patiently by, and then regale themselves upon *what is left*. The meal over, his thirst quenched by water again brought to him, he retires to his couch, there to chew betel, entertain visitors, and thus lounge the hours away until the time for retiring arrives, which is usually from eight to nine o'clock. If the weather be not too warm he retires to an inner apartment, but if very sultry he chooses the verandah, and even the sandy road-side, where he converts the dress he has worn during the day into a covering wherewith to shelter himself from dew, mosquitos, and vermin—soon relapsing into a sound slumber. A stranger, when entering a Hindoo village at an early hour of the day, is strangely affected at the spectacle—multitude of sleepers lying by the roadside, wrapped in their white clothes, and presenting the appearance of so many corpses dressed in the habiliments of the tomb. Rising at dawn, the Hindoo goes to a neighboring tank, where, with religious care he cleanses his teeth, performs his sacred ablutions, imprints the emblems of his faith upon his forehead, arm, and breast, visits the idol for morning worship, returns home to take a repast from the conge drawn off from the boiled rice of yesterday, and then is prepared for the duties of the day.

Such is a view of the dwellings and domestic economy of *respectable* Hindoos. Descending to the lowest in scale we see the *Pariar*, whose home is a small and wretched hut, with walls of mud and covering of palmyra leaves—whose food consists of a few vegetables pulled from an adjoining field, to which are added a few small fish taken from a neighboring tank, or the bones of a carcass which he divides with the carrion crow and the prowling jackall. Rising to the highest station, we see the dwelling of the rich and honored of the land, large and imposing, built of brick, and with the top terraced to allow of the morning and evening promenade. Within, the apartments are of sufficient size for domestic purposes, religious pictures decorating the walls; tables and chairs indicating an acquaintance with the more tasteful foreigner, while the meal, though partaken of in the same lowly manner, and with the same natural implements, is rendered more delicious by pickles, chitneys, and other condiments that tempt the appetite of a Hindoo epicure.

The price of a moderately-sized clay house (not including the rent of the ground) is about $15, and the annual repairs not far from $10. The repairs are usually made just before the fall rains set in, and if delayed too long, the destruction of the entire building is the inevitable result.

There are many customs respecting the locality of Hindoo dwellings, and arrangements pertaining thereto which are worthy of notice. While the building is in process of construction, there may be seen near it a pole stuck into the ground, upon which is placed an earthen jar, covered with white spots, having for its design to "*keep off the evil eye,*" which would otherwise be harmful to the builder or owner. If a person meets with misfortunes in a particular house, he concludes that some bones are buried under it, and accordingly leaves it for another more fortunate spot. When a sum of money has been stolen from a dwelling, and it is quite certain that some one among its inmates is the thief, the Hindoos, in some places, rub the thumb nails of all the persons in the house, imagining that the name of the thief will become legible on the nail of the offender. Scarcely any Hindoos attach flower gardens to their houses—in that respect differing widely from the Mohamedans, before whose doors roses and evergreens may be seen in abundance. The cause of this contrast I have never heard assigned; but the fact arrests attention in the streets of city or village. The Hindoo rents his small lot—surrounds it (except it adjoin other dwellings) with a mud wall—constructs a gate with an archway and earthen lounge—puts his house in the centre—digs his well—rears his chickens—and if he can obtain employment sufficient to meet his daily expenses, has but the smallest amount of apparent care and trouble. If his house has been paid for, a salary of $2 50 per month will amply suffice to clothe and feed himself, wife, and several children. The requisites for the table of a Hindoo are bought in the market (bazaar) and paid for daily, except milk, sugar, oil, &c., which are brought to the house by the seller, who receives his payment monthly. These articles, though cheap, do not prevent the people from being generally in debt—occasioned by expensive entertainments, gifts to Brahmins and relatives, on special occasions, marriage of children, purchase of jewelry, and the like causes demanded by custom or self-gratification. The Hindoo Shastras direct that Brahmins shall eat at two o'clock in the day and again at one in the night; but this law is at present but little heeded, though but two meals are taken by the people generally. The domestic conversation turns chiefly upon the business of the family, the news of the village, religious ceremonies, journeys to holy places, marriages, narratives of heroines and gods, with other topics not peculiar to that country in distinction from regions more enlightened and Christian. So much for the *Hindoo at home.*

# CHAPTER IX.

## HINDOO WATER CRAFT AND SAILORS.

Author's arrival at Madras—Reflections—Catamaran—Massuli-boat—War Steamer—Merchantman—Dhony—Basket-boat—Budgerow.

THE morning of March 21st, 18—, found the good ship S., after a passage of 120 days from Boston, nearing the eastern shores of India. Upon her deck stood the writer, with thirteen other passengers, gazing with no small interest upon the land, which was to be their adopted home. The mind of each was too busy with its own reflections—too full of the future, to allow of much conversation. The moment long desired, had finally arrived. The hopes of years were about to be realized, but the cup of pleasure was held by a trembling hand. A veil hung before the future, not to be penetrated by human sight, and the bright angel of Hope was accompanied by her stern companion, Fear. A silence of considerable continuance was at length interrupted by the question, " What is that object upon the water in range with the distant shore ?" While the possibility and probability of its character were under discussion, we perceived it making towards us, which served but to increase interest and multiply conjecture, till one of our number exclaimed with earnestness, "It must be a *catamaran*." "And what is a catamaran?" asks my reader. The word is compound, and means literally *tied wood*. Several logs of medium thickness, measuring from twenty to thirty feet in length, are lashed together with strong ropes, one in the centre projecting beyond those at the sides, and forming a sort of prow or bowsprit. Upon this most primitive craft three or four natives plant themselves in a kneeling posture, and with short paddles, which they ply upon alternate sides, venture far out to sea for the purposes of fishing in the deep water, and trading with the foreign vessels that anchor in the roadstead. When the state of the weather prevents the use of all ordinary means of communication, a few hardy boatmen may be seen launching forth their simple float, and braving wind and waves to keep up a connection between ship and shore. Such was the object upon which our eyes rested on the evening of that memorable day. Onward it advanced, now quite sunk beneath the waves, and presenting the strange appearance of men treading the water and performing singular evolutions in the unstable element, anon rising high upon the surface; now rolling far upon the side so as to unseat all but the most skilful and experienced, then suddenly righting to its former position, despite our apprehensions for its safety. Our fears were awakened lest the unhappy boatmen should become a prey to the sharks that infest those waters. These cannot molest them while on their floats, but the danger is imminent if they be separated from this feeble yet sure defense. Even then the case is not quite hopeless, since the shark, from the position of its mouth, can only attack them from below, and a rapid dive, if not in very deep water, will sometimes save them.

All dangers escaped, the ship was reached, while nimbly sprang up the sides three swarthy sons of the East, appropriately styled "children of nature," for they were encumbered with no articles of dress beyond the smallest cotton cloth compatible with the most lax ideas of propriety or decorum. "These are the Hindoos—these the people among whom we come to dwell!" passed from the lips of one and another of our company, as they retired to the cabin to think and weep. Immediately upon reaching the deck, one of the native comers took from the interior of a conical-shaped cap, made of palmyra leaves, and worn close upon the head, a printed document, which he gave to the captain, and which was found to contain directions as to the place of anchorage, and rules to be observed while remaining in the roads. These were sent by the "Master Attendant," the head officer of the marine department in that portion of the company's dominions. After disposing of their fish, and begging a few pice, or small coin, our visitors clambered over the bulwarks, dropped upon their restless raft, loosed themselves from the ship, and made for the shore. Thus had we gained our first sight of India—of the natives—and of that original and national craft, the catamaran. At the setting of the sun we dropped anchor; after a brief twilight, the darkness of night closed around us, and we retired to rest, that we might be prepared for the excitement and fatigue of the coming day.

The last night of a four months' voyage at sea is of short duration. It was so with our company; all were out of their berths ere the sun cast its first rays upon the beautiful city of Madras. Leaving the cabin, we found upon our vessel's deck, a multitude of natives, with various articles to sell and barter, among which, were fresh bread, butter, and eggs, with plantains and other fruits quite new to our American eyes. The places of the "catamaran jacks," were filled by another and more dignified class of native seamen, called *massuli boatmen*, so named from the craft they manned, of which three or more were lashed to our vessel's side. These may need a brief description. The waves which come rushing up the Bay of Bengal, finding their current impeded by the straitening shore, fret themselves against the Coromandel coast, especially in the region of Madras, thus causing a surf, which, in the flow of the sea, and in boisterous weather, is of a height and power entirely irresistible by any boat of European build. Hence the mussuli, which, though inelegant and unwieldy in appearance, is the only kind of vessel that can pass with safety this dangerous barrier. They are usually from twenty to twenty-five feet long, six feet wide, and six deep, stern and prow pointed, planks an inch thick, with cross bars upon which the rowers sit, having for oars long poles with heart-shaped paddles, an extra one in the hand of the strong and athletic helmsman, and supplying the place of a rudder. Upon minute examination not a nail will be discovered, the several planks being lashed or sewed together with a cordage indigenous to the country, produced from the filaments composing the husk which covers the cocoa-nut, and called *coir* (kire). Sometimes it is fitted up with a board seat in the stern, above which is suspended a canvas awning, with brushwood below, and dignified with the name of *accommodation boats* or packets—being devoted exclusively to the conveyance of passengers and their light baggage. The twelve boatmen make themselves more comely by wearing a loose jacket and turban of native cotton. Several of us having joined in providing ourselves with one of the latter craft, we quitted the faithful "S." and launched forth to buffet the rolling surges of the Bengal coast. For a short distance we moved quietly and pleasantly along, the boatmen keeping time to a wild and dismal chant, which to our ears, though strange, was not unpleasant.

But this was not long to continue. At a word from the helmsman, each oar was quiet, while a swell of the sea which had gradually been advancing in our rear was allowed to pass under us, and then the oarsmen, with renewed strength, pressed onward, that they might be out of the way before a second had time to gather and break. The next feat was to pass in safety this second wave, which is usually much higher and more violent than the first. Onward it came, swiftly rolling towards us, rapidly increasing in power, but the practiced eye of the steersman saw where it was to rear its fatal crest, and kept the boat in check just in time to let it pass under and spend itself ahead. At this point they begun simultaneously to vociferate a half Moslem exclamation, "Ulla-ulla-il ulla," thus invoking the protection of the patron prophet. The reader may be assured that strong indeed must be his nerves if he do not at this time tremble for his frail bark and its passengers. Much, however, of this stamping of feet, these frightened looks, and terrible yells, is intended to awaken additional alarm, and thus secure a promised 'douceur' in case of a safe arrival at the shore. As we neared the land the surges increased in violence, till the last wave caused our faithful bark to swing high upon the shelving beach.

I had been four months upon the sea, with not an island or rock to relieve the eye in its daily wanderings. I had passed over fifteen thousand miles of water—had doubled the Cape, and seen our largest sails torn to ribbons by the storms that make their home in those desolate regions—but during this long period, while traversing the Atlantic and Indian oceans, I had known no emotion of fear. That was reserved for the Madras roadstead, with its towering and dangerous surf. But it was passed in safety, notwithstanding our fears, and we stood upon the shores of India, that wondrous and antique land—whose barbaric pearl and gold have stimulated the cupidity of nations down the long stream of time, and whose strange vicissitudes have furnished such ample matter to adorn the moralist's and historian's pages. We had little inclination, such was the heat of the sun and the Babel sounds around us, to allow full play to the many thoughts suggested by the event of arriving at the end of our long voyage, and reaching our new home in the East. Palanquins were in waiting to convey us to the dwellings of the Rev. Mr. Winslow and Dr. Scudder, who were waiting to entertain us.

Before leaving the beach, let us look for a few moments at the several kinds of vessels riding at anchor in the roadstead. There is a *war steamer*. It belongs to the Naval Department of the East India Company's forces. Of *merchantmen* there is an abundance, each from one hundred to twelve hundred tons burden. Do you see that one with tall slim masts—of light build—sitting with swan-like ease and grace upon the water? That is the S., which I have just left. Well may her commander and crew be proud of her. It is in reference to such specimens of naval architecture, that an English gentleman, of high standing in Madras, said to me that the finest and most beautiful vessels that appeared in the road were those from Boston.

Do you see those strange objects crowded together,

with their unpainted sides—lateen sails—low masts—and square bows, the picture of uncouthness and inelegance? These are *dhonies*, or native sloops, which ply up and down the coast with cargoes of rice, timber, and various kinds of merchandise. Though, like the mussuli boats, exceedingly unwieldy and destitute of symmetry and elegance, they are useful and abundant. Were you here during the prevalence of the Monsoon, not a *dhony* would you see: these barks, unfitted to encounter wind and surge, are then housed away in some safe harbor. Foreign ships are not allowed during that period to anchor in the roadstead, and even the steamers make but a short stay, and then in the far distance from the shore. The mussula boats are undergoing their annual repair, and the *catamarans* have the coast to themselves.

Having acquainted the reader with the various kinds of boats and vessels common in the Bay of Bengal, I will now take him to the banks of the Cauvery, one of the largest rivers in the Southern Peninsula, and will there show him a craft still stranger than catamaran, mussula boat, or dhony. It is a *circular basket*, ten feet in diameter, with ribs of the strong and pliant bamboo, covered with buffalo leather. I was one of fourteen persons desirous of visiting the Seringham Pagodas upon the opposite side of the stream, and obliged to cross in this way or stay at home. Not being willing to do the latter, in we got—one after the other—ladies, gentlemen, and boatmen. The first person leaned against one side and the second on the directly opposite, to secure an equipoise, the third and fourth occupying the same relative positions, till we were all safely aboard, amid various wonderments at our curious posture, and jocose remarks about the "three wise men of Gotham, who went to sea in a bowl." "All ready?" asked the head boatman in broken English. "Aye, aye, sir," answered one of us who had not lost his sea tongue. Off we pushed, and round we went again and again, while one held her breath, another smiled to conceal his unmanly fears, and a third shrieked with alarm. "*No danger!*" called out our captain. Soon we were out of the whirlpool and in the midst of the stream. On we moved with our bow(?) at one time north, again south, not forgetting the other points of compass. A half-hour of pushing and rowing served to bring us near the opposite shore, where we were whirled once and again, as before, and landed safe upon the beach, each declaring that a *boat basket* was the most unique conveyance he had yet seen or tried, and that but one thing more was needed to give interest to such an excursion, which was, that friends across the sea might witness this strange craft, defying, as it does, the poet's pen or painter's pencil.

Were the reader passing from the Bay of Bengal to Calcutta, his attention would be ever arrested by the multitude and variety of water craft moving to and from that commercial metropolis. In addition to ships of all sizes from the British isles, and continental neighbors, and western colonies, and dhonies from the various ports of the south and east, there would be seen the *Maldivian* vessels raised to an immense height above the water by upper works of split bamboo, with lofty head, and stern immense, and crowded with a wild yet skilful and resolute crew. *Bengalee and Chittagong* vessels, with immense rudders suspended by ropes to the side, and worked by a helmsman elevated high upward ; with other crafts indicating a nearer approach to European architecture, though clumsily and dangerously rigged. If desirous of continuing his progress farther into the interior, he would do well to avoid the *pinnace* and choose the *budgerow;* the former, though safer and more commodious with respect to its interior arrangements, being less calculated than the latter to pass the shallows and sand-banks of that ever-shifting stream. "The budgerow, whose name is a native corruption of the word *barge*, is therefore usually chosen by European travellers, to whom time and expense are matters of importance. Though to a certain extent, the term *clumsy* may fairly be applied to this craft, its construction and appearance are far from inelegant; with a little more painting and gilding, a few silken sails and streamers, and divested of the four-footed outside passengers and other incumbrances on the roof, it would make a very beautiful object in a picture, and in its present state it has the advantage of being exceedingly picturesque. The greater part of the lower deck is occupied by a range of apartments fitted up for the accommodation of the party engaging the boat; these are generally divided into a sleeping and a sitting room, with an enclosed verandah in front, which serves to keep off the sun, and to stow away various articles of furniture. The apartments are surrounded on all sides by Venetians, which exclude the sun in the daytime, and let in the air at night. In front of the cabins, the deck is of circumscribed dimensions, affording only space for the boatmen, who, on descending the river, facilitate the progress of the vessel, by means of long sweeps; the upper deck, therefore, or roof, is the chief resort of the crew and the servants. At the stern, the helmsman stands, perched aloft, guiding a huge rudder; the *goleer*, stationed at the prow, ascertains the depth of the water by means of a long oar; and when the wind will permit, two large square sails are hoisted, with the assistance of which, the lumbering craft goes rapidly through the water. As the budgerow is not calculated for a heavy or cumbrous freight, a *baggage boat* is necessary for the conveyance of the goods and chattels of the party, and for the accommodation of those servants who cannot be conveniently retained on board the superior vessel. A *dinghee* or wherry, is a very necessary adjunct of river navigation, but it is not always to be procured, and when one of these light skiffs cannot be attached to the larger craft, the communication between the cook boat and the budgerow is cut off; the unhappy passengers in the budgerow, after waiting in vain for the smoking supplies they had anxiously desired, are compelled to be satisfied with a less substantial meal of coffee, eggs, and dried fish. As few persons venture to move after sunset; at day-break in the morning, the vessel being pushed out into the stream, spreads her sails like a wild swan in her flight, or proceeds more leisurely by the united exertions of sixteen men dragging at a rope fastened at the mast head. Toward the middle of the day, the boat becomes insufferably hot; both sides having received the fierce glare of the burning sun; the heat is reflected from the water, which is now too dazzling for the eye to endure without pain; the morning breeze dies away, and it requires all the patience of a martyr to sustain the torments inflicted by the scorching atmosphere, especially as the roofs of the cabins are usually too low to allow a *punka* to be hung. As the sun declines, the boat gradually cools to a more agreeable temperature; and when the welcome shadows of the woods descend upon the deck, it is delightful to sit in the open air and watch the progress of the vessel as it nears the shore, to the spot appointed as its station for the night. The moment the budgerow is securely moored, a very active and animated scene commences; the domestics whose services are not required on board, and all the crew, immediately disembark; fires are kindled for the various messes—those who are anxious for quiet and seclusion, light up their faggots at a considerable distance from the boat. The rich background of dark trees, the blazing fires, the picturesque groups assembled around them, and the tranquil river below, its crystal surface crimson with the red glow of an Indian sunset, or the fleeting tint fading away, and leaving only the bright broad river—molten silver in polished steel—as the dark shadows of the night advance, form an evening landscape always pleasing and varying with the varying scenery of the ever-changing bank." Such is a budgerow as it appears upon the waters of the sacred Ganges, conveying passengers and cargo to and from Calcutta and the upper provinces. Its place is being partially supplied by small steamers, a safer and more expeditious conveyance, though confined chiefly to Europeans and the more wealthy natives. These steam-tugs are a great convenience, for many persons undergo more fatigue, are exposed to more serious casualties, and are sometimes longer in a voyage by native craft from Calcutta, to the upper provinces, than in one from Boston or London.

## CHAPTER X.

### HINDOO LAND CONVEYANCES.

Travelling propensity of the Hindoos—Primitive mode of carrying a child—Cart and Bullocks—Canopied cart—Palanquin—Tonjon—Miscellaneous vehicles in City and Town.

RELIGIOUS festivals, marriage entertainments, funeral ceremonies and mercantile transactions, furnish occasion for the people of India often to leave their homes for long and wearisome tours and pilgrimages. When whole households thus travel abroad, the parents, if very poor, have an ingenious method of sharing the toil of carrying their helpless infant. A cotton cloth, several yards in length, is spread upon the ground, the "wee thing" placed upon the inverted folds, while, with the ends tied together, the whole is slung across a bamboo pole laid upon the shoulders of father and mother, much as two draymen carry a barrel of sugar or a bag of cotton. In passing the rice fields and seeing the mother busy at her task of transplanting the tender shoot, I have often observed her infant suspended in this manner from the bough of a neighboring tree, thus removed above all danger from reptiles and vermin, while the wind performed the important office of rocking the cradle. If pecuniary means allow, an ox trained for the purpose; or an aboriginal pony is obtained, and on it is placed the luggage, above which sits the mother, with two or more of her youthful family. A method which is deemed a grade higher in respectability and comfort, is to call into use a *common cart*, in Southern India called a *bandy*, drawn by two of the inferior class of the small but hardy bullocks. These conveyances are very serviceable in conveying travellers with their baggage and utensils—the tents and stores of the soldiery—the treasure received at the out-stations for transportation to the metropolis—with the inland products that need to be brought to the seaboard towns for exportation. When heavily laden they are drawn at the slow and wearisome rate of from fifteen to twenty miles per day.

Every Hindoo village of any importance has a set of officers to regulate and control its internal affairs. The "Headman" of this constabulary force maintains no little state in respect to dwelling, dress, equipage and attendants. His official conveyance is called a *Bowbandy*, and is formed by placing upon the axletree of a common bandy a platform about five feet square, covering which is a cushion with a pillow to recline upon, while to shield from the sun and rain, a conical-shaped canopy of cotton cloth rises to the height of four or more feet, surmounted by a gilded ball, glittering in the rays of the resplendent sun. Much taste is displayed in the ornaments by which this vehicle is decorated, the axletrees and beams being painted of various hues, while the depending tassels of parti-colored silk are graceful and imposing, if not in all respects tasteful and elegant. These carriages are drawn by large milk-white bullocks, with bells about their necks, several footmen running by their side and in the rear, while a crier precedes the cavalcade, blowing at intervals a long trumpet, and informing the people that the "great man" is coming, and that they must do him reverence.

The vehicle in use among the higher classes of Hindoos, and almost wholly so among foreign residents, is the *palanquin*, which, from its importance claims a particular description.

Not long before leaving Madras, I found it necessary to visit the neighboring village of S. Having sent to the nearest place of rendezvous, the maistry, or headman of a set of bearers, soon entered my presence with a low salaam, when the following colloquy passed between us: "Well, maistry, I wish to go to S. Have you a neat palanquin and a set of good booies (bearers) all ready?" "Yes, sir—we can go at any moment the Reverend order." "How far is it?" "Four kathams," (anglicè, forty miles). "How many bearers will be needed?" "If the Reverend wishes to go through in one night, a full set of twelve men—a mussalchee, (torch-bearer) and cavardy cooly. At what time does your Reverence want to leave?" "At six o'clock. Be here all of you at that hour, and I shall be ready. But stop a moment—tell me first what you are to charge." "The Reverend knows what the government rates are, but for *master's favor* (making a low salaam,) we will go for one rupee (about fifty cents) apiece each way." "Well, I will give it if you do well—remember now, a good palanquin and good practiced fellows." "How could I do otherwise for the Reverend?"—with which flattering expression he salaamed himself out of my presence, and went about making ready for the excursion. At the hour appointed, the whole set came gliding into the yard, the empty palanquin being brought leisurely along by four persons, who placed it before the door, while each in turn made his obeisance. "Well, maistry, are your men all here?" "The Reverend count and see." The whole twelve were then passed in review. "The *mussalchee*, where is he?" "There, your Reverence," and I immediately recognized this important personage by his long stick with cotton cloth wound round one end, which, in journeying he carries in his left hand, and keeps saturated with oil from a flask in his right. This torch-man is always considered necessary, though the light of the moon may render his flambeau quite uncalled for. "And the *cavardy cooly*, where is he?" Upon which there stepped forward a short, thick-set man, all muscle and sinew. "Well, now, let us look at your palanquin." And had the reader stood by my side he would have observed that the singular conveyance submitted to his examination is shaped like an oblong box, in length six feet—in depth and width four. A strong pole extends from either end about five feet, which is fastened by means of four rods to the body of the vehicle, and in case of a long journey an additional rope attached to one pole passes under to that of the opposite. These arms, the frame-work, panneling, &c. are made of teak or other pliant wood, with sliding doors and Venetian blinds. Within, upon a rattan bottom, is placed a mattress covered with chintz or morocco, which forms the traveller's seat and bed. Passing from one of the inner sides to the opposite, is a wide leathern strap, against which he leans, while a small pillow lies loose upon the cushion, by which his knees can be a little elevated and relieved from the tediousness of a horizontal position. Just over the spot where the feet are to be placed, there is a shelf, where books, medicine, &c., can be deposited, near which is a watch pocket, and many other little contrivances essential to one who anticipates a journey far from home. The whole is painted green, and on the top is a large cotton cloth to shield the occupant from the dust, and colored blue or black, according to the taste of the owner. As my maistry has brought a superior article, the reader will remark that it has a few extra conveniences. There is a second top, raised about four inches above the first, thus admitting a current of air, and tending to produce greater coolness and comfort. Upon this second covering is a tin box, painted black and called an *imperial*, which forms a receptacle for those articles of clothing that cannot find room in the main body of the vehicle. A *gurglet* (earthen bottle) for water, is nicely encased in a wicker-work basket, and fastened upon the end of the pole next the body of the palanquin; and in the same position upon the opposite sides, are bottles for oil and medicines.

Such was the conveyance brought for my night's excursion. In the first place, two square tin boxes were filled, one with necessary clothing, and the other with table furniture, cooking utensils, "curry stuffs," bread, and other et ceteras. These were given to the cavardy cooly, who fastened one upon each end of a strong bamboo, and having slung them upon his shoulder started off immediately, that he might be at the end of the stage before my arrival.

Now for the *palanquin*—in went one article after another, the poor bearers beginning to think that the Reverend's money and favor were to be obtained at the expense of no slight fatigue.

But their complaints were little noticed. Just so much must go, and in this way only. The last article being stowed away, the maistry was told to call his men for a departure. Slowly they rose from their recumbent posture upon the verandah or sand, where they had seized a few moments to refresh themselves in preparation for the fatiguing duties before them. Their first act of making ready was to aid each other in winding around the body a long cotton cloth, by way of imparting greater strength to the frame. Then followed the taking of their stations, each being supplied with a small pad to prevent the shoulder being injured by the friction of the pole, while those of a shorter size were furnished with a second or third to bring the palanquin upon a level. "All ready, maistry?" "All ready," was the reply—a parting salutation to the friends I was about to leave, and in I crept, when first the rear, then the forward beams were slowly placed upon the shoulders of my men, and off I hastened, while the shout began with which they kept time and directed their tread. To a griffin (*alias*, a new-comer), this sound is rather frightful, and I have heard of a young man who was informed that so soon as his bearers began to make a noise he must jump out and run for his life. He did as he was directed, not a little to the surprise of the innocent natives and amusement of his jocose friends. Being accustomed to these sounds, they neither alarmed me by their strangeness or troubled me by their apparent expressions of pain—for I knew them to be necessary to equality of tread and the preservation of courage and good spirits. At times these responses have no meaning, being a simple "*he he, ho ho*," while again they have reference to the size and weight of the person they are carrying, of which the following is a significant illustration:

"Oh what a heavy bag, Ho, ho,
He is an ample weight, " "
Let's let his Palkee down, " "
Let's set him in the mud, " "
No, but he'll be angry then, " "

Aye, and he'll beat us then, " "
Then let us hasten on, " "
Jump along, jump along," " "

If a *lady* be the passenger, such expressions as these may be heard:

" She's not heavy, Putterum (care)
Carry her softly, "
Nice little lady, "
Here's a bridge, "
Carry her carefully, "
Carry her gently, "
Sing along cheerily, "
" Putterum, Putterum."

When passing through the streets of a town, they are accustomed to dignify the traveller with the noblest titles.

" Here is a great man, Ho, ho,
He is a Rajah, " "
She is a Ranee," " "

for the reason that their own importance will be enhanced by an attendance upon so noble a person.

When approaching home the theme is changed. The benevolence of the traveller is then the burden of song. The ear is saluted by complimentary expressions like these:

" He is a charity man, Ho, ho,
He loves to do good, " "
She is benevolent, " "
She won't forget us," " "

the object of which is to remind the one they are carrying, that in case of a safe arrival at home, a little extra pay will not be at all unwelcome.

As I passed beyond the city limits, the face of the country presented little to interest, and my confined position allowed but a glance at any object as I passed. To while away time that began to hang heavily, I availed myself of the remaining twilight to read a book, brought for that purpose. This was difficult, for the tread of the bearers, though usually regular, caused a motion of the conveyance more tremulous than that of a railroad car. I succeeded tolerably well, however, though such a mode of testing the strength of the eyes is contrary to the advice of the wise and prudent.

But of all the vehicles in which I have yet had the fortune to be conveyed, the palanquin is the most lonely, and least attractive or agreeable. It is eminently useful, and here your praise of it must end. Carrying but one person, there he must sit and think and speculate, while there is just enough about him to divert attention, and thus to forbid a very profitable and connected train of reflection. Such being the case, I was right glad to perceive that it was late enough to conclude upon retiring to rest. Having accordingly told the men to set me down, which was willingly done, I removed the end of the strap behind, and arranged my pillow; then making my necessary toilet, I reclined at full length, hoping for a quiet repose of a few hours. The bearers again under way, I was visited by the nocturnal goddess, though I could not say with the poet "Kind nature's sweet restorer, *balmy sleep*," the state I was in being little entitled to the appellation "sleep," and still less to that of "balmy." Once I was aroused by inhaling an odor quite foreign to the *spicy* land of Ind. A breeze had sprung up, and my torch-man had taken shelter under the leeward of my palanquin, giving me an opportunity of quaffing the fumes of burning cotton and rancid oil. Having intimated to him, in very decided terms, that he must leave that locality, he trotted ahead, while I relapsed into my former repose, from which I was again awakened by a dream which was "not all a dream," to wit that I was again doubling the Cape of Storms. When a little aroused, I called for information respecting the very disagreeable motion of the conveyance, when I was told that a new man had taken hold. I requested the maistry to defer all experiments of apprentices until some other person (or thing) was their traveller than myself. My request was heeded, and again all went smoothly onward.

After journeying a few miles further, the maistry was at my elbow with the intelligence that we were near a river, the water of which was deep, and that we might find some difficulty in crossing.

Such interruptions are not uncommon in that land of drought and torrent. That which now presents to the eye but an extended waste of arid sand, becomes in a few days the bed of a navigable stream. At these times the journeyer does best to trust himself to the judgment and experience of his bearers, instead of himself directing what shall be done. When the water is very high and the current strong, prudence dictates a patient delay upon the bank till the "river runs by," which it sometimes does in a few hours, especially if the monsoon have not fully set in. In other cases the course is adopted which was pursued in the present instance. The torch-bearer went ahead into the middle of the stream, holding his flambeau above him in one hand, while with the other he carried a long pole, cautiously measuring the water's depth just before him. After finding that the river was fordable, he returned and reported to the maistry, who directed one-half of the men to place the bottom of the palanquin (cooly like) upon their heads, and the other merely to walk near their fellows, that they might be at hand in case of danger. Thus we entered the river cautiously, slowly, with just enough of the "ho ho" not to let courage fail or spirits flag. Deeper and still deeper sunk the bearers, and nearer to my person approached the rapid waves. I looked ahead and there was the mussalchee, his light borne aloft, and his turbaned head just appearing above the surface of the water. I thought much, but said nothing. At the moment in which it seemed that another step downward would have brought the raging stream into my vehicle, I felt a slight elevation. The danger was past, cheerful sounds were again heard from the men, and with buoyant steps I was carried safely to the opposite bank, hardly less pleased at my arrival than when the mussuli boat landed me on the sandy beach of Madras.

The bearers placed the palanquin upon the ground, to allow themselves a little rest after their tiresome march, while the maistry made his appearance, in their behalf, at my door with a low salaam, which was answered by a commendation of their skill and an intimation that a more valuable expression of my good will was in store for them. With a few other interruptions, which I will not weary the reader by narrating, we reached the village of S. at sunrise, having been twelve hours running forty miles, including the delay in crossing the river. Reaching the bungalow, I very happily found it unoccupied, and therefore had the suite of rooms to myself. My palanquin was brought within, so as to be sheltered from sun and rain. My bearers having received the means of purchasing a sheep, and thus enjoying an extra dish of curry, were dismissed for the day, with directions to be at the door before sunset. I threw myself upon a cot—with one or more of which, and a table and chairs, these caravanseries are furnished, and seized a little rest, while tea, toast and eggs were in course of preparation for my breakfast. So much for a night's excursion in a palanquin, which although, as before suggested, very lonely and very distasteful to many, is of eminent utility in a land where stage coaches, canals and railroads are unknown.

The *ton-jon* is a conveyance much used in the cities and large towns of India for shopping, calling, and evening airings. It resembles the palanquin in having a pole of three and a half feet length before and behind, and in being carried by bearers. In the form of the body, and in its rising and falling top, it is like the chaise, the seat being only of sufficient size for one adult. The sides are left open, but are provided with extended brass wires, upon which are hung curtains of green silk that may be drawn at pleasure. It is light and airy—suited only for short distances, as the posture is upright instead of reclining.

The value of a *palanquin* varies from fifty to a hundred dollars; and that of a *ton-jon* from thirty to seventy-five dollars, according to their size and elegance of finish. The wealthy, and those in high official station, retain a set of bearers for their personal use—the expense for eight persons (enough for short distances and with no baggage,) being about $20 per month, housing and feeding themselves. When not needed in carrying the vehicle they run upon errands, pull the punkah, assist the ayah in amusing the children, watch the premises, introduce visitors, and the like employments of which the foreign resident has sufficient to engage many attendants.

In Calcutta, Madras and Bombay, almost every conceivable mode of conveyance is in use among the various classes of inhabitants. Take your position at six o'clock in the evening (the hour for Indian drives,) at some prominent point upon the thoroughfare of either of the above-named cities, and the scenes you witness will alternately awaken your admiration and

F. Michelin lith. 111 Nassau St.

HINDOO TONJON

excite a smile. Here comes a carriage. "Europe-built"—well proportioned and highly though tastefully ornamented—four native troopers are riding ahead to clear the way—postillions are mounted upon magnificent Arabian steeds, with other attendants running at the side with ornamented dress and glittering spear. Within is the Governor or Chief Justice—high in rank and authority among the foreign residents. There goes a plain, substantial carriage, drawn by a pair of strong though not showy horses, also of Arabian origin—the reins in the hands of an English gentleman, who is taking his family to breathe the invigorating sea air after a day's confinement within his house or office. This again, is a civilian or one of the higher class of commission merchants, and his sallow countenance indicates that his constitution cannot much longer endure the demands made upon it by his daily seclusion, cares and fatigue. There go two young men, boys almost, in military costume, upon animals they can hardly manage, dashing along at a breakneck pace, laughing, bowing, and attracting not a little attention from passers-by. These are cadets just from shipboard—graduates at Addiscombe, and sent to India to make their fortune. One of two destinies is before them—either they will find an early grave in that strange land, or, if they pass unscathed through the ordeal of griffinage, and have time and disposition to profit by experience, they will become eminent and useful.

But look again—yonder approaches a hackery,

drawn by a lank animal, which has seen all the service that should be demanded, but is doomed to spend its last days in drawing those East Indians, or foreign sailors from place to place—to see—be seen—and enjoy their rude life.

What a beautiful palanquin that is, coming. The bearers, how well dressed, and their spears how bright and gaily tasseled! Within is a wealthy Hindoo, who owns his millions of rupees, and lives in Eastern luxury. And that *ton-jon*—how light and airy. There is an Ayah and child—the mother is in the carriage that just went by. Standing at this point, what a strange and motley mixture of persons and vehicles. People of every hue, dress, and grade and business—civil, military and commercial—English, European and native—honored, respected and despised—eminent, indifferent and ignoble—drawn by horses from Arabia, Cape, Pegu, Acheen—in coaches, buggies, drays, carts—carried in palanquins and ton-jons—all upon the same general errand of breathing the delicious sea breeze, and thus preparing for the evening's repast and a night's rest.

In the up-country stations, the same may be witnessed though on a smaller scale.

# CHAPTER XI.

## HINDOO LITERATURE.

Languages of India—Antiquity of the Sanscrit—The Vedas—Shastras—Pooranas—Ramayanum, Analysis of, and Quotation from the Poem—Remark by Dr. Duff—Institutes of Menu, and other Works on Hindoo Jurisprudence—Ethics—Extracts from the Cural and Ovviyar—Miscellaneous Proverbs—Puncha tantrakathy—Moothory—Nannery—Nalladiyar—Hindoo Poetry.

India abounds with languages, there being not less than eighteen in habitual use throughout the Peninsula. In the provinces which constitute *Northern Hindoostan*, we find the Kashmeeree, and Khasee or Purbuttee;—in *Hindoostan Proper*, are the Punjaubee, Hindostanee, Sindee, Mahrattee, Kuchee, Goojratee, Runghee, Bundulkundee, Moogadkee, Bengalee, and Bhootiya;—in the *Deccan*, the Mahrattee, Gondee, Teloogoo, Oorya, and Canarese; while in *Southern India*, are the Canarese, Teloogoo, Malayalim and Tamul, which last is also vernacular among the inhabitants of North Ceylon. Had these languages a *common origin*, if so, what was it? are questions which have engaged a large share of attention, from men of letters in England and on the Continent.

Adelung, an eminent oriental scholar, asserts with much confidence, that "the *Sanscrit* may be considered, with the exception of a few mountain dialects, as the parent of all Indian languages, from the Indus to the farthest part of Arracan, and from Cape Comorin to Chinese Tartary." To this opinion Halhed, Sir William Jones, Colebrooke, Rev. Dr. Carey, and other oriental scholars have expressed their assent. While there is much to favor such a sentiment in regard to the languages of the north, the proof is not equally conclusive respecting those of the extreme south. It is supposed by some oriental scholars that the "Tamul is the original source of the Malayalim, Canarese, Teloogoo, Mahrattee, and Oorya, it being known to have attained a highly finished form some time prior to the introduction of the Brahminical system, though, together with other dialects, having since received a large admixture of Sanscrit."

But, though denying to the Sanscrit the undoubted right of being the root of which the other Indian languages are the branches; or the fountain of which these are the streams, most justly does it claim the homage of high antiquity. The Hindoo gives to it a Divine origin, and calls it *Deva-Nagari*, the "writing of the Gods." This is no matter of surprise when we see that it is the depository of his religion, and organ of the national institutes; for it is entirely natural for a people like the Hindoos, to attribute a celestial character to that which is the medium of conveying the Divine will, especially if it have much of intrinsic excellence to command admiration and homage.

Sir William Jones speaks of it as "of wonderful structure, more perfect than Greek, more copious than Latin, and more exquisitely perfect than either," in which high eulogium Halhed, Talboys, Adelung, and others fully concur. Though long since disused in all parts of the country, it retains a large place in the veneration of the people.

The dialects of the various hill tribes are still, for the greater part, distinct from the others, and have no written character.

Waiving farther remarks upon the Indian languages in general, I proceed to illustrate the subjects of which they are the honored vehicle.

Foremost in the vast array of Indian *literature* stand those ancient, voluminous, and sacred writings, the *Vedas.*

These are regarded as an immediate revelation from heaven, and as containing all that man needs to know respecting the character of God, and His claims upon the rational world.

The term is derived from the Sanscrit *Ved,* (the law,) and includes four classes of works, of which the first is called the *Rig-Veda,* and treats of the first cause of all beings and things, the creation of matter, the formation of the world, of angels and the soul, rewards, punishment, corruption, and sin.

The second, or *Yajur-Veda* contains instructions respecting religious exercises, the castes, feasts, purifications, gifts, building of temples, ceremonies at birth, marriage, and death, and of the kind of animals required in sacrifice.

The third, or *Sama-Veda*, comprises hymns in praise of the Supreme Being, and to the honor of subordinate deities.

The fourth, or *Atharvan-Veda* which treats of mystic theology and metaphysics, is supposed by some to be of less authority than the preceding threc, from this circumstance, among others, that while they are derived successively from the *fire*, *air*, and *sun*, this last has no such important parentage.

These four classes are regarded as the fountain of all true religion, and thc primeval sources of every other species of useful knowledge. They are believed by the community at large to have proceeded direct and entire out of the mouth of the Creator himself, and therefore as challenging the most implicit faith and profoundest reverence. When the various portions of the universe, the gods and men, were issuing from the different parts of the body of Brahma, these holy works, fairly and fully written, dropped from his four mouths. After meeting with sundry disasters by falling into the sea and like places of danger from which a miracle alone saved them, they were finally placed in the hands of Vyasa and other learned men to methodize and arrange, and from them have they come to our day.

Let a single quotation illustrate the character of

these works. It is taken from the third or Sama-Veda :—

"Possessed of innumerable heads, innumerable eyes, innumerable feet—Brahm fills the heavens and earth, he is whatever was, whatever will be, his command is as the water of life, he is the source of universal motion, he is the light of the moon, the sun, the fire, the lightning. The Veda is the breath of his nostrils, the primary elements are his sight, the agitation of human affairs is his laughter, his sleep is the destruction of the universe. In different forms he cherishes the creatures; in the form of air he preserves them, in the form of water he satisfies them, in the form of the sun he assists them in the affairs of life, and in that of the moon he refreshes them in sleep, the progression of time forms his footsteps, all the gods to him are as sparks of fire. To him I bow, I bow."

These sacred hymns are arranged in metre, and sung with much taste and melody.

Sir William Jones fixes the date of the Vedas at 1500 years before the birth of Christ, which Mr. Colebrooke and others consider as far too modern a period. After long and arduous efforts, a complete collection of these sacred books has been found and now lies in the British Museum; bound in eleven folio volumes.

Parts of these treatises have been translated into the English and Continental languages, but the obscurity of their style, the obsolete dialect in which they are composed, their voluminousness, and the comparatively limited interest taken in the study and reading of such subjects, will probably prevent for years, and perhaps for ever, a full translation of their contents.

Extracts from the Vedas have been made, and may be found in the "Journal of the Asiatic Society," "Ward's View of the Hindoos," Colebrooke's Essay," and other works on the East.

Next in importance to the Vedas the various *Shastras* hold a place. Rishes and sages are their authors, and their themes less sacred than those of the Vedas. These teach respectively the science of architecture, law and logic, moral philosophy, astrology, and medicine. Being the great books of Hindoo science, they are used in schools and colleges, and present a formidable array of metaphysics, morals, and philosophy, "falsely so called."

Next in order of importance are the *Pooranas*, which are in Hindoo literature what the Vedas are in theology, and the Shastras in science. They are mythological poems and of great popularity and interest the nation over. Under this title are arranged those gigantic poems *Bhagavata*, a history of Vishnu who bore that surname, the *Mahabharat*, an epic poem of more than 100,000 slokas or couplets, the subject of which is the history of a race of beings descended from the great Bharata, who was banished the city Hastinapad, and wandered about a long time in misery; but at length, by the assistance of Krishna, regained his crown and re-enjoyed prosperity. It is compared for its beauty, to a deep and noble forest, abounding in delicious fruits and fragrant flowers, shaded and watered by perennial springs.

Last named, but first in public esteem, is the *Ramayana*, the work of the poet Valmiki, in the introduction to which it is said that, "He who sings and hears this poem continually, has attained to the highest state of enjoyment, and will finally be equal to the gods."

The great celebrity of this work, and the completeness with which it exhibits the strength of oriental genius, induces me to lay before the reader an outline of the poem, and an extract from its voluminous pages. "At different times, Bhoodeir or the earth is represented as oppressed with monsters and demons. Unable any longer to bear their enormities, she enters the presence of Vishnu, entreats his interposition, and receives his promise that he will become incarnate and destroy her enemies. Hence the many incarnations of that second of the Triad, as fish—tortoise—boar—man-lion—and an ox. After describing these six incarnate forms of Vishnu, the author proceeds to the seventh as *Rama*, son of Dusarutha, king of Oude. His wife is born a princess, and in process of time they are united in marriage. His father Dusarutha becomes old and infirm, and wishes Rama to take the reins of government into his hands. Rama replies, 'It cannot be—I have not been born for such a worldly purpose as this. I must call my wife Seeta, along with me, we must reside like ascetics in the desert, and it will presently transpire for what purpose I appear among men.' He does so. They build a hermitage, and spend their time amongst the beasts of the forest. The giant Ravenna, king of Lunka in Ceylon—the monster with ten heads, and as many arms, and to destroy whom it is the design of the incarnation, hears this intelligence, and is determined, in the struggle, to give Rama as much trouble as he can. Having the power of changing his form, he assumes that of an ascetic, and whilst Rama is absent from the hermitage, he appears at the door, and entreats Seeta to give him alms. When approaching to bestow the bounty desired, he seizes, carries her off, and puts her in prison. On returning to the hermitage, Rama cannot find his wife, sinks into a sea of grief, utters the most piteous cries, and passes through those deep emotions of sorrow which characterize Eastern nations. To assist him in his conflict with the giants, the angels are represented as becoming incarnate in *monkeys*, and Hunumunta is their leader. As the latter is worshipped in every town and almost every village of India, it is evident that he is a deity of no small consequence. Finding Rama in a state of despondency, he becomes his prime minister, and undertakes to visit Lunka and find out the circumstances of Seeta. He assumes the form of a rat, and pursues his circuitous route through the houses of the enemy, till he discovers the prison where Seeta is confined. Like a faithful servant he delivers to her the message of his master, and receives from Seeta her answers in return. After having emerged from the prison, he assumes his proper form—is seen scampering over the walls and houses—and excites much alarm among the giants in Lunka. Whether his visit was an omen of good or evil they could not understand. At length they seized him as a prisoner, and brought him to the court of Ravenna to be examined. As they would not give him a seat, but compelled him to stand, he took his tremendous tail, and coiled it, cable-like, till it rose to such a height as enabled him to sit down on an equality with the throne of Ravenna. In reply to the question put to him by the king respecting his name, parentage, design in visiting Lunka, &c., he gave such shrewd and ingenious answers, that he sets the whole court in bursts of laughter against the sovereign. Ravenna is frantic with rage, and asks what is to be done with this monkey? Some proposed one thing, and some another; but all agreed in the suggestion, that he made such a boast of his tail, that it ought to be set on fire. Accordingly, all the old clothes, the rags, and paper to be found in Lunka, are put in requisition, to make a flambeau of this tail. They cover it with tar and pitch, and other combustibles—set it on fire—and then liberate the prisoner, that they may have a day of frolic. No sooner does Hunumunta regain his liberty, than he commences a race—now through the fields of corn, and sets them on fire—then through the farm-yards and over the hay-ricks, and puts them in a blaze—then over the walls and through the houses, and kindles a fire which is not easily extinguished. Never did such an incendiary visit Lunka before. To save their city from destruction, the giants now pursue him to put out the torch which they had lighted. Hunumunta ascends the tower of a temple, and hides himself in its summit; and when he finds it well filled with giants, he throws it down with violence, and destroys them all. He makes his escape—dips his tail in the sea—and returns to Rama. After reporting the exploits of his embassy, they assemble an army of monkeys—throw a bridge across the sea (gulf of Manaar) from the Continent to Ceylon—and lay siege to the fortress of Ravenna. The war is commenced, and prodigies of valor are performed on both sides, till Rama kills the monster Ravenna, liberates his wife Seeta, and delivers the earth from the giants, whose enormities cause her to groan." Such is an outline of this famous epic; but the poetry, figures, and illustrations are not to be translated. There is no describing the intense interest with which the millions listen to the recitation of this Poem by the bards who wander up and down the country. The first time I witnessed this scene was in the city of Madura, when passing through a wide street, in company with the Rev. Mr. Cherry. There was a large pandal built in front of the dwelling, beneath which sat the reader, upon an ornamented mat; lamps above, attendants at his side, and thousands crowding the street before him. We stopped to listen, and though we could understand but little, yet the melody of his voice, the distinctness of his enunciation, and the force of his recitation, produced an impression, even upon us, not to be effaced.

Add to this an understanding of the sentiment, and an appreciation of the style, and no wonder that the multitude of half-clad and illiterate Hindoos sat entranced with wonder and admiration, while the moments sped as on eagle's wings.

While, as before remarked, there is no conveying to those of another nation and language the beauties which a Hindoo sees in this Poem, I shall venture to insert a few lines as illustrative of its more pathetic style.

When Dusarutha was told by Rama that he would not gratify his wishes in the matter of succeeding him upon the throne of Oude, but must retire to a forest, the old man protested against his daughter's accompanying him. Under these circumstances she addressed her husband in the following most dutiful and affectionate manner:

Son of the venerable parent! hear,
'Tis Seeta speaks. Say, art thou not assur'd
That to each being his allotted time
And portion, as his merit, are assign'd,
And that a wife her husband's portion shares?
Therefore, with thee this forest lot I claim.
A woman's bliss is found, not in the smile
Of father, mother, friend, or in herself:
Her husband is her only portion here,
Her heaven hereafter. If thou indeed,
Depart this day into the forest drear,
I will precede and smooth the thorny way.
O chide me not; for where the husband is,
Within the palace, on the stately car,

Or wandering in the air, in every state,
The shadow of his feet is her abode.
My mother and my father having left,
I have no dwelling-place distinct from tnee.
Forbid me not. For as a gay recluse,
On thee attending, happy shall I feel,
Within this honey-scented grove to roam,
For thou, e'en here can'st nourish and protect;
And therefore other friend I cannot need.
A residence in heaven, O Raghuvu,
Without thy presence would no joy afford.
Therefore, though rough the path, I must, I will,
The forest penetrate, the wild abode
Of monkeys, elephants, and playful fawn.
Pleased to embrace thy feet, I will reside
In the rough forest, as my father's house.
Void of all other wish, supremely thine,
Permit me this request—I will not grieve—
I will not burden thee—refuse me not,
But shouldst thou, Raghuvu, this prayer deny,
Know, I resolve on *death*—if torn from thee.

Thus much upon the Vedas, Puranas, and Shastras. Their characteristics are *number*, *antiquity*, and *bulk*; upon the last feature of which I shall quote the language of Dr. Duff:

" The Æneid of Virgil extends to about twelve thousand lines, the Iliad of Homer to double that number; but the Ramayana of Valmiki rolls on to a hundred thousand, while the Mahabharat of Vyasa quadruples even that sum! Many of the other sacred books exhibit a voluminousness quite as amazing. The four

Vedas, when collected, form eleven huge octavo volumes, while the Puranas extend to about two millions of lines ! In one of these it is gravely asserted, on divine authority, that originally the whole series of Puranas alone consisted of one hundred kolis, or a thousand millions of stanzas ; but as four hundred thousand of these were considered sufficient for the instruction of man, the rest were reserved for the gods. Well might Sir William Jones say, "Wherever we direct our attention to Hindoo literature, the notion of infinity presents itself; and sure the longest life would not suffice for a single perusal of works that rise and swell, protuberant like the Himalayahs, above the bulkiest compositions of every land beyond the confines of India."

Next in order are works on the subject of *Jurisprudence*, among which the *Institutes of Menu* occupy a place altogether pre-eminent. The author is "known in the Puranas as the son of Brahma and one of the progenitors of mankind." His Institutes, in twelve volumes, though inferior to the Vedas in antiquity, are held to be equally sacred ; and, owing to their being more closely united with the business of life, have tended much to mould the opinions of the Hindoos. Sir William Jones places the publication of these ordinances about 880 B. C. The work has been translated by the great Orientalist, and published once and again in London and Calcutta.

The Law-books of India, or Smritee Shastras, as they are called, are very numerous. In addition to many which have been lost, there are now extant *seven* works on the duties of kings, *thirty* on inheritance, *seventy-five* relative to the Canon Laws, *twenty* on offerings to the manes of ancestors, and above *ninety* on vows, oaths, marriages, and various other subjects pertaining to private welfare and the public good. These Smritees contain eighteen titles of law, which are declared to be the "ground-work of all judicial procedure in this world." I would close what might be illustrated at greater length respecting the law books of India, with the important enactment that "the preservation of the kingdom from thieves, or vigilance in punishing theft, secures Paradise to the magistrate."

The literature of the land abounds with volumes on *ethics* and *casuistry*, variously expressed in the language of poetry, proverb, fables, narrative, and didactic counsel.

While many of the sentiments contained in these works are greatly defective, and in some cases ruinous in their practical tendency, it must be admitted that very much is true, and worthy of commendation and practice. At the head of this class of authors stands *Tiruvullavar*, deemed an incarnation of wisdom, to whom the Hindoos are indebted for that extraordinary production, the *Cural*. Though more than fifteen hundred years old, this rare collection of precepts, conveyed in the style of unequalled poetry, has lost none of its original favor among the people. In one hundred and thirty-three chapters it treats of almost every variety of subjects pertaining to the relations and duties of life, forming a text-book of indisputable authority. Portions of this work have been translated into English by several oriental scholars, from one of which, made by Mr. Ellis of the Madras civil service, I have selected the following stanzas, by which the reader may form an opinion of the whole production :

As ranked in every alphabet the first,
The selfsame vowel stands, so in all worlds
The Eternal God is chief.

Of virtue void, as is the palsied sense,
The head must be, that bows not at his feet,
Whose eight-fold attributes pervade the world.

As the hook rules the elephant, so he
In wisdom firm his earthly passions rule
Who hopes to flourish in the soil of heaven.

No greater gain than virtue canst thou know,
Than virtue to forget no greater loss.

Refer not virtue to another day ;
Receive her now, and at thy dying hour
She'll prove thy never-dying friend.

Know that is virtue which each ought to do,
What each should shun is vice.

If love and virtue be thy constant guests
Domestic life is blest, and finds in these
Its object and reward.

Before their scornful foes
Bold as a lion those dare never walk,
Whose fame is sullied by their wives' base deeds.

Of all the world calls good, no good exists
Like that which wise and virtuous offspring give
I know no greater good.

Sweet is the pipe, and sweet the lute they say,
They who have never heard their children's tongues
In infant prattle lisp.

What bolt can love restrain? What veil conceal;
One tear-drop in the eye of those thou lovest,
Will draw a flood from thine.

To honor guests with hospitable rite,
Domestic life with all its various joys
To man was given.

Though courtesy rejoice the heart, yet words
Of kindness which dress the face in smiles
Will more avail.

Discourteous speech when courteous may be used,
Is like the sickly appetite which culls
Fruit immature, leaving the ripe untouched.

Small as a grain of millet
Though it be, large as the towering palm
A benefit to grateful eyes appears.

Though every virtue by his hand expire
Yet may he live ; but by the stroke he dies,
When murdered gratitude before him falls.

That virtue which in all relations holds
Unchangeable its nature, that alone
Deserves the name of justice.

It is the glory of the just to stand,
Like the adjusted balance, duly poised
Nor swerve to either side.

Though unrestrained all else, restrain thy tongue,
For those degraded by licentious speech
Will rue their tongues' offence.

The wound may heal, though from a burning brand,
And be forgotten, but the wound ne'er heals
A burning tongue inflicts.

As vehicles for the conveyance of ethical precepts, *proverbs* are very popular among the people of India, and form an important part of the national literature. Before me is a volume containing nearly two thousand of these concise and pithy sentences, many of them having their origin in the wisdom of remote antiquity, but retaining a place in daily usage the country over. From this volume I have selected the following, as illustrative of the class:

If taken to excess even nectar is poison.

The crow imitating the gait of the swan, lost even its own.

Ambrosia at the tip of the tongue, but poison at the root.

To the timorous, the atmosphere is filled with demons.

If distant, even enemies are friends.

Is it difficult for one to swin a *tank*, who has swam a *river*?

When the elephant is given, shall a dispute ensue about the goad?

Does the hand that has caressed the elephant, caress the sheep?

It will happen in its time—it will go in its time.

Is the fold to be placed where the sheep may wish?

Though you go a begging, go decently attired.

If on entering you are obliged to swim, how will you reach the opposite shore?

Bullets do not fly in your battles.

Though a little bird soar high, will it become a kite?

Is he a friend who helps not in adversity?

Your friendship is sincere, it is true—yet do not put your hand in my sack.

Are all men, *men*? or are all stones, *rubies*?

Are we not to milk when there is a cow?

No one knows all things, and no one but knows something.

Is it necessary to add acid to the lemon?

The flower which is out of reach is dedicated to God.

No matter what becomes of others' affairs, attend to your own.

Though a man may remove to the distance of fifty miles, his sin is still with him.

If *one* only knows the matter it is a secret, if *two* it is public.

Learn even to thieve, but *forget it.*

What the eye has seen, the hand may do.

If the ass be beaten with a bundle of sugar-cane, will he thereby taste its sweetness?

Time passes away, but sayings remain.

Winnow while there is wind, and turn the mill while there is sugar-cane.

Of what use can the news of the country be to a frog in a well?

Even the monkey thinks its own young precious as gold.

A guilty breast is always agitated.

Will the barking dog catch game?

When faults are scrutinized, relationships cease.

It is easier to procure eight oxen, than to find one that has strayed.

Infatuation precedes destruction.

They who give, have all things; those who withhold, have nothing.

Truth will conquer, but falsehood will kill.

Even a small rush may be of use as a tooth-pick.

Taxes and gruel will continually grow thicker.

The effect of moral action will terminate on the actor.

A demon will laugh at a destructive thought.

The fellow walks on foot, but his words are in a palankeen.

The deeds of a bad man will burn himself.

He is most eloquent, when none is found to dispute.

A swan in his own, and a crow in a foreign country.

While we meditate one thing, God determines another.

Marry the daughter on knowing the mother.

Friction removes not the scent of the sandal wood.

Favors silence the tongue.

To roast a crab, and set a fox to guard it.

A dog is courageous—in his own kennel.

Will there be smoke where there is no fire?

To destroy an enemy make friendship with him.

His rank entitles him to a palankeen, but he has no strength to enter it.

First at the feast, and last at the battle field.

Insanity has left me—bring the rice pounder, that I may gird myself.

Did ever any one become poor by giving alms?

Desert not old friends for new ones.

Will the young of the tiger be without claws?

Taciturnity makes no blunders.

Forbearance is stronger than the ocean.

Even the blind may shoot—if a mountain be the target.

A prudent youth is better than an old fool.

When a dog barks against a mountain, which is injured, the dog, or the mountain?

Stumbling is the excuse of a lame horse.

Can he that prospers not by truth, succeed by lies?

There is no flower that insects will not visit.

The greatest enmity is preferable to uncertain friendship.

The dam must be made before the flood comes.

No one was ever ruined by speaking the truth.

Under the general head of *ethical literature* we find several *fabulous works*, in which the adventures and discourses of animals are narrated with a view to the entertainment and instruction of the people. By far the most popular of this class is a volume entitled the *Panchatantrakathy*, being a systematic arrangement of fables, or apologues, arranged after the style of Æsop, and found in all the languages of the country. The plan of the work is briefly this: in the city of Patilaputra, Sudarsana, the reigning king, had three adult sons, who seemed to vie with each other in coarseness of disposition and manners. The good prince, in great affliction, having convened his council, addressed them thus: "What benefit is there in children who are neither learned nor virtuous? or of what use is the feeding of the buffalo that never gives milk? An unbecoming son is a discomfort to the family. Youth, wealth, authority, and ignorance, are each of them a source of ruin; and what will be the wretchedness of him in whom all these four are united? Is there a man to be found who will be able to regenerate my sons, who are born to have merely a name, and wander in the paths of error?"

The Brahmin *Somajanma* at once arose and offered his services to the king, being willing to undertake the reformation of the princes, and that within a few months. The offer was joyfully accepted, and the wayward youth put under his care. The Brahmin, with great patience and toil, succeeded at length in his enterprise, and subdued the habits of his royal pupils; and all through the medium of five principal fables, each embracing a greater number of subordinate ones. These fables compose the *Pancha-tantra*, or five points of industry. They are five romances, which are entitled instructive, although their morality is not very sound; sometimes conducing to what is evil, rather than teaching the means of avoiding it. The *first* story explains how dexterous knaves contrive to sow divisions between best friends. The *second* teaches the advantage of true friends, and how they should be selected. The *third* explains how one is to destroy an adversary by artifice, when he cannot do it by force. The *fourth* shows how a man loses his property by misconduct, and the *fifth* exhibits the bad effects of thoughtlessness and precipitate decision. These narratives are so constructed as that one fable, before it is completed, gives rise to another, and that onward, to the close. It is impossible to determine the age of these fables, no authentic document of their era being extant. The Hindoos rank them among their oldest productions; and the estimation in which they are held throughout the country is a proof of their antiquity. Their resemblance to the fables of Æsop is very close and striking, but whether either was debtor to the other, is a question involved in the deepest obscurity. Originally composed in verse, they have been translated into the language of every part of the Peninsula; and as a text-book in the daily schools of the land, exert a great influence in moulding the sentiments, and thus forming the character of Hindoo youth.

From a large class of proverbs with which these tales abound, the following are appropriate specimens :

Courage is tried in war, integrity in the payment of debt and interest, the faithfulness of a wife in poverty, and friendship in distress.

He who in your presence speaks kindly, but in your absence seeks to injure, must be rejected like a bowl of poison covered with milk.

It can never be safe to unite with an enemy ; water, though heated, will still extinguish fire.

A wise man will never be the leader of a party ; for if the affairs of the party be successful, all will be equally sharers, and if unsuccessful, the leader will alone be disgraced.

He who removes another from danger, and he who removes terror from the mind, are the greatest of friends.

The truly great are calm in danger, merciful in prosperity, eloquent in the assembly, courageous in war, and anxious for fame.

Little things should not be despised ; many straws united may bind an elephant.

He who seeks the company of the wise, shall himself become wise ; even glass inserted in gold partakes of its color.

Truth, contentment, patience and mercy, belong to great minds.

Happiness consists in the absence of anxiety.

A gift bestowed with kind expressions, knowledge without pride, and power united to clemency, are rare but excellent.

Every one looking downwards becomes impressed with the

idea of his own greatness; but looking upwards feels his own littleness.

A wise hearer is not affected by the *speaker*, but by the *oration*.

The deceitful have no friends.

It is the essence of riches to corrupt the heart.

It was through these and like media, that the Hindoo sages conveyed instruction to their pupils and readers respecting the manifold duties of life. While their thousands of pages contain much that is true and admirable, the value of their teachings is often impaired, and in some cases neutralized, by the absence of a proper motive of moral conduct, the edifice being based on selfishness. This, however, is certain, that a habit of regarding the excellent counsel given respecting truth, integrity, benevolence, and virtue, would quite change the face of India society.

I have also before me a small volume containing "Extracts from the writings of Tamul Moralists," compiled and published by a civilian of Madras, for the use of schools. From the first, entitled *Moothoory*, let two illustrations be drawn. "Consider not the smallness of a man's body: the sea is vast and all its water bad, while the little spring is pure and tasteful." "Imagine not that the brethren of your household will be, of course, your protectors; disease born with you will destroy you, while the medicine in the far off and lofty mountain will be your cure and life."

From the "*Nannesi*." "An affectionate wife and

her lord should perform their domestic duties without disagreement, even as both the eyes look at the same object." "The worthy will rejoice at the approach of the good, and grieve at the sight of the wicked: on the approach of the south wind, the sweet mango-tree will put forth its tender leaves, but it will be troubled at the coming of the whirlwind.

From the "*Nulvurle.*" "If people are ready to be liberal, like a milch cow giving out fresh milk, all the world will be their near relatives."

From the "*Nèthĕnărĕvĕrlukkăm.*" "The world are led according to the taste of the warrior king. What else does the boat that is borne along the river current?" "A man who, without malice, takes up and dwells upon the faults of others only to excite laughter, is like a man who would kill his neighbor that he might see his body quiver in death."

Others might be added from *Naladiyar*, &c., but these must suffice.

The Hindoo mind has ever been distinguished for brilliancy rather than depth and strength; hence they have devoted more time to *literature* than science, and very much to *poetry*. The Abbé Du Bois remarks: "There is no country on earth where poetry was more in vogue than it was in former times in India. It seemed impossible for them to write but in verse. They have not a single ancient book that is written in prose; not even the books on medicine, grammar, and the like matter-of-fact themes. All Hindoo books not in verse are modern; at least it is so in regard to the Tamul, Teloogoo, and Canarese, and so far as I can learn, the country over."

Hindoo poetry, as we might infer from the intellectual and moral state of the nation, abounds in the most extravagant metaphors, and often very licentious images. As to the former feature, let a few instances suffice :

"Your glory so far exceeds the splendor of the sun, that his services are no longer necessary." "Thou art the greatest of plunderers. Other thieves purloin property which is worthless : thou stealest the heart. They plunder in the night ; thou in the day." "That person has discharged his arrow with such force, that thought cannot pursue it." "If there had been no spots on the moon, his face might, perhaps, have borne a comparison with thine."

A leading defect in their poems is, that the descriptions are too long and too minute. When describing a beautiful woman, they are never contented with drawing her likeness at a single stroke, as a European would do, but the writer must particularize the beauty of her eyes, forehead, nose, cheeks, and expatiate upon the color of her skin and her many ornaments. Not a part of her visible frame will escape his scrutiny and recital ; each will be represented in finished detail often with great power of expression, but frequently much to the weariness of the reader.

# CHAPTER XII.

## SCIENCE OF THE HINDOOS.

**The Hindoos not a barbarous People—Arithmetic—Geometry—Algebra —Trigonometry — Astronomy — Geography— Chronology— Natural Philosophy— Chemistry— Mineralogy —Botany— Geology—Doctors —Medical Institutions at Calcutta—Polytechnic Institutions—Lawyers—Present state of Learning in the land.**

Those of my readers who have been accustomed to regard the Hindoos as a semi-barbarous, illiterate people will have read, with some surprise, the statements and extracts of the preceding chapter. Were more needful to correct this erroneous impression, the necessity would be fully supplied by an illustration of the past and present character of *science* in that land. The limits assigned to this volume require brevity upon these topics, though it is intended to say enough to justify an assigning to the natives of India a high rank in the world of letters.

In all the sciences which contribute towards extending our knowledge of nature in mathematics, mechanics, and astronomy, *arithmetic* is of elementary use.

In whatever country, then, we find that such attention has been paid to the improvement of arithmetic as to render its operations easy and correct, we may presume that the sciences depending upon it have attained a proportional degree of perfection. Such improvement we find in India. While among the Greeks and Romans, the only method used for the notation of numbers was by the letters of the alphabet, which necessarily rendered arithmetical calculation extremely tedious and onerous, the Hindoos had, from time immemorial, employed for the same purpose, the ten ciphers or figures, and by means of them performed every operation in arithmetic with the greatest facility and expedition. The Arabians, not long after their settlement in Spain, introduced this mode of notation into Europe, and were candid enough to acknowledge that they had derived the knowledge of it from the Hindoos." Arithmetic is one of the few studies pursued in all the schools of the land. It is almost wholly *mental*, the operations being performed with extraordinary facility and correctness. It is interesting to observe a palanquin-maistry, for example, replying to your question, "how much he will ask to carry you to a distant place?" so many bearers—so many miles—so much for extras, &c.—he thinks, his lips move—a figure is noted upon the ground—again he thinks, and with less time than I have taken to write this sentence, he tells you the amount, and if his data be correct, you will find nothing wrong in the result.

The Hindoos are, as a nation, very correct accountants.

About the year 1150, of the Christian era, a learned sage of India wrote a work, which, in honor of his daughter, he called *Lilavati.* This volume contained treatises on *arithmetic* and *geometry*, and begins thus: "Having bowed to the Deity (Ganesa), whose head is like an elephant, whose feet are adored by gods, who, when called to mind, restores his votaries from embarrassment, and bestows happiness on his worshippers, I propound this easy process of computation, delightful by its elegance, perspicuous with words, concise, soft, and correct, and pleasing to the learned." The rules are then given in verse, and the language, when most technical, is often highly figurative. The *geometrical* part of this work contains the celebrated proposition that the square of the hypothenuse of a right-angled triangle is equal to the squares on the sides containing the triangle. And among other propositions the one which discovers the area of a triangle when the three sides are known. Geometry is not at present pursued in the common schools, and is but little understood among the most erudite of the land.

The author of Lilavati wrote a learned system on *algebra*, which had great repute, and was translated into various eastern languages, and finally in the year 1813, into the English. Another Hindoo work on algebra, had for its author Arya Bhatta, who lived in or before the fifth century of the Christian era, and was almost as ancient as the Greek algebraist, Diophantus, though the Hindoo treats the science with a completeness far beyond the Grecian; especially such points as the resolution of equations containing several unknown quantities, resolving indeterminate equations of at least the first degree, &c. Upon the question, "was the science of algebra known long before, and by what degrees of improvement did it advance, until the time of Arya Bhatta?" there is a division of opinion, the late Professor Playfair contending that the science had a commencement prior to both Grecian and Hindoo, while Delambre and others give to these sages the credit of originating it. "It appears," says a modern writer, "from the Hindoo treatises on algebra, that they understood well the arithmetic of surd roots, the resolution of equations of the second degree, a general solution of indeterminate problems of the first degree, and a method of deriving a multitude of answers to problems of the second degree, when one solution was discovered by trial—which was as near an approach to a general solution as was made until the time of Lagrange. They had not only applied algebra both to astronomy and geometry, but conversely applied geometry to the demonstration of algebraic rules." The ripe scholar and learned orientalist, Colebrooke has instituted a comparison between the Hindoo and Grecian algebraist, and finds reason to conclude that, in several most important respects, the *latter is very far behind the former.*

*Trigonometry* was also studied at a very early

period, as appears from the *Surya Siddhanta*, which contains a very rational view of this system.

From motives of curiosity, usefulness, and religion, the *heavenly bodies* have secured the interested and earnest attention of the thoughtful in all ages and nations. The most ancient and universal of all sciences is *astronomy*. The history of its rise in any country can never be absolutely determined, since it goes back far beyond all recorded annals, and is lost in the darkness of antiquity. The Brahmin tells you, with all gravity, that this science was first made known to the people of his land, in a volume called the *Surya Siddhanta*, a divine revelation, received 2,164,899 years ago. The learned Bailly was willing to allow that Hindoo astronomy had its origin more than 3000 years before Christ. Little was known of the state of this science in India until after the incursions by the Mohamedans. But during the last half century, much attention has been given to the subject by several English and French philosophers. It is impossible, in a work of this kind, to present a complete view of a subject so large, subtle, and scientific as this. With a few observations I must commend the reader to the History of British India, vol. iii. Chapter 13, Ward's View, &c., Part iii. sect. 35, and the appendix of "Robertson's History, Par. V. The latter writer says: "It may be considered as the general result of all the inquiries, reasonings, and calculations, with respect to Hindoo astronomy, which have hitherto been made public, that the motion of the heavenly bodies, and more particularly their position at the four epochs of 21st March, A. D. 638, 10th March, A. D. 1491, A. D. 1569, and one which extends back far before the Christian era, of which tables have with great labor been obtained, are ascertained with much accuracy; and that many of the elements of their calculations, especially for remote ages, are verified by an astonishing coincidence with the tables of the modern astronomy of Europe, when improved by the latest and most nice deductions from the theory of gravitation. The Brahmins, who annually circulate a kind of almanac containing astronomical predictions of the more remarkable phenomena in the heavens—such as the new and full moons, eclipses of the sun and moon—are in possession of certain methods of calculation, which, upon examination, are found to involve in them a very extensive system of astronomical knowledge. But though skilled in the use of the rules contained in his treatise, the Brahmin has no acquaintance with the mode of their structure. Seated on the ground with his shells before him, he repeats the enigmatical verses which are to guide his calculation, and from his little tablet of palm-leaves takes out the numbers that are to be employed in it, obtaining the result with great certainty and expedition." These tables have, as their threefold use, to compute the places of the sun and moon—to calculate the localities of the planets—and determine the positions of eclipses. It may be known to the reader that, according to the Vedas, the eclipses are occasioned by attacks upon the sun and moon by the monster Rahoo, because of a grudge he has against those orbs. It will not do for the Hindoo astronomer to declare that sentiment false, for it is found in a sacred book. He therefore avoids the difficulty by saying, that "certain things might have been so formerly, and may be so still; but *for astronomical purposes, astronomical rules must be used.*" And as to the teaching of the Shastras, that the earth is supported upon the heads of monsters, &c., these are explained to mean the moon's nodes and latitude; and thus an unity is preserved between the deductions of Science and the instructions of Revelation.

There are several points of oneness between the astronomical systems of the eastern and western continents. Both have distinguished that portion of the heavens in which the motions of the sun, moon, and planets are performed from the rest of the celestial sphere. There is an almost perfect identity between them in the number and names of the zodiacal signs. In both systems time is divided into periods of seven days (the Hindoos reckoning our Friday as their first day), and the ecliptic is divided into three hundred and sixty degrees. With these general remarks I must leave the interesting subject of Hindoo astronomy, except it be to say that *astrology*, a false branch of the noble science, is studied with much earnestness, great use being made of it for purposes of superstition—the "*star*" under which an event occurred, having much to do with its successful or adverse progress and completion.

A few sentences must suffice upon the science of *Geography*. "As nothing but actual observation could make the Hindoos acquainted with the surface, contents, and dimensions of the globe, and as their laws and institutions discourage the disposition to travel, as well as the translation and perusal of the enquiries of other nations, they have therefore, in this department of knowledge, completely failed." According to the Puranas, "The earth is circular and flat, like the flower of the water-lily, in which the petals project toward each other. Its circumference is 4,000,000,000 miles. In the centre is Mount Soomeroo, ascending in height 600,000 miles; at the base 128,000 in circumference; and 256,000 wide at the top. On this mountain are three peaks formed of gold, pearls and precious stones, where Vishnu, Siva, Indru, Ugnee, Yumu, and other deities, reside. The clouds ascend to about one-third of its height, while at its base are the mountains Munduru, Sundhu-madunu, Vipoolu, and Sooparshwu; on each of which grows a tree 8,800 miles high. On each side of the mountain are several countries, divided by ranges of mountains, the furthermost of which is bounded by the salt sea. Beyond this sea are six other seas—the sea of sugar-cane juice, of spirituous liquors, of clarified butter, of curds, of milk, and of sweet water, each surrounding a separate continent; beyond all which, is a country of gold as large as the rest of the earth; then a circular chain of mountains; and then the land of darkness, or hell. Gunga, proceeding from the foot of Vishnu, fell on Soomeroo; from thence on

Mount Vishkhumbu ; and thence on the head of Meha-Deou ; and thence divided into four large streams of great sanctity. If any one, though overwhelmed with sin, hear the name of Gunga (Ganges), or desire, behold, and touch this goddess, or bathe in her stream, taste of her waters, pronounce her name, call her to recollection, or extol her merits, he instantly becomes holy, and ascends to the heavens of the gods. When the sun, in its annual course, continues for six months in the northern hemisphere, the gods on Mount Soomeroo enjoy its rays, of which they are deprived when it passes to the southern hemisphere ; hence the doctrine that one year of mortals is equivalent to a night and day of the gods. In the centre of the globe is Patalu, where the darkness is dispelled by the splendor which issues from the pearly heads of the hydras. There the Usoorus and hydras remain ; there the daughters of the hydras, of exquisite beauty, sport with each other ; and there reside the immortals, enjoying the splendor of their own forms, brilliant as gold." The reader rightly judges that this description has little to commend it beyond the ingenuity of its imaginative author.

The system of *Hindoo Chronology* has, from different causes, excited much attention in the literary world. The *Măhă Yoog*, or great divine day, through which mankind are now passing, consists of four human ages, the last and worst of which is now revolving. These ages, of unequal and continually decreasing length, are the

| | |
|---|---|
| Satya Yoog, which lasted | 1,728,000 years. |
| Teeta Yoog | 1,296,000 " |
| Dwapar Yoog | 864,000 " |
| Kālĕ Yoog, which is to last | 432,000 " |

Of the dark era in which we live, only about five thousand years have already passed. Of the Satyayoog, the golden age of innocence, there remains only a dim and pleasing tradition, the great flood said to have occurred, at its close, swept away all its memorials. This vast sum of years has been eagerly seized upon by the opponents of the Bible as an argument against the Mosaic records. But the power of this deistical argument is broken by the fact, that but thirty-six kings are alleged to have reigned during the second, and forty-seven during the third period ; and as seventeen, or some say twenty years, is the average reign in a long series of kings, the Hindoo dynasties will not pass beyond our established chronology. The commencement of the Kālĕ Yoog does not materially differ from the Mosaic date of the creation.

As to natural philosophy, chemistry, mineralogy, botany, geology, and like departments of knowledge, there is no evidence on record of their having been pursued by the Hindoos as separate sciences. They, undoubtedly, engaged considerable attention, but no treatises upon these subjects are extant, so far as my information goes.

India abounds with *Doctors*, or to speak with more truth, with empirics and quacks since we have the authority of Sir Wm. Jones, for saying, that "physic appears in that country to have been, from time immemorial, as we see it practised at this day by Hindoos and Mohamedans, a mere empirical history of diseases and their remedies." The Shastras having affirmed, that, in the human body, there were certain defined elements, the student inferred from thence that all diseases were owing to the diminution or increase of these essential ingredients; and to reduce these elements when superabundant, and increase them when wanting, he had recourse to a series of medicines obtained from the bark, wood, roots, fruit, or flowers, of different plants or trees, or from a course of regimen supposed to be suited to the circumstances of the patient. Fevers they starve away by keeping the patient fasting from one to ten and even twenty days. They never bleed a patient, for the life is in the blood. Inoculation for the small pox has long been customary in India, the virus being introduced just above the wrist. The Hindoo depends, however, as much upon charms, and prayers for restoration to health, as upon medicines. The physician expects to receive his fee before prescribing, which varies, according to the ability of the patient, from a few pence to hundreds of dollars. While Hindoo practitioners decry the European 'Faculty,' they allow their superiority as *surgeons*, and borrow from them much knowledge respecting the stopping of bleeding, and setting of limbs. It is well for the poor Hindoos that the simplicity of their diet gives their blood uncommon purity, so that their wounds recover with wonderful expedition, otherwise the sufferings they would receive from the unskilful hand of the Hindoo surgeon could not be borne. The happiness of any community being so greatly dependent upon the character of its medical advisers, every philanthropist finds it a cause of gratitude and joy that *Medical Colleges* have been established under the direction of the English government at Calcutta, Madras, and Bombay. To each of these institutions are attached professors of high attainment, and native prejudice has so far yielded, that there is no lack of pupils, who are pursuing their studies with great diligence and zeal, and who will thus, ere long, supply India with sound medical assistance. I would here remark that *extensive hospitals* have been established in all the large cities and towns of the country, which are presided over by an European physician, with several Eurasian and native assistants. *Polytechnic institutions*, in which lectures on the sciences, especially chemistry, with modern discoveries in steam, galvanism, electricity, &c., have been established, and have thus far been attended with good results. When the foreigner tells a Hindoo that news can be transmitted a thousand miles a moment, the astonished listener professes to believe the statement, because "His Honor," or "the Reverend" says so, but *he would much like to see it done.*

If truth and justice do not triumph in India, it is not for want of Lawyers, any more than sickness and suffering are caused by lack of doctors. An injured person may, at any moment, obtain the services of one who is, by profession, learned in the law, and who promises to secure for him his rights of property, character and peace. If he be disappointed it is no more than falls to the lot of multitudes in this land, who trust to the like "uncertainty." But few natives are wealthy enough to retain an English barrister; most cases, therefore, are entrusted to a class of persons called Vakeels, who are little superior in knowledge and principles to the pettifoggers of an English or American court.

It is believed that no thoughtful reader of the preceding pages will deny to the Hindoos of former times the praise of much intellectual cultivation. "The variety of subjects upon which they wrote, prove that almost every science was cultivated among them, while the contents of their philosophical and law books indicate the depth of wisdom possessed by their authors compared with the writings of any nation flourishing at that time. In these respects the deterioration has been great and general throughout the country. The decay of Hindoo learning may be dated from the Mohamedan conquest. The heaviest blow struck was when Madura, eminent as the seat of a University famed the country over, became a prey to the ravages of the bigoted and unsparing conquerors. Up to that time, such was the celebrity of that city, in a literary and religious point of view, that multitudes congregated here annually from the most remote parts of the peninsula for instruction in science ; and here, too, Mr. Bell obtained an acquaintance with that mode of instruction which he carried to Europe, and immortalized his name. But as elevated as was the height, so deep has been the fall of national science in that country. A few Brahmins at Benares, and in connection with native colleges, read parts of the Shastras, Smirtees, Vedas, &c., and venture to publish editions of the same, with explanations. But no original works of note have appeared during the last century. In the library of a learned Hindoo may be found one of the grammars, a dictionary, five or six volumes of poetry, a few law books, a popular work on astronomy, portions of the Puranas, a few abridgments on the common religious rites and ceremonies. The Hindoo youth possesses a capacity for study and erudition by no means inferior to the young of other lands, but so soon as the elements of knowledge are acquired, he is removed from school to assist in supporting his family, and there his education closes. Hence the want of intelligence among the mass of the people, the necessity being urgent for those institutions of learning with which the benevolence of Christendom is furnishing that land ;—institutions which, while seeking as their ultimate and important end to sanctify the heart, are intended to enlighten the national mind upon the works and ways of the Divine Creator.

# CHAPTER XIII.

## ARTS AND OCCUPATIONS OF INDIA.

Introductory Remark—Agriculture—Modes of Cultivation—Native Plow, Harrow and Threshing Machines—Cultivation of Rice, Wheat, Barley, Indigo, Opium, Sugar, and Tobacco—Fabrics—Native Loom—Glass—Potter—Carpenter—Blacksmith—Goldsmith—Shoemaker—Brassfounder—Barber—Confectioner—Florist—Shopman—Washerman—Oilman—Milkman—Fisherman—Distiller—Palanquin Bearer—Difficulty of introducing Modern Implements—Public Buildings—Descriptions of Temples at Elephanta, Seringham, and Madura—Droogs—Reflections upon beholding these Ruins.

One cannot live long among the Hindoos without observing the vast discrepancy between the results of their industrial occupations and the means by which they are accomplished. In many departments of art India knows no superior, the world over, and yet the machinery employed is of the most simple and primitive kind; such, indeed, as no European artisan would use in forming the rudest structure or the coarsest fabric. By way of illustration, the reader's attention is requested to a review of the leading occupations and implements of the country. *Agriculture* stands foremost among the pursuits of native Hindoos. Two modes of cultivation are practiced, *wet* and *dry*, the former being devoted principally to rice and indigo, the land requiring to be watered by means of tanks with their strong, high embankments, and wells from twenty to three hundred feet deep, while upon the dry lands are the sugar cane, barley, wheat, and various other grains, fruits, and vegetables. The plough used by the farmer consists of two rude sticks, or one if sufficiently crooked, with an iron spike at the end, as a share which the ploughman guides with one hand, while he uses the other in directing the movements of the cattle; thus making a rut or scratch in the field similar to the movement just beneath the soil of a strong finger. Entering a village at an early hour of the day, you will see the farmer going to his toil, bearing upon his shoulder yoke and plough, which he steadies with one hand, while with the other he holds the rope-reins fastened to his tiny bullocks. The sowing is as clumsy as the ploughing. The common drill-machine has three pieces of sticks, that make scratches about an inch and a half in depth, and the seeds drop into the scratches through three hollow bits of bamboo, that are immediately behind the scratching sticks. These bamboos are united to one rude vessel at the top, containing the seeds. The larger seeds are sown by means of a bamboo fastened to the drill by a string, and having a little cup upon the end. A woman attends to this bamboo, holding directly over any one of the three scratches, into which she wishes the seed to fall with one hand, and dropping the seed into the cup with the other. The *covering plough* follows, which is a horizontal stick drawn along by two bullocks, and by being pressed against the ground, covers the seed with mould. The operation of sowing requires the attention of four persons and the labor of four bullocks. The business of the *harrow* is performed by an instrument like a ladder, on which the husbandman stands, while rough bushes attached to it assist smoothing the ground. Instead of threshing machines, the rice is beaten out of the husk, the pulse trodden out by the cattle, and the small grain threshed with a staff. These implements are the same that have been in use throughout the land, from time immemorial. Good *rice* lands in Bengal yield about forty bushels per acre, and in Mysore about forty-five; fifteen bushels of produce to one of seed being considered a fair return. In the rich districts among the Ghauts, there are often two crops a year, and at times three. In Guzerat, Malwa, and Allahabad, *wheat* is sown, which yields about fifty bushels per acre. In the hilly districts of the north *barley* is the bread-grain. India is famed for its *indigo*, which grows wild in the neighborhood of the Ganges and Jumna, but largely cultivated throughout Hindoostan Proper. *Opium* is the product of Bengal, Bahar, Allahabad, and Malwa, yielding from thirty to forty pounds to an acre of poppies. *Sugar* is very abundant in the Circars, and with due encouragement might furnish the market of all Europe. *Tobacco*, of excellent flavor, grows throughout the midland districts. Did my limits allow a complete exhibition of the mode of cultivating and gathering and perfecting these products, a like simplicity would appear in the system pursued, and implements used as before named. The same holds in respect to the productions of the *loom.* What fabrics more durable and beautiful, too, than the Arnee and Decca muslins, Malabar checks, Bengal chintz, with the silks of Burdwar, carpets of Ellore, flannels of Patra, the calicoes of Coromandel, the embroideries of Delhi, and shawls of the North and North-west. When examining the irregular texture, and fineness of thread and beauty of color, I have hardly known which was predominant, admiration of their superior excellence, or wonder at the places and modes of their formation. The weavers reside in villages, and when the article they make is in demand, a busy scene arrests the attention of the traveller. Man, woman, and child are all employed in one way or another. And all *in the open air*, except silk weaving, which is done in a cellar or low basement like room. The loom is rude enough, consisting of four forked sticks set in the ground,—two pieces across these sticks, to which the ends of the web are attached, for the warp is not rolled on a beam, as with us. The hiddles are but sticks and strings, which are fastened to the tree which shelters the weaver, and he gets a foot into each of the two loops at the bottom, and with this contrivance, upon which an European could not manufacture the coarsest canvas, the Hindoo perfects his delicate and beautiful texture. Bleaching, coloring, &c., are all done in the same simple but perfect manner. *Glass* is made in the Mysore district, but soft and opaque, being principally used for rings and bracelets. *Pottery* is rude and coarse, though abundant, a necessity being found in the fact that almost all the idols and cooking utensils are made from clay. The Hindoo *carpenter* knows no other tools than the plane, chisel, wimble, a hammer and hatchet. The earth his shop-board, his foot the hold-fast; but he will "turn out" an article which (in all respects but brilliancy of finish) will bear a comparison with the like productions in any English or American city. The *blacksmith* sets up his forge before the house of the person who calls him, and with the clay oven at hand, makes a wall, before which he places his hearth, and behind which are two leather bellows, kept in motion by his attendant apprentice; his anvil a stone, and his apparatus a pair of pincers, hammer, mallet, and file. Here he makes to order bill-hooks, spade, hoe, weeding-knife, ploughshare, nails, locks, keys, &c., as may be needed. The *goldsmith* also carries his shop with him. His furnace is an earthen pot—an iron pipe his bellows—while his crucible is made upon the spot, and thrown aside when no longer needed. Who would suppose, when admiring the "Trichinopoly watch-chains," with the gold and silver ornaments of Vizagapatam, that the utensils employed in their manufacture are thus simple and rude. The females of India being excessively fond of ornaments, the workers in the precious metals have constant and profitable employment. The *shoemakers*, though very important members of community, are esteemed among the lowest in the land. In social position they are below the Soodras, and are employed as executioners of criminals, and for carrying away dead bodies. A knife and awl are their tools. The leather is made after the shoes are ordered, and the article is cheap and inferior. To these may be added *brass-founders*, *shell ornament makers*, *barbers*, who may be seen at the road-side, shaving the head, shaving or plucking the beard. *Confectioners*, with the hundred different sweet meats, principally composed of sugar, molasses, flowers and spices, of which all natives, adult and young, are excessively fond. *Sellers of flowers*, who prepare wreaths for the bride and groom, with the other appendages to a marriage procession. *Shop-keepers* of various grades. *Washermen*, who make sad havoc of the clothes put in their charge by beating them upon a flat board or stone till cleansed, and then pounding with a mallet till made smooth and fit for use. *Bankers*, or money-changers, who are ever ready to accommodate you with funds at 10 to 40 per cent. interest. *Oilmen*, who furnish an excellent article pressed from the cocoanut shell and castor bean, either of which emits a clear, strong, and steady light, with no unpleasant odor. *Milkmen*, who will, if well watched, bring to you for a reasonable sum this needful accompaniment of an evening's meal, and of a character superior to any just anticipations upon seeing the poor condition in which the animals are kept by their owners. *Fishermen*, a hardy, industrious, but illiterate class of persons, who find a ready market for an article of food which but few, even among the most religious Hindoos, need reject. *Distillers*, who make *arrack* from rice, molasses, water, and spices ; and a species of rum, made from the bark of several trees steeped in water ; and, finally, *Palanquin-bearers*, a laborious and useful class, referred to in a preceding chapter.

Such are some of the trades and occupations of native Hindoos, with the implements of their industry. "But why," asks my reader, "do not foreigners introduce the machines and implements of the western continent?" To a limited extent this has been done ; but it is a precept of that land most faithfully heeded, that "ancient custom is irreversible law." The English officer who had in charge the district of Madura during my residence in that city, imported from England several ploughs and hoes, with an admirable loom for weaving cotton. "To please His Honor," the complaisant farmer used the plough for a little time, but soon found a plausible pretext for returning to the time-honored scratcher ; while the other implements met a no more fortunate reception. We made every effort to induce the woman who swept our rooms to use the brooms we carried from this country, instead of the bunch of grass tied in a brush-like form, which was to the highest extent wearisome : but, no, custom prevented. The same obstacle opposes all advances in cotton cultivation, and like improvements.

"Our fathers did so, and so will we," say the people all the country over. The native Hindoos excel as copyists. Their painters will give the most faithful representations of any object that is set before them; their craftsmen will build a carriage or construct a piece of furniture the fac similie of any given model; and their tailors never fail in making a garment precisely according to the pattern. They excel in this species of accurate imitation rather than in originating any new device or unattempted contrivance. In this connection may be introduced a few remarks respecting the *public buildings* of India. These are of two kinds, those consecrated to the offices of religion, and fortresses built for the security of the country. To the former are given the general names of *temples* and *pagodas*, and indicate by their vast dimensions and high degrees of finish, a state of public sentiment, as well as skill and energy, which belonged to a race scarcely within the range of known history. Let three suffice by way of illustration. The pagoda, in the island of Elephanta, near Bombay, has been hewn by the hands of man out of a solid rock, about half way up a high mountain, and formed into a spacious area nearly one hundred and twenty feet square. In order to support the roof and the weight of the mountain that lies above it, a number of massy pillars have been cut out of the same rock, at such regular distances as on the first entrance presents an appearance of great beauty and strength. Much of the inside is covered with human figures in high relief, of gigantic size as well as singular forms, and distinguished by a variety of symbols representing, it is probable, the attributes of the deities whom they worshipped, or the actions of the heroes whom they admired. In the Isle of Salsette, still nearer Bombay, are excavations in a similar style, hardly inferior in magnificence, and destined for the same religious purposes. The first pagoda I visited was that on the island of Seringham, near the city of Trichinopoly, and my memory still retains a vivid impression of its vastness and magnificence. It is composed of seven square enclosures, one within another, the walls of which are twenty-five feet high and four thick. These enclosures are three hundred and fifty feet distant from one another, and each has four large gates with a high tower, which are placed one in the middle of each side of the enclosure, and opposite to the four cardinal points. The outward wall is nearly four miles in circumference, and its gateway to the south is ornamented with pillars, several of which are single stones thirty-three feet long, and nearly five feet in diameter; and those which form the roof are still larger. In the inmost enclosure is the chapel, which vies with Benares and Ramisseran for sanctity and efficacious power to bless the unnumbered pilgrims who flock to it from the remotest distances to secure absolution and heaven. Few places in India have obtained greater or more permanent celebrity than the city of Madura. In this connection I name the single feature of a large edifice (called a choultry) built by Trimal Naig, an ancient king of great wealth and power. This building is in the form of a parallelogram, three hundred and twelve feet in length, by one hundred and twenty-five in breadth. It consists of one vast hall, the ceiling of which is supported by six rows of columns twenty-five feet high, most of which are formed of single stones, and the whole composed of hard, grey granite. On the second pillar to the right of the spectator as he enters, is the figure of the founder of this gorgeous structure, in a group with six of his wives, one of whom has a large gash below the hip on the left side, the result of a blow by her royal lord, because she told him tauntingly that the edifice was far inferior in splendor to her father's stables. Beyond this column are other statues, commemorative of remarkable events in the respective reigns of his ancestors. The same prince erected a palace but a short distance from this choultry, which the present ruins show to have been a noble structure. Rising from the immense plains of India are eminences and rocks, of which the natives early took possession, and fortifying them with works of various kinds, rendered them almost impregnable stations. Of these fortresses, or *droogs*, several still remain near the city of Benares and in the Deccan, which must have been constructed in very remote times, and repelled almost any amount of force which could have been brought to bear against them. India abounds with the magnificent remains of temples, palaces, pagodas, forts, mausoleums, and walls, which indicate the past existence in that land of a wealth, power, ingenuity, religious zeal, and enterprise, which forms a sad contrast with what now appears in the sentiments and feelings of the nation. The person who would have his heart filled with strong, delighted, sorrowing, and wondrous emotions, let him go to Delhi, to Benares, to Mysore, to Madura, and he will return satisfied so far as feeling is concerned, but still perplexed with questions to which no replies have been returned, and which will remain forever veiled in the darkness of remote antiquity.

# CHAPTER XIV.

## POPULAR AMUSEMENTS OF INDIA.

Hindoos not fond of work—Card-playing—Backgammon—Dominoes—Checkers—Chess—Quoits—Marbles—Cock-fighting—Dancing—Story-telling; Tale of the three deaf men—Theatrical Exhibitions—Hunting—Gymnastics and Jugglery, illustrated by descriptions of wondrous feats—Remarks.

"*Labor ipse voluptas*," conveys a sentiment with which the Hindoo has no practical sympathy. When he works, it is from necessity, not choice—to satisfy a demand, not to gratify an inclination. In place of the motto, "labor is itself pleasant," he would substitute this, "*work* when you *must*, *be idle* when you *can*, eat, drink, and be merry." My reader may suggest that this is human nature the world over. Grant it, but in regions within the tropics the instinct is less easy of resistance than in our more vigorous clime, while with greater simplicity of dress and diet the necessity is not so urgent for laborious exertion of mind and body. The Brahmins, not in government offices, do little after completing their daily routine of ceremonies than recline, talk, and while away the weary hours in modes more pleasing than profitable. Upon the afternoon they may be seen upon the front verandahs of their dwellings, the picture of contentment, self-satisfaction, and indolence. If one member of a Hindoo family secure a situation which yields a salary sufficient to maintain the household, even the husband, son, or brother, deem it in no way unbecoming to look to that source for their daily subsistence. It is in reference to customs such as prevail throughout India that the saying of the wise man holds true :—" If riches increase, they increase who eat them." To these remarks there are honorable exceptions—but such is the *habit* of the nation.

To be wholly unemployed is wretchedness, therefore the Hindoo relieves this ennui by attendance upon religious festivals, the number of which is great and the parade attractive and imposing—presence at marriage ceremonies, with their showy and brilliant accompaniments—and participating in or witnessing amusements, shows, sports, which are by turns mirthful, tragic, and deeply exciting. Many of these find their counterparts in our own country, while others are adapted to Eastern taste and habits. Hours are wasted at the *card-table*, with the common yet sad results of property, character, and peace, sacrificed at the shrine of this ensnaring game. *Backgammon* is attractive to many, together with the less intellectual *dominoes* and *checkers*. *Chess* is reserved for the few who are willing and disposed to think long and intently. By the highway may be seen youth and adults playing at *quoits* and *marbles*, with much skill and earnestness. *Cock-fighting* is confined to the Mohamedans or lower class of Hindoos, and is pursued with all the refinements of cruelty common to that heartless sport.

*Dancing* is restricted to the females, and of these to a class among whom virtue and modesty have no abode. The movements of the Hindoo "dancing girl," whether before the idol or in the presence of nobility and wealth, are wholly free from those vehement pirouettes, extravagant contortions of limb, dizzy gyrations, and pedal dexterity, which made the name of Fanny Ellsler, Europe and America famed. The Nautch girl advances gracefully before her audience, her arms moving in unison with her tiny naked feet, with little variety but much grace, and with an expressiveness of motion both understood by, and gratifying to those who sympathize with the actress in moral sentiments, though suggestive of sorrow and disgust to one of high and pure emotions. The ornaments worn by these dancers are often of great elegance and high value. The throat is encircled with several necklaces, sometimes composed of pearls, and often of gold richly chased. A large jewel hangs from the right nostril, suspended by a plain gold ring. On the forehead, between the eye-brows, an ornament is worn, which has, no doubt, given rise to the sevigné, gracing of late the European belle. Their symmetry of form, modesty and elegance of attire, gracefulness of attitude and motion, contrast most sadly with their habitual habits and feelings. The most abandoned of their sex, captives to licentiousness, you can in no way more directly insult a Hindoo female than by calling her a *dancing girl.* On this account India Nautches are decreasing in popularity, and will do so in proportion to the progress of high-toned morality among the European residents. The time has gone by when a civilian or military officer would take his wife and daughter to these entertainments, and yet the dances, generally speaking, are much more decent, than those encouraged in the theatres of Europe, which young and innocent girls are permitted to behold and applaud without a blush.

*Story-telling* and *hearing* consume a great deal of a Hindoo's time. Some of these tales are accounts of marvels performed by deities and heroes, while others are entirely fictitious. By way of illustrating the latter class, I will insert a "*Tale of Four Deaf Men*:"

"A deaf shepherd was one day tending his flock, near his own village; and though it was almost noon, his wife had not yet brought him his breakfast. He was afraid to leave his sheep to go in quest of it, lest some accident should befall them. But his hunger could not be appeased; and upon looking around, he spied a Talaiyari, or village hind, who had come to cut grass for his cow, near a neighboring spring. He went to call him, though very reluctantly, because he knew that though those servants of the village are set as watchmen to prevent theft, yet they are great thieves themselves. He hailed him, however, and requested him just to give an eye to his flock during the short time he should be absent, and that he would not forget him when he returned from breakfast. But the man was as *deaf as himself;* and mistaking his intentions, he angrily asked the shepherd, "What right have you to take this grass which I have had the trouble to cut? Is my cow to starve that your sheep may fatten? Go about thy business and let me alone." The deaf shepherd observed the repulsive gesture of the hind, which he took for a signal of acquiescence, and therefore briskly ran towards the village, fully determined to give his wife a good lesson for her neglect. But, when he approached his house, he saw her before the door, rolling in the pains of a violent colic. Her sad condition, and the necessity he was under to provide breakfast for himself, detained the shepherd longer than he wished; while the small confidence he had in the person with whom he left the sheep, accelerated his return. Overjoyed to see his flock peaceably feeding near the spot where he left them, he counted them over; and finding there was not a single sheep missing, 'He is an honest fellow,' quoth he, 'this *Talaiyari*, the very jewel of his race! I promised him a reward, and he shall have it.' There was a lame beast in the flock, well enough in other respects, which he hoisted on his shoulders and carried to the place where the hind was, and courteously offered him the mutton, saying, 'You have taken great care of my sheep during my absence. Take this one for your trouble.' 'I,' says the deaf hind, '*I break your sheep's leg!* I'll be hanged if ever I went near your sheep since you have been gone, or stirred from the place where I now am.' 'Yes,' says the shepherd, '*it is good and fat mutton*, and will be a treat to you, your family, and friends.' 'Have I not told thee,' replied the Talaiyari in rage, '*that I never went near thy sheep;* and yet thou wilt accuse me of breaking that one's leg. Get about thy business, or I will give thee a beating.' And by his gestures he seemed determined to put his threat into execution. The astonished shepherd got into a passion also, and assumed a posture of defiance. They were just proceeding to blows, when a man on horseback came up. To him they both appealed to decide the dispute between them; and the shepherd laying hold of the bridle, requested the horseman to alight just for a moment, and to settle the difference between him and the beggarly Talaiyari. 'I have offered him a present of a sheep,' said he, 'because I thought that he had done me a service; and, in requital, he will knock me down.' The villager was at the same time preferring his complaint, that the shepherd would accuse him of breaking the leg of his sheep, when he had never been near his flock. The horseman, to whom they had both appealed, happened to be *as deaf as they;* and did not understand a word that either of them said. But seeing them both addressing him with vehemence, he made a sign to them to listen to him, and then frankly told them that he confessed that the horse he rode was not his own. 'It was a stray animal that I found on the road,' quoth he, 'and being at a loss, I mounted him for the sake of expedition. If he be yours take him. If not, pray let me proceed, as I am really in great haste.' The shepherd and the hind, each imagining that the horseman had decided in favor of the other, became more violent than ever; both accusing the umpire of partiality. At this crisis there happened to come an aged *Brahmin.* Instantly they all crowded around him—shepherd, Talaiyari, and horseman—each claiming his interposition, and a decision in his favor. All spoke together, every one telling his own tale. But the *Brahmin had lost his hearing also.* 'I know,' said he, 'that you want to compel me to return to her (meaning his wife), but do you know her character? In all the legions of evil ones I defy you to find one that is her equal in wickedness. Since the time I first bought her, she has made me commit more sin than it will be in my power to expiate in thirty generations. I am going on a pilgrimage to Kasi (Benares), where I will wash myself from the innumerable crimes I have been led into, from the hour on which I had the misfortune to make her my wife. Then will I wear out the rest of my days on alms in a strange land.' While they were all venting their exclamations *without hearing a word*, the horse-stealer perceived some people advancing toward them with great speed.

Fearing that they might be the owners of the beast, he dismounted and took to his heels. The shepherd seeing it was growing late, went to look after his flock, pouring out imprecations, as he trudged along, against all arbitrators, and bitterly complaining that all justice had departed from the earth. Then he bethought himself of a snake that had crossed his path in the morning, as he came out of the sheep-fold, and which might account for the troubles he had that day experienced. The Talaiyari returned to his load of grass; and finding the lame sheep there, he took it on his shoulders, to punish the shepherd for the vexation he had given him, and the aged Brahmin pursued his way to a choultry not far off. A quiet night and sound sleep soothed his anger in part, and early in the morning, several Brahmins, his neighbors and relations, who had traced him out, persuaded him to return home, promising to engage his wife to be more obedient and less quarrelsome in future."

With stories like these, the memory of the Hindoo is full, and it requires but a brief residence in the country to observe the use made of them, in relieving the tedium of long journeys by night, and unemployed hours on the verandahs of their dwellings.

*Theatrical exhibitions* are common throughout the country, especially during the four months when the deeds of Krishna, Rama, Siva, and Doorga are to be recalled and celebrated. These entertainments occur at night, and are often continued until near morning, the spectators being affected with grief and joy to as great a degree as those who behold the tragedies and comedies of the European stage. Many of these scenes having reference to alleged and recorded events in the life of the lascivious Krishna, produce a very deleterious effect upon the morals of the spectators—especially the young, to whom the drama proves a curse and ruin.

*Tiger and elephant hunting* once engaged a large share of public attention. After much and long preparation, the nabob would sally forth with the retinue of a thousand strong, to attack the noble tenants of the jungle and forest. He was not unfrequently attended by the European resident, from whom a voyage across the sea had not taken a love for the chase. But those scenes belong to the past, hunting being confined to the northern districts and conducted upon a limited scale and with diminished zeal.

The Hindoos delight in the *marvellous*, as appears from their fondness for such tales as that before named, and others akin to the "Arabian Nights." On this account it is not surprising that the country should have become famed for its *gymnastics* and *jugglery*. Both are carried to a perfection that defies all competition. The eye must witness their feats of agility and cunning ere the mind can really believe them possible. I am aware that this is a trite topic, and yet some of my readers may not have in their memories the precise methods in which the Hindoos show their skill, and for their benefit I will name a few instances, some of which have come under my own observation, and all are authentic. The jugglers and gymnastic performers journey in companies, carrying their poles, ropes, baskets, jars, &c., with them, and perform wherever they can secure profitable spectators. You are sitting on the verandah, and a company enters the yard. If you do not bid them away they will begin something in this manner: A woman takes a bamboo twenty feet high, places it upright on a flat stone, and then, without any support, climbs to the top with surprising activity. Having done this, she stands upon one leg on the point of the bamboo, balancing it all the while. Around her waist she has a girdle to which is fastened an iron socket;—springing from her upright position on the bamboo, she throws herself horizontally forward with such exact precision, that the top of the pole enters the socket of the iron zone, and in this position she spins herself with a velocity that makes you giddy to look at; the bamboo appearing all the while as if it were supported by some supernatural agency. She turns her legs backward till the heels touch her shoulders, and grasping the ankles in her hands, continues her rotation so rapidly as to appear like a revolving ball. Then sliding down the pole she balances it on her chin, then upon her nose, and finally, projects it a distance from her without the application of her hands.

This over—a man comes forward, places his head downward, with his heels in the air, raises his arms and crosses them upon his breast, balancing himself all the while upon his head. A cup which he projects upward, containing sixteen balls is now placed in his hands; keeping the whole sixteen in constant motion, crossing them, and causing them to describe all kinds of figures, and not allowing one of them to reach the ground. A small man then climbs up his body, and stands upon the inverted feet of the performer. A second cup, containing sixteen balls, is handed to him, who commences throwing them until the thirty-two are in motion. The whole being caught in the cups, the upper man jumps to the ground, and the other as nimbly springs to his feet.

Such feats being over, a performer comes near you, spreads a cloth upon the ground about the size of a sheet. After lying still for some time, it seems to move upward, and upon being removed you see several *pine-apples* growing under it, which the performer presents to you as proof that they are the genuine article. I have witnessed this trick many times, and yet it is to me wholly inexplicable.

Does the reader "see through" that, well here is one. A man takes a large earthen vessel, with a capacious mouth, fills it with water, and turns it upside down, when all the water flows out. The moment, however, it is turned mouth upwards, it is full again. He allows you to take it. You do so. You examine it. By his permission you break it in pieces, and yet you are no wiser than before.

Here is another: A basket is produced, under which is put a lean *Pariah dog*; after the lapse of a minute the basket is removed and she appears with a litter of seven puppies. These are again covered, and upon raising the magic basket a *goat* is presented to view. Then comes a *pig*, in the full vigor of existence, and when covered a little time it is presented with its throat cut, and again it is restored to life.

But here comes what children call "hocus pocus." A man takes a small bag full of brass balls, which he throws one by one into the air to the number of thirty-five. None of them appear to return. After a little pause, and a significant, guttural call, they are seen to fall one by one until the whole of them are replaced in the bag.

But I must not continue these illustrations farther, for I am occupying space which might be devoted to more practical topics. I might allude to the snake catchers and charmers, and other feats of legerdemain, but these must suffice. As to the reality of such performances there is no room to doubt, as to the explanation, I can but refer the reader to the performers themselves.

Such are some of the amusements by which the Hindoo beguiles the weary hours, and gratifies his taste for the mirthful, tragic, and marvellous. Accustomed as they are to deeds of mystery, the argument in favor of the Christian system drawn from *miracles* is almost powerless upon their minds. Over against one miracle upon the Gospel record, multitudes are contained in their sacred books, and performed before their eyes. Their judgment may tell them that it is jugglery, and so say they may have been those of the Founder of Christianity. To pluck up mountains and hurl them to and fro at will—to cut off parts of the moon, and cast them to the earth—to fish up sacred books from the bottom of the sea—these are but a few among the deeds of the Hindoo deities, and what more of miracle can any religion allege. This objection against the *special* divinity of Christianity is often and skilfully used by the Brahmin, to parry the blow aimed against his favorite creed, and to gain for the system he teaches a stronger hold upon the faith of its credulous and attached devotees.

# CHAPTER XV.

## MUSIC OF THE HINDOOS.

Remarks on the universal prevalence of Music—Antiquity of Hindoo Song—Remarkable statements by Sir William Jones—"No accounting for tastes"—Hindoo Gamut—Extract from Abbé Du Bois—Names of musical instruments—Style illustrated by Stanzas from the Poem of Arumuga Tambiran, sung at his baptism—Two verses written in English by a Convert at Calcutta—Authors of "Spiritual Songs" in Southern India.

"The practice of music is universal. There appears no nation upon the face of the earth to whom it is not familiar. It is, so to speak, the vernacular idiom of nature, and may be considered to be coeval with creation." India, in its past and present attachment to song, illustrates the truth of these well-advised remarks. Music accompanies all Hindoo festivals, all their processions whether solemn or gay, many of their religious ceremonies, and is almost daily resorted to the country over, as an evening recreation of the social circle. And so has it been from the earliest period, for, as another has eloquently said, "When the war songs of the Germans in the time of Tacitus, were pealed from hill to hill, like the cry of the Scottish gathering, or echoed through the dark tracts of their primeval forests, over which, perhaps, the waters of the deluge had poured their devastation, the Vina of the Hindoos was heard among the palm-groves of the East, tuned to scientific measures, and sharing with the nightingale the admiration of man."

The celebrated Orientalist, Sir William Jones, in an article on Hindoo music, uses this language.

"A learned native told me that he had frequently seen the most venomous and malignant snakes leave their holes upon hearing tunes on a flute, which gave them peculiar delight. And an intelligent Persian, who repeated his story again and again, and permitted me to write it down from his own lips declared that he had more than once been present when a celebrated lutanist, surnamed Bulbul, was playing to a large company, in a grove near Shiraz, when he distinctly saw the nightingales trying to vie with the musician, sometimes warbling on the trees, sometimes fluttering from branch to branch, as if they wished to approach the instrument whence the melody proceeded; and at length dropping on the ground in a kind of ecstacy, from which they were soon raised by a change of mode."

I feel no disposition to question the truth of these statements or to derogate ought from the fame of Hindoo musicians—but if these things were as Sir William and others tell us, the Hindoos have indeed

"Fallen from their high estate."

It is true that the natives of that country will allow the superiority of foreigners in almost all respects except *in musical skill*—it is true that, as I have myself observed, if upon the esplanade at Madras, the Governor's band is discoursing its finest strains at one end of the field, and half-dozen tom-tom and cymbal beaters are performing on the other end, the natives will flock to the latter with expressions of surprise that any musical ear could not perceive the superiority of India over England—but it is hard to make the foreigner hear in the clash and clangor of Hindoo trumpets, cymbals, and drum, ought but *noise*, "et præterea nihil." Were the reader to be where the writer has often found himself—in a village bungalow —trying to get a little rest after a day's toil, he will wish that the tom-tom and horn were anywhere else than within his hearing—so discordant, harsh, unmelodious.

I shall be doing the Hindoos injustice if the impression be left upon the reader's mind that the music of India is performed, even at this time, without skill. The gamut has been known among them from the earliest time, and the Abbé Du Bois thinks that it has been borrowed from them by other nations who now use it. "It is but in modern times," he says, "that it has been introduced into Europe by the Benedictine monk, Guido Aretino, who adapted it to the seven signs, *ut*, *re*, *mi*, *fa*, *sol*, *la*, *sa*, which are the first syllables of some words contained in the first strophe of the

Latin hymn composed in honor of John the Baptist, which runs thus :—

> “ [1]Ut queant laxis [2]resonare fibris
> [3]Mira gestorum [4]famuli tuorum
> [5]Solve polluti [6]labii reatum
> [7]Sancte Joanes.”

The Gamut of the Hindoo is the same as ours, being composed of the same number of notes and arranged the same way.

What renders the music of India so unwelcome to a cultivated ear, is the limited number of their tunes, and therefore constant reiteration of the same notes, and the small variety of their instruments together with the imperfect manner in which they are played. Dr. Ward of Serampore mentions about forty kinds of instruments, of which twelve are different species of *drums*, four of *tabors*, four of *violins*, with the *cymbal*, *reed*, *horn*, *hautboy*, *flute*, *&c.* The most common article, and one that is dinging in your ear wherever you go is the tom-tom—which is nothing more than a half-tanned sheepskin, drawn, when damp, over a wide mouthed earthen or iron vessel from six to twenty or more inches across, and when dry beaten with a stick or leathern thong. This is often accompanied by a pair of sharp-sounding cymbals. A funeral procession is preceded by two persons, blowing each a long horn which emits a doleful and prolonged note of a distinctive, and at times very plaintive and sorrowing character. There are horns also at marriage festivities, but of different shape and note. Scattered over the country, are pensioned or dismissed band-men, formerly attached to European corps who are not unfrequently present at funerals, and amid the clangor of cymbal and horn, you distinguish the notes of the "Dead March in Saul," upon the drum and fife. A strange medley which provokes a smile though in the presence of death.

Every pagoda of any note, has a band of musicians; who are obliged to attend at the temple twice every day, to make it ring with their discordant sounds and inharmonious airs. A portion of the musicians execute the vocal part, and sing hymns in honor of the gods.

The singing of native Hindoos is much in the style of a chant—with prolongation of the sound at the end of each line. I am desirous of illustating this topic of Hindoo songs, but find a difficulty in selecting a piece entirely appropriate. I have concluded, however, to insert parts of a poem which was written by a religious mendicant, when renouncing Hindooism and embracing Christianity. He sang it at his baptism. It describes in detail, the means he had successfully used to secure pardon and heaven.

1. High places ascending, sitting painfully cross-legged
as a Yogee and meditating . . . Enough, enough.
Now the majestic Jesus who came to
save me . . . . . . Behold ye, behold ye.

2. The sacred Sadi, with entangled hair Rut-
tracham, necklaces and beads . . Enough, enough,
Now—Jesus who delivers me from trusting
in such things . . . . Behold ye, behold ye,

3. Dressing in yellow robes and rubbing ashes on
the body . . . . . . . Enough, enough.
Now—the Lord Jesus who saw me and
saved me . . . . . Behold ye, behold ye.

4. Bathing in holy-waters and visiting Siva
temples . . . . . . . Enough, enough.
Now—Jesus, the God of gods who
sought me and saved me . . Behold ye, behold ye.

5. Wandering to holy places and bowing to
images . . . . . . . Enough, enough.
Now—the Divine Jesus who discovered
and saved me . . . . Behold ye, behold ye.

6. Of feast days and following idol
cars . . . . . . . Enough, enough.
Now—Jesus the Lord of worlds who pow-
erfully saves me . . . . Behold ye, behold ye.

7. Wearied with long pilgrimages to Casi,
fainting and forlorn . . . . Enough, enough.
Now the excellent Jesus who gov-
erns me by his grace . . . Behold ye, behold ye.

8. Carefully performing prayers, rites, and
sacrifices . . . . . . Enough, enough.
Now—the salvation of the loving Jesus,
to which He has called us . . . Behold ye, behold ye.

9. Gathering sacred flowers, and plucking ears of
the Vilvum to perform idol
worship . . . . . . Enough, enough.
Now—the sweet salvation of the
Supreme Jesus . . . . Behold ye, behold ye

10. Dropping holy oil into the sacred fire;
then whispering senseless mantras into
the ears of deluded disciples . . Enough, enough.
Now—to the pure baptism of Jesus
who fills all . . . . Come ye, come ye.

11. Cymbals, brass plates, and bells sound-
ing in every street . . . . Enough, enough.
Now—to the prayers and praises of the
God Jesus . . . . Come ye, come ye,

12. Dancing before idols, hands clapping,
and prostrations . . . . Enough, enough.
Now the rightly instituted worship of
the High Priest Jesus . . . Come ye, come ye.

13. Adorning with garlands, heathen vest-
ments and necklaces . . . Enough, enough.
Now—to the high praises of the
heavenly Jesus . . . . Come ye, come ye.

14. Wearing the Branim string and
saying daily mantras . . . . Enough, enough.
Now—to the holy sacrament of
the spotless Jesus . . . . Come ye, come ye.

15\. Studying the Vethams and Shastras
to obtain salvation . . . . Enough, enough.
Now—to the true Gospel of the
exalted Jesus . . . . Come ye, come ye.

16\. To leave wordly, lying, heathen-
ism . . . . . . Strive ye, strive ye.
Now—to the doctrine taught
by God's ministers . . . Come ye, come ye.

The reader may gather from these stanzas some impression as to the manner in which the Poem is constructed. It was sung in a slow tone, with a dwelling upon the chorus "Enough, enough.—Come ye, come ye."

The native style of singing is not retained in places of Christian worship—hymns having been written to the tunes common with us, as "Old Hundred," "Mear," "St. Thomas," and the like. That the Hindoo can adapt himself by practice to the European stanza is evident from many examples that might be given. Here is one which was written by a Hindoo, a proficient in English, and sung at his baptism.

"Long sunk in superstition's night, by sin and Satan driven,
I saw not, cared not, for the light which leads the blind to heaven.
I sat in darkness, reason's eye was shut, was closed in me,
I hastened to eternity, o'er error's dreadful sea.

But now, at length, thy grace, O Lord, bids all around me shine,
I drink thy sweet, thy precious word, I kneel before thy shrine.
I've broke affection's tenderest ties, for my dear Saviour's sake,
All, all, I love beneath the skies, Lord, I for thee forsake."

The reader will rightly conclude that the writer of those verses could easily compose hymns to our metre.

The Tamil churches of Southern India are much indebted to the late Mr. Rhenius and to my esteemed friends, the Rev. Messrs. Spaulding and Hutchings, with contributions from the lamented Lawrence and others for the "spiritual songs" sung in missionary chapels.

A hymn-book, used by the Canarese Christians of the Mysore district, lies before me, chiefly from the pen of the Rev. Messrs. Rice and Campbell, of the London Missionary Society.

The German missionaries have always taken a leading part in this department of Christian literature.

This is as much as my limits will allow me to say on the music of the Hindoos.

# CHAPTER XVI.

## PECULIAR CEREMONIES.

Two circumstances that impart importance to the birth of a Hindoo—Hindoo names, whence derived, and the ceremony of giving them—Hindoo Marriages—Courtship—Desirable qualities in a Wife—Kooleen Brahmins—Death—Exclamations of a Mother over a Dead Child—Strange Comforters—Nuisances on the Ganges—Burning of Bodies—Singular custom in the Northern Districts—Parsee mode with their Dead—Mohamedan Cemeteries—Also Roman Catholic—Graves of Foreigners—Superiority of the Gospel over Brahminism in the Dying Hour.

Connected with the birth, naming, marriage, and death of a Hindoo, there are ceremonies of a distinctive character, with which the reader may find an interest in becoming acquainted.

There are two circumstances which impart peculiar interest to the natal hour, of which the first is the *position of the heavenly bodies* at the time the event occurs. Respectable Hindoos keep an astrologer in waiting, who, so soon as informed of the birth of the infant, "casts its nativity, and opens the roll of its fate." Having drawn up a paper minutely describing what of weal or woe is to befall the young stranger during his present, and sometime his future life, he hands the same to the father, who deposits it in his house for reference when good or ill happens to his child. These family records are often of real value in the settlement of legal questions. The *sex* of the infant is the second feature of interest, and one that awakens no little anxiety in the mind of a native Hindoo. As the male members of a family can alone perform the funeral rites of a parent, the birth of a son awakens far different emotions than than that of a daughter; the one being an occasion for chagrin and sorrow, the other of gratitude and delight. When the father first goes to see the child, if a rich man, he puts a silver coin in its hand, as do other wealthy relatives. The Hindoo mother, both before and after confinement, is treated with the highest consideration by her family, she and the infant being supplied with everything which will conduce to their comfort and health.

When the child is a few days old, the parents *give to it a name;* generally that of a *deity*, for the alleged reason, that "the repetition of the names of the gods is meritorious, and operates like fire in consuming sin." The names of the lads under my instruction were often such as these, Krishnun, Rama, Narraiyanun, Gopalu, and the like, all the appellatives of celestials; while others were honored with the titles of Pareya Swamy (great god), Chinna Swamy (little god), Chinna Tumbe (little brother), &c. Females are named after the goddesses; as Kalé, Doorga, Lukshmée, Gunga; as also titles descriptive of some prominent excellence, as, the "Beloved of Vishnu," the "Water-lily," and the "Beautiful." Some parents give an unpleasant name to a child born after repeated bereavements, as Dookhee (sorrowful), Haranu (the lost); the reason they assign for which is, that the former were such pleasant children, and had such sweet names, that they died through the envy of others. The Hindoo stands in constant awe of the bad passions of those around him. If a rich man become poor, the exclamation is at once heard, "See how sharp men's teeth are! He is ruined entirely because men could not bear to see his happiness." That the family descent or place of birth may be remembered, it is common for a Hindoo child to annex the name of father and residence to his own. Thus, Moothor Haruppina, the son of Pareyaswamy, Narrayanun, the child of Madras. "Some Hindoos place two lamps on two names beginning with the same letter, and choose that over which the lamp burns most fiercely. The name of the stellar mansion under which the child was born, is often added to its common name." The ceremony of naming is brief and simple. The parents being seated on the ground, the mother having the infant in her arms, the officiating Brahmin hands to the father a plate of raw rice, upon which he writes the name of the child, and the name of the ruling star at its birth. The former is pronounced three times, and the ceremony closes with an offering to the god of the dwelling, together with a dinner and fee to the priest. Greater or less degrees of éclat attend this occasion, according to the wealth and importance of the family. The name of the son and the daughter (though married) remains unchanged through life.

As it is intended to give, in the following chapter, a full description of a Hindoo wedding, the statements now to be made will concern only native marriages in general. A learned work on civil and canon law mentions eight kinds of marriage, 1. When the girl is given to a Brahmin without reward; 2. When she is presented as a gift, at the close of a sacrifice; 3. When two cows are received by the father in exchange for a bride; 4. When the girl is given at the request of a Brahmin; 5. When money is received in exchange for a bride; 6. When a marriage takes place by mutual consent; 7. When a bride is taken in war; and 8. When a girl is taken by craft. A Hindoo, except he be grown up, as in a second marriage, never chooses his own wife. Two parents, with a view to the junction of their estates or honors, determine upon a union of son and daughter, while both are but infants. The espousals take place while the parties are but children, frequently before either has reached the sixth year, when the affianced youth are taken to their parents' home, little aware of the bearing which the gaudy scene through which they have been conducted is to have upon their earthly peace. If there be no special reason for another course, the parent employs a person, called a Ghutuku, to find a suitable boy or girl for his child. "Many of these men are notorious flatterers and liars, and in making matrimonial alliances endeavor to impose in the grossest manner upon the parents on both sides. If the qualities of a girl are to be commended, she is declared to be beautiful as the full moon, of a fine figure, sweet speech, has excellent hair, walks gracefully, can cook, fetch water," &c. In this way persons are united in wedlock with the greatest possible difference of disposition and habit; and, as a consequence, happiness is sought for elsewhere than at home, and the hours they are compelled to pass together are filled with recriminating words and acts. The pressure of this evil is greater upon the wife than the husband, for if she die, the survivor can marry again, and usually does within a few months after the decease of his spouse; while she must occupy that most unhappy of all positions, Hindoo widowhood; or must allow herself to be burned with his lifeless corpse. If the young man be of an age, and in circumstances to make personal choice of a wife, he must have an eye to these, among other commendable qualities, "She must not be of a family where the prescribed acts of religion have been omitted—or a family in which there have been no sons—or a family in which the Veda is not read—or a family that has been subject to disagreeable ailments of any kind. Her form must be, so far as possible, without defect—she must have an agreeable name—she must walk gracefully, *like a young elephant*—her teeth must be moderate in size and quantity—her lips must be like the leaves of a mango tree—and her voice like the *sound of a cuckoo!*" As to mental and moral qualities, they are not deemed of sufficient importance to deserve a place in this catalogue of desirable qualities in a bride. As her only duties are to cook food—clean the house—and take care of the children, it matters little to a Hindoo whether his wife is amiable or morose, wise or ignorant, engaging or repulsive. Subserviency to the inclinations of the stronger sex is her supreme duty. *Divorce* is unknown among the natives of India. Marriages once solemnized can never be dissolved among persons of a reputable caste, particularly among Brahmins. A Hindoo may reject his wife on account of her incontinency, but he is obliged to support her as long as she lives, and wearing the *tahli* (an ornament answering to the marriage ring) marks her as a wife. *Polygamy* is not usual in that country. "Where persons live with several females, but one is considered a lawful wife, and her children alone legitimate. The law excludes the offspring of the others from any share in their father's property, if he die without a will" (Du Bois). There is in the northern district a class of Brahmins with whom a matrimonial alliance is considered so desirable, that multitudes of females are willing to attach themselves to one of them, though at the risk of being left a hopeless widow, and with children to provide for by laborious and unwearied exertion. A writer before quoted mentions the names of five of these *Kooleen Brahmins*, who had in all three hundred and twenty-one wives, and two hundred and sixty children! It often occurs in these cases that a parent does not know his own sons and daughters.

*Death* comes to the Hindoo with all its natural repulsion and dismay, unrelieved by any of the consolatory reflections by which the gospel of Christ assuages the sorrows of the fatal hour. If the Hindoo die with calmness, it is often as the effect of narcotic drugs by which mistaken kindness would enable him to sleep away his being, or the yielding to an omnipotent necessity, and not a cheerful submission to an all-wise decree. Resignation, such as the Christian feels in sorrow's darkest hour, is foreign to the creed as it is a stranger to the heart, of an idolatrous Hindoo. Hence, when a friend dies, the mourner uses language of reproof to us most strange and repulsive. Instead of raising his weeping eye upward, with the language of the patriarch, "The Lord gave, the Lord hath taken away, blessed be the name of the Lord," he turns to the lifeless form with words of upbraiding and censure. "Why," exclaims the weeping widow, "why, oh my husband, hast thou forsaken me? What did I do to drive you hence? Was I not a faithful wife? Was I not attentive to all your household affairs, cooking your food, taking care of your children, defending your character? Oh, why, why did you desert me thus cruelly, my departed one!" This she does with her hair dishevelled, dress carelessly thrown on, and beating her breast with her palms, as if she would drive the very breath from her frame. A mother overwhelmed with grief for the death of her child, will express herself thus:

"Ah! my child! where is he gone? My child!
My child!

My golden image, who has taken? My child!
My child!
He played around like a golden top. My child!
My child!
Like his face I never saw. My child!
My child!
Let fire devour the envious eye. My child!
My child!
It ever was calling, Mother, mother. My child!
My child!"

It often occurs that after lamenting in this manner for some time, a female comes, and putting the end of her garment on the mouth of the mother, tries to comfort her by such strange arguments as these: "Why do you weep? why destroy your health? If the child had been designed to be yours, it would not have died. This is the fruit of children; they come to give us sorrow. *Perhaps in a former birth you stole somebody's child, and now your own is gone.* You set the highest value upon him, and therefore you weep; but if he had been worth any anything, he would not have left you. Go, go into your house, and comfort those that are left. He was *not your son*, but an *enemy* sent to bring sorrow upon you. Why weep longer for him!"

Passionate exclamations of a similar kind to these fall upon your ear almost daily, as you move through the streets of a Hindoo city or village. They are confined almost exclusively to the female mourners and the mourning women (hirelings called in to keep up the lamentation when the strength of the real mourner is exhausted.) If the person reside sufficiently near the Ganges, the dying one is carried to that sacred stream, that by breathing his last upon its bank, and then being immersed beneath its flood, he may secure remission and heaven. The multitudes committed to that stream are sources of great annoyance to the ships at anchor in the river, across whose bows and hawsers they are daily entangled; and still greater nuisances are they to the residents on the banks, who often retain among their servants one whose sole office is to thrust into the stream any dead body which may float ashore. The Hindoos usually *burn* the dead, which is attended with a variety of ceremonies very tedious and childish. I have stood for an hour observing these ablutions with water and oil, offerings of butter, honey, sugar, money, &c., genuflections and prayer, until my patience was exhausted, and my curiosity gratified to satiety. The rich mingle sandal wood with the other fuel of the pile, and even the poor strive to put in a little. This cremation, with the attendant ceremonies, is considered by the great mass of religious Hindoos as necessary to happiness after death. A few, here and there, follow the example of Europeans and Mohamedans in *burying* the dead. In some of the mountainous districts the inhabitants have a singular mode of disposing of a corpse. They first carefully wash the body, and after having prepared it for the principal process by a variety of ceremonies, they cast it into a huge mortar, where they reduce it, bones and all, to a thick pulp, which is rolled up into small balls. These are taken to a spot consecrated for this particular purpose, and strewed upon the ground, when they are instantly devoured by kites, which always hover about these places of interment in great numbers. The Parsees, on the Malabar coast, have a mode of burial hardly less peculiar than the one just named. A circular uncovered building is erected, sometimes from fifty to sixty feet in diameter, and thirty feet high. It is built up within, leaving a parapet about one and a half yards high, the interim space sloping with a gentle convexity to the centre, where there is a well five yards broad. Immediately around this well are grooves, in which the bodies of the dead are deposited, and left exposed to the vultures. As soon as those voracious birds have stripped the bones, the surviving relatives return to the cemetery, and cast them into a well, whence they are removed at certain periods by means of subterranean passages, and flung into the sea. The Mohamedans have large cemeteries in which they bury their dead, erecting a neat mound of clay, or more durable material, over each grave, with a triangular indentation in it for a small lamp, which is often kept burning during a long succession of years. Near the city of Madras is a Mussulman burying-ground, several miles in circumference, which presents a very attractive appearance at night from the light of numberless small lamps scattered over the extended plain. A similar care of their dead is taken by the Roman Catholics in India as elsewhere, decking them with flowers, and erecting a cross at the head.

The country is covered with white marble slabs, sometimes in thick clusters (as in the cemeteries of large towns), again, isolated at the roadside, in the field near the choultry, in the village, denoting the resting-place of an English officer, or wife, or child, or a missionary who had suddenly fallen a victim to that insalubrious climate, or bowed before the fearful pestilence,

> " While foreign hands their lonely graves adorned,
> By strangers honored and by strangers mourned."

No thoughtful person can once listen to the hopeless lamentation of the Hindoo when the fatal foe enters his dwelling;—can once see the weeping eyes, and dishevelled looks, frantic beatings, and hear the heart-piercing outcries attendant upon that event, without turning with gratitude and joy to that Gospel which has brought "life and immortality to light;" which enables its disciple to say in view of his own departure "Oh, death, where is thy sting—for me to die is gain, I long to depart and be with Christ," and constrains the mourner to part with the heart's best beloved, knowing that "he is not lost, but gone before."

We are told that a Hindoo of a reflecting turn of mind, lay on his death-bed. As he saw himself about to plunge into the boundless unknown, he cried out, "What will become of me?" "Oh," said a Brahmin who stood by, "you will inhabit another body." "And where," said he, "shall I go then?" "Into another," was the reply. "And where then?" "Into another, and another, and thus on through millions of years." Darting across this whole period, as though it were but an instant, he cried, "And where shall I go then?" But paganism could not answer; and he died with the inquiry on his lips, "where shall I go then?"

Reader, have you in your hand the Gospel of the Son of God? Be grateful for its possession and so follow its precepts and imbibe its spirit—that when the summons reach your ears, "This night thy soul shall be required of thee," you can say with heart-felt gratitude and joy, "welcome death—welcome heaven"—or when called to mourn the departure of a beloved friend, you can repeat those words of delightful resignation—

"Unveil thy bosom—faithful tomb
Take this new treasure to thy trust,
And give these sacred relics room
To slumber in the silent dust."

# CHAPTER XVII.

## WOMAN IN INDIA.

Importance of Female influence—Facts illustrating the relative position of women in India: (1) Grief at their birth; (2) Subjection exacted; (3) Not to mention their husband's name; (4) Not to speak of her husband's excellencies; (5) Not to be seen walking with him; (6) Not to take food with him; (7) Is not inquired after by guests; and (8) Is not taught even the rudiments of knowledge—Remarks by a Hindoo writer—Life and self-immolation of Hollee Lutchema—Suppression of Sutteeism—Lord William Bentinck—Appeal.

It were difficult to name a triter theme than that of *female influence.* What mothers, and sisters, and wives, have it in their power to accomplish, and what they do actually effect in the formation of national character, is one of the leading topics of the day. This is as it should be. "There are general laws which affect the whole community; there is a common source from which every running stream is supplied; there is a river, the streams whereof pervade and moisten the whole social soil." That primary and all-pervading principle, that common source of power, that ever-flowing fountain of good or ill, is female character and influence. The philanthropist and Christian will deem a volume on India very defective that makes not distinct and somewhat extended mention of the relative position of the females of that land. The subject is one upon which a volume might be written, while I am limited to a few pages only. My plan will be to state in paragraph form several facts respecting the relative attitude, social and public, of this part of Hindoo society, closing with a biographical illustration.

1. The birth of a daughter, in comparison with that of a son, is a *domestic calamity.* Her mother has to endure ten extra days purification. No rejoicing attends her natal hour, as does that of her brother, and she shares not the blessing which is invoked from the Divine Benefactor for his prosperity and happiness. An English gentleman at Bombay was called upon by an intelligent native, who came, as he himself expressed it, to condole with him that the little stranger that had just joined the family circle was a daughter instead of a son.

2. The supreme duty of a Hindoo female is *obedience.* It is a popular sentiment the country over, that a "woman can never be independent." Says an ethical writer of elevated standing, "In childhood a female is to be subject to her father—in adult years to her husband—in old age to her sons." We have before seen that she is to exercise no volition in the important matter of marriage, and so it is to be with her through life.

3. A Hindoo wife is never, under any circumstances, to *mention the name of her husband.* "He"—"The Master"—"Swamy," &c., are titles she uses when speaking of, or to her lord. In no way can one of the sex annoy another more intensely and bitterly, than by charging her with having mentioned her husband's name. It is a crime not easily forgiven.

4. When in the presence of others, it is not for a Hindoo wife to be talking about her partner, either by way of censure or commendation.

5. A Hindoo and his wife should never be seen walking together in the streets, or exchanging expressions of affection in the presence of others. The sight of European ladies walking arm in arm with their husbands, strikes a native of India with surprise and disgust.

6. The female members of a family never take their food in company with the more honored sex. They sit patiently by while father, husband, brother, are eating, and then relieve their hunger with what remains. There is no "family table," around which all the household, adult and young, meet to enjoy the blessings of Divine Providence.

7. A guest never inquires after the health of the wife of his host. If absent, she is not asked for; if she enters, no salutations greet her; if present, she is unnoticed. The more respectable the family for wealth and rank, the more rigid is the observance of this rule.

8. Hindoo females are allowed to remain in profound

ignorance of all literature and science. India abounds with schools for boys, but *none for girls.* It is a popular adage that if a woman learn to read, she will become a widow! This may have been invented to deter her from so doing, as she would avoid what might by any possibility lead to that deepest evil—*widowhood.* Another and the real reason for this prohibition is, that they may feel' their inferiority and be kept more easily in subjection Pitiful, indeed, is the sight of persons, beautiful in figure, graceful and engaging in attitude and movement, yet so profoundly ignorant as not to understand the first letter of the alphabet, and unable to converse upon any subjects but those of the most physical and commonplace character. The Shastras themselves declare that a woman has nothing to do with the text of the vedas: all her duties being comprised in pleasing her husband and cherishing her children. A few (like Ovviyar, sister of Tiruvaluvar, author of the Cural), have arisen above this national prejudice and become quite eminent in the world of letters, but the instances are very few.

9. The directions and statements of the sacred books of India cannot but exert a destructive effect upon her in respect to all attempts at mental and moral elevation. They are such as these: "A woman is not allowed to go out of the house without consent of her husband; nor to laugh without a veil over her face; nor to stand at the door; nor to look out at the window. She is like a heifer on the plain, that still

longs for fresh grass. Infidelity, violence, deceit, envy, and viciousness are all her's. She was made for servitude to her husband. She has no fitness for his equal companionship." These are indices of the native mind upon the social position of the female sex.

From all these circumstances arises the state of female society, so well described by a native Hindoo in a late prize essay: "The Hindoo mother is incapable of conferring on her children, in any measure, the blessings of education, and never dreams of training them up in 'the way they should go.' As to exercising a salutary influence and discipline over them—her own ideas of moral responsibility being vague—she expresses no solicitude about their actions being governed by principles; and since scarcely any of those crimes to which humanity is most prone, are held disreputable in Hindoo society, she seldom feels anxious to guard them against leading impure lives. She allows them to strengthen and grow up in immoral habits (such as lying, obscene language, and the like), and can form no idea of subjecting them to a course of moral restraint. Nor are her children only *passively* suffered to grow wild in a moral and intellectual point of view, but they are actually taught things which their tutors would afterwards have them unlearn. She scruples not to avail herself of false promises and threats in the management of them; and is not very cautious in avoiding the use of indelicate language in their hearing." Such is the picture drawn by a Hindoo's pen. The writer, a person of high caste—one well-instructed in the books of his nation, and well-advised as to the opinions he uttered.

I will now invite the reader's attention to an abridged sketch of female character, drawn by an eloquent writer—Dr. J. Massie—himself, for several years, a missionary at Bangalore

Hollee Lutchema was the daughter of parents comparatively affluent. Her infancy was succeeded by a few short years of ripening childhood, which rapidly glided away; and, during which, all the education she received, was limited by the pitiable circle of childish amusements and domestic duties. She was taught to speak, to wash her teeth, to bind on her cloth, to walk gracefully, to ornament the entrance of the dwelling;—an embellishment, in which great pride is felt, and which is performed according to various heathen devices designed on the earth with consecrated powder, skilfully dropped through the fingers. It was a period of undisturbed mental gloom; no means were used to inspire her with a love of knowledge—no plans were followed to expand her mind. If she had few sorrows to endure, or sufferings to remember, she had, also, few pleasures to anticipate, and few hopes to cherish. Over her future years hung a cloud of mingled and obscure uncertainty; nor was there any friendly hand to lift the veil or shed a light upon her path. Once she heard some communings and negotiations about marriage; but the matter was altogether unintelligible to her, and the personal feeling, she could experience at the moment, was so uninteresting, that she had no anxiety to know her destined bridegroom, or be introduced to his family and friends. Her time passed heedlessly over, and as the period drew near when a woman's feelings and predilections took possession of her bosom, she learned that her hand had been bestowed, and her affections bartered for a piece of gold. The ceremony of marriage, in the preliminary stage, was now performed, and the alliance ratified by the accustomed rites; she was presented, but not yet rendered up to him, who was to be vested with the dominion of her person, and entitled to her homage and subjection. There had been no exercise of choice on either part, nor mutual affection—designed to be a slave, she had not been wooed as the object of a tender attachment. She remained now as the betrothed wife, in her father's house, and in subjection to her parents, till convenience or caprice led to a consummation of the domestic union.

Youthful and pleasing, with certain undefined ideas of marriage, but no relative sympathy and reciprocal confidence, she was conducted through the pageantry and ceremonial of the festive day. Many and tiresome were the ceremonies observed at her espousal. While her bridegroom was being received, by her father, with all the rites of hospitality, three vessels of water were emptied on her head, and accompanied by prayers, usual to the occasion, but too indelicate for insertion here; their hands then, having been rubbed by an auspicious drug, were placed, hers in his, and bound, by a matron, with sacred grass, amidst the sounds of cheerful music. The attendant priests were directed by her father to utter their acclamations, while he poured water from a vessel, containing fragrant grasses, upon the hands of the united pair; and pronouncing their names, as well as his own, he appealed to "God the Existent," and said, "I give unto thee this damsel, adorned with jewels, and protected by the Lord of creatures;" to which the bridegroom replied, "Well be it." The father of Hollee here presented Soobarao with a piece of gold, a text from the Veda was recited, and the affianced parties walked forth, while the bridegroom addressed to her the first expressions of their intercourse,—"May the regents of space, may air, the sun, and fire, dispel that anxiety which thou feelest in thy mind, and turn thy heart to me. Be gentle in thy aspect, and loyal to thy husband—be fortunate in cattle, amiable in thy mind, and beautiful in thy person—be mother of valiant sons—be fond of delights—be cheerful, and bring prosperity to us and ours." The skirts of her mantle were knotted together with his by her father, who enjoined them to "be inseparably united in matters of duty, wealth, and love." Fatiguing and trivial were the many subsequent ceremonies Sacrificial fires were lighted up, jars of purifying water were arranged, handsful of rice were prepared, and many formalities of expression were recited, while the bride was clothed with a new waist-cloth and scarf; oblations of clarified butter were made to the fire, the moon, and the world, during which the bride was first made to stand, and then to sit upon a mat prepared for the purpose. A stone being placed before her, she, with her hands joined in a hollow form was made to tread upon it with the toes of her right foot, during this address of the bridegroom, "Ascend this stone—be firm like this stone—distress my foe, and be not subservient to my enemy." The rice, which had been previously consecrated, was now repeatedly placed in her hands and mixed with butter; and she according to direction opened her hands allowing it to fall into the fire. Now followed the most emphatic symbol of the ceremony—being conducted to the bridegroom, he directed her to step successively into seven circles, while seven texts were repeated, and the moment in which the seventh circle was trod upon, was declared the consummation of the nuptial bond, which was now complete and irrevocable. A friend holding one of the jars of water, approached them, and poured the contents upon him and her; again were their hands joined and sanctioned by sacred texts. Such a marriage verily required the prescriptions of a ritual and the spiritual directions of a priest. Surely if oblations and the precise observance of prescribed ceremonies could have insured happiness and prosperity, Hollee Lutchema might have looked forward to many days of uninterrupted enjoyment and peace; but alas! how vain and delusive.

The natural reserve and restraint of her temper under circumstances so novel, at first perceptible in her intercourse with him who had taken her into such intimate relationship, gradually subsided; freedom of manner toward him, however, could never be accompanied with mutual confidence. She had not been trained to be an intelligent associate, and he had not sought an helper and equal who would accompany him in the ways of wisdom, and cheer him in affliction. The playfulness of sprightly youth, and the soft sweetness of so young a female, were soon abated, familiarity, characterized by their intercourse, speedily rendered unattractive her blandest smile. Caprice, selfishness, and an undue estimate, either of the female character, or of the circumstances under which Hollee had been tutored, the low standard fixed for woman's attractions or merits, and the example which had been exhibited in his father's house, conspired, along with occasional disappointments, to subvert any youthful affection which had primarily been excited under auspices such as we have described. Unaccustomed to rule her own spirit, or to seek the enlargement of her own mind, the first interview had showed her to the most advantage, and there remained no hidden excellences to be developed—no resources of enjoyment which had not at the first moment been presented. Ill-informed himself, her husband had not calculated on unseen defects, or the partial exhibition which a mere exterior would furnish amidst the peculiar circumstances of their first acquaintance. He soon became discontented, irritable, and violent; his requests were uttered with authority, and his commands were enforced with the severity of exaction. Speedily the connexion became one of bitter rule and reluctant subjection; while the untoward captive could ill-brook the lordly despotism which governed her as a slave. Yet there were moments in which the iron yoke relaxed, and when the silken cords of love were felt; when woman's power held captive the imperious tyrant; the bond of natural affection and the sympathies of our better nature prevailing, realized to them the sweets of domestic union. Such were, however, like angel visits, few and far between. Years rolled on, the freshness of youth decayed, the cares of a family accumulated upon them, and became a burden more to the mother than to her professed companion. There had been in her a natural ardor and a genial kindness of disposition, which, had they been cherished by education and religion, might have expanded into the fair fruits of a generous, benevolent, and useful character. She often had felt a clinging to him as the stay of her youth; and even in the hours of discord would the yearnings of her heart be toward him who should have proved the kindred associate of her riper years. She had no knowledge of anything for which she should live better than her husband and her personal enjoyment; but death waits not our pleasure and convenience. His pale face invades the dwelling of the Hindoo with even more hasty steps and appalling look than where a better religion prevails. Hollee's husband was visited with sickness, which, despite her earnest prayers and the skill of the village doctor, made fearful inroads on his strength. She attended him with incessant care—wept and made supplication to her gods—but all in vain; for when least prepared for the event, he expired! It required at that moment but little external excitement or persuasion to awaken a wish that she had died with him. She knew the dreary widowhood before her—no resources had she to sustain her agonized mind—no friend to say to her, Live! She looked on the right hand, and the priest was standing to direct her to the only refuge he deemed accessible—the holy funeral pile! She looked to the left, and there those who superstitiously imagined they might share in the benefit of her immolation and the honor of her sacrifice, or otherwise be burdened by her maintenance, were waiting, nay pressing forward to urge her adoption of the priestly counsel. She looked forward, but gloom impenetrable hung over her path. She cast her eyes upward, but the heavens were sackcloth, and the sun blood. She turned within, and here bewildered with agitation, overwhelmed with grief, flesh and heart failed her, and in her paroxysm of sorrow she embraced the purpose, and uttered the irrevocable vow of immolation. Now the priest thanked Nurraian; the relatives expressed their joyful gratitude; and the means of sustaining her resolution, of lulling her fears, and strengthening her attachment to the deceased, were lavishly employed. Her children were removed from her sight, stupifying drugs were abundantly administered, her body was perfumed, her hair saturated with oil, her head covered with sandal dust, garlands of flowers were presented as her ornaments, and she was hailed a favorite of the gods! A crier was employed to announce her pious resolution, and the time of the sacrifice. The intelligence was sent to me, with a solicitation from a friend that I would attend. It was an hour and a half before sunset when we reached the place of ungodly sacrifice. The husband was covered with clothes, and laid upon a bier made from unpeeled branches of trees, and without ornament. It had been carried thither on the shoulders of men, and placed in a circle formed by tho officiating priests, the victim, the near relatives and kindred, and such as were approaching to obtain the last benediction of Hollee. She was attired in a salmon-colored cloth, and her skin was deeply tinged with saffron. She was bent forward, as if laboring under an oppressive burden; or rather, as if inward anxiety and anguish had bowed her down; yet she seemed to smile. It was the smile of sorrow—the expression of a heart which had conquered nature and burst the bonds of life itself. A red line was drawn from the root of her hair to tho ridge of her nose; it seemed to me the mark of suicide. Beside her were bunches of flowers, clothes, cocoanuts, pounded spices and money, which she distributed to the female friends who came soliciting her favors. She was attended by two Brahmins, one of whom held an ölla book, from which he read sentences for her direction and comfort, at times assisted by his associate. While the poor woman and priest were thus engaged, others were employed in preparing the pile, which was constructed of dried wood in the shape of an oblong square, upon which were heaped combustible faggots to the height of four feet from the base. A stout branch of a tree was fixed in the earth at each corner, which suspended a canopy of heavy boughs at about three feet elevation. After the corpse was placed upon the pile, Hollee was led around it by a priest, and then walked twice around it alone; kneeling by the right side a few seconds, and then mounted and lay down to the left of the deceased. Deliberately she composed herself; her infant child was placed in her arms for a moment and embraced; she saluted her mother, and called her sister to whom she delivered her jewels; then having loosened her garments, she drew her cloth over her head and laid herself down beside her husband with such calmness as if it had been but for a night's repose. They then covered her with straw, and poured oil and melted butter over all parts of the pile, the extremities of which were now lighted by the eldest male relative of the family. The straw fanned by the wind was at first suffered only to roll thick volumes of smoke over her, and then the suspended canopy, cut down by the attending officers, fell upon her with its heavy crushing weight! The poor woman had hitherto remained silent, but when the flames had reached her she shrieked and screamed for help with piteous and heartrending exclamations. The Brahmin assured the people that *she was now in communion with her god,* while the forlorn mother, overwhelmed with grief, was rolling herself, tearing her hair, beating her breast, and leaping with frantic bursts of passion, striving to throw herself on the altar of her daughter's sacrifice and destruction. The scene was closed by the fierceness of the flame, which drove the bystanders to a distance, and forced even the priests to retire, while the victim was yet uttering the moan of helpless suffering. Thus was offered upon the altar of that sanguinary superstition the infatuated Hollee Lutchema."

Such scenes as this, but ofttimes far more sickening in their detail, have been enacted throughout India from a period that goes back into the unknown past. While the subject of its suppression by British authority was under discussion, and means were being taken to arouse the public mind of England to the character of the custom, steps were pursued to ascertain, with all possible precision, the number of annual immolations. From official returns for the year 1818, it appears that *eight hundred* were thus sacrificed during that year alone; making, with the addition of the other two Presidencies, and the vast Punjaub, which was not then under British rule, at least *three thousand!* It was not till Lord William Bentinck ascended the vice-regal throne of India, that the mandate was issued against these scenes of suicide and murder.

"Yes, child of Brahma, then was mercy nigh,
To wash the stain of blood's eternal die;

Peace did descend to triumph and to save,
When noble Bentinck crossed the Indian wave."

And yet, though the instances are far less numerous and the exhibitions less public than they once were, it is known that the funeral pile still sends up its lurid flame, and the trembling wife still submits to its fatal torture in many parts of the country. And so will they till the Sacred Scriptures come in to supplant the Vedas in their teaching and spirit. And who would not pray for the coming of that time? Reader, will you? And to your prayers will you add your endeavors to put them in possession of that volume which says, "Leave thy fatherless children and I will protect them, and LET THY WIDOWS TRUST IN ME."

# CHAPTER XVIII.

## HINDOO CASTE.

Definition of Caste—Four-fold division—Origin and duties of Brahmins, Kshatiras, Veishas, and Soodras—Pariars—Six facts illustrating the evil influence of Caste upon its adherents—Its anti-social and anti-benevolent character—A barrier to the progress of Christian truth—A convert at Calcutta—Apology by Abbé Du Bois—Early Views of Swartz, Bishop Heber, &c.—Action of Bishop Wilson and Modern Missionaries—Caste doomed, and what is now expected of all converts to Christianity.

THE word *caste* is a Portuguese term, which has been adopted to denote the different divisions of Hindoo Society. These are four in number—*Brahmins*, *Kshatiras*, *Veishas*, and *Soodras*, with various subdivisions under each general class. A brief explanation of each order, with a few remarks and facts illustrative of the whole subject, is all that can now be given.

At the time the Vedas dropped from the mouth of the exalted Brahma, there were produced from the same facial orifice, the *Brahmins*; indicating thereby that their position in community was to be preeminent in sacredness and honor, and that their duties were to concern religious doctrine and ceremony. The Smritees assign to Brahmins the offering of sacrifices; the offices of the priesthood; the study of the Vedas; explaining the Shastras; giving alms; and receiving presents. Such is their exalted position, that to injure a Brahmin, was the last of pardonable offences. Whatever part of the body was used in harming one of the privileged class, that part was, at once, to be removed; while to do a beneficent act to this deified personage, would atone for almost every sin, and secure the highest commendation and merit. Such was their exalted position, that the Peishwa, at the head of the Mahratta confederacy, who held the most commanding station of any Indian sovereign, was long excluded from eating at table with any Brahmin of high caste. Their peculiarity of dress is the *poita*, or sacred string, which all of this class wear over one shoulder and under the opposite arm, and which none but the hands of the "*twice born*" are allowed to touch.

There has been a wonderful lowering of Brahminical pride and dignity since the conquest of the country by Europeans. While thousands are attached to the temples, and subsist upon the revenues of ecclesiastical lands, others are employed in courts of justice, as pundits to foreigners in the acquisition of the language, as merchants, accountants, and even as farmers and soldiers. But, still, as a class, they stand, by universal acknowledgment, *first* in Hindoo society.

From the *arm* of Brahma sprang the *Kshatiras*, who were created to "protect the earth, the cattle, and Brahmins." Kings, governors, all to whom are entrusted civil and military affairs, belong to this class.

Then followed the *Veishas*, who were produced from the *thighs* of the Supreme, and have, as their assigned vocation, to provide the necessaries of life by agriculture and traffic. They are the farmers and merchants of the land.

While last of the four, are the *Soodras*, the offspring of the *feet* of Deity, as denoting the servile pursuits to which they are to devote themselves.

In addition to these, there are the *Pariars*, who are esteemed the "outcasts of society, the refuse of mankind,—the men of infamy and degradation—persons with whom the least of any of the preceding castes will have no intercourse, being consigned to ignominy and subjection forever."

"Is caste a civil or religious institution?" Both, I answer; but eminently the *latter*. The distinctions it establishes are of Divine decree, and subjects of sacred record. Its effects upon all social relations are immediate and direct, but without the religious element it could not have retained its vitality so long, and produced such results as we now witness.

In the place of farther didactic statement, I will present the reader with several facts and occurrences by which he may judge of the strong hold this system has upon the Hindoos, and the inhuman results with which it is often attended.

I. "I once happened to be present when a sepoy of high caste, falling down in a faint, the military surgeon ordered one of the Pariah attendants of the hospital to throw some water upon him, in consequence of which, none of his class would associate with him, because he had forfeited the privileges of his clanship. The result was that, soon after, he put the muzzle to his head, and blew out his brains."

II. "I once saw a high caste Hindoo dash an earthen jar of milk upon the ground, and break it to atoms, merely because the *shadow of a Pariah had fallen upon it as he passed.*"

III. "As I entered the dwelling, I saw, lying upon the centre of the floor, a man of middle age, apparently near his end, while at a little distance was his wife, much in the same state. A little girl was kneeling at their side, asking, in an earnest, bitter tone, for rice. I called to a servant, who had accompanied me, to bring a basket of provisions, which I opened before the child, when the unhappy father, turning his eye upon me with a look of horror, threw out his arms like a maniac, seized the famishing creature, dragged it from the polluted food, and fell back dead."

IV. "Shortly after our arrival at Bangalore, the roof of our house was under repair; and one of the bricklayers fell from a great height, and was much injured. To relieve the sufferer, we called upon the workmen, standing near, to run to the well and bring some water. Not one of them would stir; for, said they, that *man is not of our caste*, and we are not allowed to give him water."

V. A Kshratiya, whose son had rejected caste, sought an asylum at that son's house, just before death; yet so strong were the prejudices of caste, that the old man would not eat from the hands of his own son, but crawled, on his hands and knees, to the house of a neighbor, and received food from entire strangers, rather than from his own child, though, then, on the brink of eternity.

VI. Several buildings were on fire in Madras, and which threatened a general conflagration of the city. There were several wells near at hand, but the Brahmins forbade the use of the water, lest a person of lower caste than themselves, should approach, and thus pollute them.

These instances might be greatly multiplied, but they are sufficient for the purpose now in hand. They illustrate the dissocial, selfish, and unmerciful character of this institution. Some have supposed that the system is productive of benefit, as it respects mechanical operations; because an employment descends from father to son, through successive generations; but experience disproves this theory. The fabrics and ornaments of India are, many of them, very beautiful, and justly admired; but there have been no improvements for centuries past. There is no invention, no discovery, no progress in workmanship throughout that country, as in lands where no such system exists. Caste is a foe to all generous and noble feeling. It binds, in chains of adamant, a large portion of every community, saying to them: "You proceeded from the feet of Brahma; you are created for servitude." It limits the social circle to a comparatively few persons, to the careful exclusion of all the rest, however worthy in character and commendable in deportment. A Brahmin would sooner see a Soodra die than give him food, if, in so doing, he must touch the body or clothes of the debased one. It is said that a company of the professed teachers of right and duty will stand upon the river's bank, and see a boat load of Pariars go to the bottom, rather than use any personal effort to save them from death. And how ungodlike, unchristian, too! The Bible directs that we "do to others as we would have them do to us;" and commends the Samaritan, who bound up the bleeding sufferer, while it condemns the Levite, who, (Brahmin like,) would let him die of his wounds. Caste has done more than aught else to make India what it is, a land of limited attainments, selfish propensities, and grovelling aims.

"If a Brahmin break caste, can he regain it?" Not generally, but it has been done. After the establishment of the English power in Bengal, the caste of a Brahmin was destroyed by an European, who forced into his mouth, flesh, spirits, &c. After remaining three years an outcast, great efforts were made, at an expense of 80,000 rupees, ($40,000,) to regain his rank, but in vain. After a time, an expense of two lacs more, ($100,000,) were incurred, when he was restored to his friends. About the year 1802, a person, in Calcutta, expended in feasting and presents to Brahmins, 50,000 rupees, ($25,000,) to obtain his lost rank. Other methods have of late been discovered, but the lapsed ones never become what they formerly were in public estimation, sanctity and honor. The stain, though not so visible as before these gifts and atonements, is not wholly washed out. "In some parts of the country, the inhabitants do things with impunity, which in other sections would cause the loss of caste. In the upper provinces, the regulations regarding eating, are far less regarded than in Bengal; while other features are guarded with greater anxiety."

It will occur to my reader that caste presents a formidable barrier to the progress and triumph of Christianity in India. It does so; one of the most formidable that can be named or conceived. It prevents the Christian teacher from gaining that free and familiar intercourse with the people, so important in securing for the truth deliberate examination, and an impartial judgment. All foreigners are considered as belonging to the lowest class, and are, therefore, forbidden that social intercourse at the table and in the family, which furnishes so favorable an occasion for giving a personal direction to his public instructions. The state of heart produced by this institution is unfavorable to the reception of Bible doctrine and spirit. When a Hindoo enters a place of worship, his first object is to secure a seat where he shall be sure of avoiding a contact with persons of a lower grade than himself. He is solicitous, in the extreme, to allow no part of his dress to touch that of one descended from less honored parentage. How opposed is such a disposition to that humble and contrite spirit with which the Most High delights to dwell!

It presents a formidable barrier in the way of confessing the name of Christ and becoming his disciple. To "*lose caste*" is, to the native of India, one of the most dreaded of evils. It is renunciation of friendships, intimate and long existent, of honors enjoyed through a succession of years, and, until lately, an entire of the paternal estate and inherited wealth. A person may be wicked, profane, devoid of every good principle, and an abandoned profligate, and yet, as a Hindoo, may enjoy all the privileges of his caste; but the moment he violates any of its rules by eating with one of another class, by journeying to a distant country to extend his observation of men and things, by dealing in articles which the Shastras prohibit, by examining into the claims of another system of religious belief than his own and then espousing it—that moment he exposes himself to the most dreadful denunciations. "No persons can receive the miscreant into their houses, or hold any intercourse with him; every one agrees to cover him with ridicule, contempt and disdain; to be seen with him would be deemed a crime worthy of reprehension; the woman to whom he was betrothed would not be allowed to marry him; all denounce him as the veriest vagabond, and his parents and friends must be the first to disown him, and shower curses on his head." The barrier this opposes to an examination of the truth, and, above all, to its espousal, will occur to every reader. If a Hindoo be convinced that the Bible is Heaven-descended, he must become a martyr the same hour he becomes a public and declared believer. He must literally "forsake all," to become a Christian. While this has, no doubt, kept back many from making a profession of faith and attachment, who would otherwise have become formalists and hypocrites, it has deterred others who are sincere inquirers after truth from pursuing their investigations, and, farther still, from obeying the decisions of their judgment, and convictions of conscience. A single case must suffice, by way of illustration :—"Naraputsingh, a convert in Bengal, during the days of his heathenism, lived like a nabob, with his train of servants, and splendor of oriental equipage. But the moment he submitted to the ordinance of baptism, and embraced the truth, his relatives seized upon his property, to the amount of $40,000, since which time he has been laboring for the support of himself and family, at $5 per month. The Abbè Dubois has a long chapter in advocacy of this system, as that by which India kept up her head when all Europe was plunged in barbarism, preserved and extended the arts, the sciences and civilization;" but the farther my observation extended, when a resident of that country, and the more I have learned, through the remarks and pages of others, the more deeply I am convinced that it is an evil, with scarcely a feature to relieve its bitterness—with hardly a ray to cheer its darkness. For a time, it was to an extent allowed in the Christian churches, from the impression of its social character, and therefore beyond the pale of direct ecclesiastical direction. The eminent Swartz and his colleagues, and the amiable Heber, were so disposed to regard and treat it. But when we see one communicant refusing the sacramental cup because it had touched the lips of one of lower birth—or a Christian catechist declining to call upon a fellow disciple, only because of his less honored origin—or a professed follower of Christ absenting himself from a "love feast," only because the food may have been prepared by the same person who served his own religious teacher, it is surely quite time for the Church to interfere, and say, with kindness, yet decision, these things ought not, cannot so remain—this is not the spirit of the Gospel, and must be eschewed by all who "name the name of Christ." And such is the present decision and action. The Bishop of Calcutta, Dr. Wilson, has spoken boldly, and with authority—some may say, with a little too much severity—and yet other churches are coming round to his views. As a system, it will henceforth find no favor with the promoters of Christianity in that land. He who would become a Christian must renounce caste heartily and practically. Not that he will be compelled to intermarry with those of lower social grades, or be upon terms of familiar intercourse with Soodras and Pariars—but he will not regard himself as by right of birth their superior in moral excellence, or entitled by a divine decree to immunities and prerogatives which they are forever denied. He must be willing to say, with conscious honesty, YE ARE MY BRETHREN—ALL.

# CHAPTER XIX.

## RELIGION OF THE HINDOOS.

Design of the Chapter—Brahm—Brahma—Vishnu—Siva—Ganesa—Supramunman—Doorga—Kaléé—Latchmi—Sarasvati—Munmuthan—Indru—Sooryu—Kartikeya—Pavuna—Vuroona—Yumu—Weakness of them all—Immorality—Character of the worshippers—What can elevate India—Appeal to the Reader.

It is intended, in the present chapter, to present the reader with a brief view of Hindooism, as a system of revealed religion. India has its sacred Vedas and Shastras, which claim to communicate all that need be known regarding the character of the Supreme, with the modes of performing acceptable worship, and of securing the divine blessing. These ancient and voluminous records teach the existence of one universal Spirit, the fount and origin of all other beings, animate or inanimate, material or immaterial. To this supreme Divinity is given the incommunicable name of Brahm; a noun in the neuter gender, as indicating the negative mode of his existence, and to be distinguished from *Brahma*, the distinctive title of the first in the Hindoo Triad. Of this great, self-existent, independent, and eternal One, we are told in the Shastras that he resides in perpetual silence, takes no interest in the affairs of the universe, finding his happiness in undisturbed repose. They add, that though all spirit and without form, he is devoid of qualities, without will, without consciousness of his own existence, immersed in an abyss of unrelieved darkness and gloom. He is ONE, say they, not *generically*, as possessed of a divine nature; not *hypostatically*, as simple and uncompounded; not *numerically*, as the only actual deity, but the sole entity, whether created or uncreated. "His oneness is so absolute, that it not only excludes the possibility of any other god, co-ordinate and subordinate, but excludes the possibility of aught else, human or angelic, material or immaterial." He is thus, as one well says, an "*infinite negative*—an *infinite nothing*." This is the supreme deity of that land, mysterious, unapproachable, indescribable—in truth, unintelligible; and whom deists and infidels have boastfully referred to as the counterpart of Jehovah; but from whom, by the absence of all moral qualities, all supervision of human affairs, all intelligent and worthy attributes, he is placed at a remove immeasurable, infinite. The Hindoos are not atheists in the sense of a chance creation of all beings and things. Their system is rather, in its original state, refined and sublimated *Pantheism*, all visible things being but manifestations of his essence. With a verbal change, we may adopt the poet's couplet:

> "All are but parts of this mysterious whole,
> Whose body nature is, and *Brahm* the soul."

The authors of the Hindoo system, like the Grecian philosophers, found a difficulty in conceiving how pure spirit could exert any energy, and especially an energy sufficient to form a world. When, therefore, the supreme Brahm willed to create the world, he drew forth from himself three hypostases, to which were given the names of Brahma, Vishnu, and Siva. These constitute the celebrated Hindoo Triad, of whom the sacred books declare that "They were originally united in one essence and from one essence were derived, and that the great One became distinctly known as three gods, being *one person and three gods.*" It may interest the reader to have a fuller acquaintance with the history of these divine personages.

### BRAHMA.

This deity is usually represented as a man with four faces, riding on a swan, and holding in one of his four hands a portion of the Vedas; in the second, a pot of water; while the third is raised upward to indicate protection; and the fourth declined downward, as bestowing a gift. He is variously styled the "self-existent" (falsely though, for he sprang from Brahm), the "great father," the "lord of creatures," and, more appropriately, the "creator." He is reputed to have had originally five heads, having lost one for a reason upon which his biographers are divided in opinion. That given in the Skanda Purana is as follows: "The linga (or sacred symbol) of Siva fell by the curse of a Rishi from heaven, and increased in such height that it filled heaven and hell. In order to see it, Brahma, Vishnu, and the other gods assembled, and in the midst of their wonder they called out, "Who can reach to its extremity?" Vishnu descended to hell, and Brahma went upwards; but neither search proved successful. Brahma, under the influence of shame, hired the cow kama and the tree ketaku as false witnesses, and asserted three times that he had seen the end. The gods, knowing the falsehood of his declaration, deprived him by their curse of all worship, and Siva cut off one of his heads." Be the cause what it may, there is but one temple to his honor erected in the land, and he receives less direct reverence than almost any of the celestials.

## VISHNU.

This second of the Trimurti, or Triad, appears as a blue man, riding on a skate, and holding in his four hands a war-club, conch shell, a weapon called chakra, and a water-lily. He has other names, as Náráyaná, Prumahl, &c., and is worshipped as the Pervader, or the personification of the preserving principle. The Puranas mention ten avatars, descents, or incarnations of this god, of which nine are these, a *fish*, a *tortoise*, a *boar*, a *man-monster*, a *dwarf*, a *giant*, *Rama* (hero of Ramayanam), *Krshna*, *Budha*, and the tenth, which is still expected, a *white horse*. On each visit wonders were performed, which we cannot even allude to for want of room. His moral (?) character appears from this incident. When the sea was churned to recover the ambrosia (Mount Mandra being the churning stick, a five-headed snake, Vaysooke, the rope, and the demons called Asuras the workmen), Akabai and Lakshmi, two maiden sisters, arose at the same time. Vishnu perceiving Lakshmi to be the more beautiful, wished to marry her; but not being able to accomplish the object until the elder was disposed of, he deceived the Rishi Uddakala as to Akabai's beauty and excellences, which induced him to marry her, while he espoused the woman of his choice. The followers of this divinity form one of the twofold divisions of Hindoo society—the Vishnuvites.

## SIVA.

This *destroyer* of mankind is seen as a silver colored man, with five heads and eight hands, in six of which are severally a skull, a deer, fire, an axe, a rosary, and and an elephant rod, while the seventh is open in the attitude of blessing, and the last of protecting. He has a third eye in his forehead, with perpendicular corners, ear-rings of snakes, and a collar of skulls. At the end of each series of the four yoogas, Siva drowns, and then remodels the earth; his name being more properly the new-modeller, or reproducer. One form in which this deity is worshipped is as the *lingum*, which the classical reader will understand when I say that it resembles the phalli of the Greeks. It is exposed to public view the country over. Siva has a vast number of worshippers, some of whom deem him superior to Brahma himself. One of his consorts is the sanguinary Kaléé, another is the more pacific Doorga, of both of whom we shall speak before concluding tho chapter. The disciples of this deity are entitled *Sivites.*

This triad has given birth to a great number of additional deities, some of whom are held in scarcely less reverence than the original. Of these *three hundred and thirty millions of divinities*, I will notice but a few of the more prominent.

*Ganesa* is the elder son of Siva and Parvuti. With his elephant face, big belly, and four hands, he presents a strange and repulsive appearance. But for all this, no deity is more often named than he. Being esteemed the *work-perfecter*, or, one who can place and remove obstacles, he is always invoked at the commencement of any undertaking or enterprise. Before a journey, writing a letter, studying a book, and the like, *Ganesa* is upon the lips of the traveller or student. This eminent position was given to him as a compensation for the strange head he wears, which was put upon his shoulders when he lost his own, in infancy, by a look of the celestial Shunèè.

*Subramunman*, the Hindoo Mars, &c., special guardian of the Brahminical order, is represented with six faces, twelve arms, riding on a peacock, and holding in his hands severally a bow, an arrow, a conch, a circle, a sword, a rope, a trident, a diamond-weapon, fire, a dart, a crescent-shaped weapon, and a drum. He is specially worshipped at Secandar Mali, near Madura, Trichendoor, Pyney, Tiruerugaram, and all the hill country.

*Doorga*, who combines the characteristics of Minerva, Pallas, and Juno, is one of the wives of Siva. Her original name was Parvuti, but, having, by a display of extraordinary valor, defeated a giant named Doorga, she was thenceforth dignified with the name of her conquered foe. This monster is supposed by some to be a personification of *Vice*, and Doorga, of *Virtue;* while the struggle typified the action and reaction of good and evil in the world. The festival in honor of this goddess, celebrated in the month of September, has no superior for magnificence of entertainment and imposing appearance in the country. At the celebration of one festival, a wealthy Hindoo has been known to give 80,000 lbs. of sweetmeats, 80,000 lbs. of sugar, 1,000 suits of cloth garments, 1,000 suits of silk, 1,000 offerings of rice, plantains and other fruits. In the single city of Calcutta, it is supposed that *half a million pounds sterling* are annually expended on the Doorga festival alone.

*Kaléé*, another of Siva's wives, is the Moloch of the land. Her appearance indicates her character. She is represented as standing with one foot upon the chest of her husband, Siva, whom she has thrown down in a fit of anger; her tongue, dyed with blood, is protruding from her mouth; she is adorned with skulls, and the hands of her slain enemies are suspended from her girdle. The blood of a tiger delights her for ten years;—of a human being for one thousand years. If any of her worshippers draw the blood from his own person, and offer it her, she will be in raptures of joy; but if he cut out a piece of flesh for a burnt-offering, her delight is beyond bounds. But, though thus sanguinary and malevolent, Kalée is one of the favorite deities among the Hindoos. The Swinging Festival and other observances, to be alluded to in detail hereafter, are in her honor—being designed to avert her wrath, or secure her blessing. She is the especial friend of thieves and murderers, who invoke her blessing before entering upon their deeds of violence and death.

*Latchmi*, the goddess of fortune, is the wife of Vishnu, before alluded to. Painted yellow, she sits upon an expanded water-lily, holding in two hands the lotus, while the others are employed in protecting and blessing. She is worshipped in a manner the opposite of the fiendish Kalée.

*Sarasvati*, patroness of learning and music, is wife of Brahma. Dressed in white raiment, with a garland of diamonds, she holds in her four hands a part of the Vedas, a string of crystals, a musical instrument; while, with the fourth, she seems to be illustrating some problem. She is the peaceable Minerva of Greece and Rome, inventress of the fine and useful arts. Festivals in her honor are largely attended by those especially who need her peculiar blessings.

*Munmuthan* is the Indian cupid; the "beautiful son of Brahma, who bears the five flowery arrows which inflame with love the inhabitants of the three worlds."

He is represented, allegorically, as conveyed by females so united as to form the body of an elephant—thus expressing the illusion which he causes—and as having his quiver at his back, and in his hand his bow of sugarcane, with a string composed of honey bees, and arrows of flowers.

To these may be added *Indru*, king of heaven, with his thousand eyes, a thunderbolt in his right hand, and bow in his left ; *Sooryu*, with his red face and three eyes, and four arms, whose followers never eat till they have seen the sun, and fast if he be obscured by clouds ; *Pavuna*, god of the winds and messenger of the celestials , *Vuroona*, god of the waters ; *Yŭmŭ*, judge of the dead, who sends to hell or heaven as the case demands ; and scores of others with whose names, duties, and characters I will not weary my reader. While I have attempted to be brief, it was demanded by my subject that I make a somewhat complete mention of leading persons in the pantheon.

Two features in the character of this entire class of celestials arrest attention ; their limited physical and mental faculties, together with the entire absence of all moral qualities. In illustration of the first point, look at Brahma. He is said at one time to have performed a long course of ascetic devotions to secure a desired object, and after all *failed of success ;* whereupon he he sat down and wept from very chagrin and sorrow. As to morality, there is not the first element of truth, modesty, or goodness in one of them. See Brahma in in a fit of intoxication attempting the virtue of his own daughter, and Vishnu telling a palpable falsehood to secure his favorite object, and Siva worshipped under an emblem too immodest to be named, and *Krishna* sporting with milkmaids in a state of shameless nudity.

I pause at this point, and ask my reader to form his own judgment as to what must be the religious institutions acceptable to such beings, and what the state of morals in a land of such divine personages. The characteristic features of the Gospel system are *holiness* and *mercy*, because these are the leading attributes in the Being adored. "Be ye holy, for *I am holy.*" "Love one another, for *God is love.*" "Be ye merciful, even as your *Father in heaven is merciful.*" View the gods of India, false to their word, thievish licentious, ambitious, murderous, all indeed that is repellant, malignant, and vile, (their own writers being judges,) is it surprising that there is perjury, and injustice, and wickedness the land over? Ah no! The people are bad, many of them *very* bad; but they do not and cannot equal their own gods in wickedness. Their deities must be changed ere their moral condition can be materially and generally improved. The Bible must supplant the narratives of their false divinities; their temples, covered now with sculptures and paintings which crimson the face of modesty even to glance at, must be demolished; the vile lingam must be levelled to the ground; the festivals, in which are re-enacted shameless events in the lives of Krishna, and others like him, must be abolished; the scenes now passing before the eyes of that nation, sanctioned by divine example, must cease. Then will India rise from her deep moral depression.

Reader, is not this a desirable result? While perusing these pages, has not the thought occurred, "Oh, that they knew what I do of the true God?" It is a generous emotion, becoming you as a philanthropist and Christian. Stifle it not, but resolve that if the Hindoos remain longer in the bonds of ignorance, the fault shall not be yours.

# CHAPTER XX.

## HINDOOISM IN PRACTICE.

Facts indicating the Religious tendency of the Hindoos—Car Drawing—Sailing—Hook Swinging—Passing through the Fire—Other and like Observances—Quotation from Bishop Heber respecting the Moral Character of the Hindoos.

HAVING treated of Hindooism in theory, and as taught in the sacred Shastras, the reader's attention is now requested to this religious system as acted out by its disciples. The native of India does not consider it enough simply to express his assent to certain dogmas, and with that be satisfied; but to a verbal confession of Brahma and his faith, is added a consecration, personal, self-sacrificing, and fearless, to his will and claims. A thoughtful traveller in that country will be ever ready to exclaim, with one of old, "*I see that ye are very religious.*" When the Hindoo appears in public, he carries upon his forehead and arms the symbols of his faith; when he passes a temple or a religious teacher, expressions of reverence are seldom forgotten; the ceremonial of the morning is scrupulously practiced; and he omits no part of the long and ever-recur-

F. Michelin lith. 111 Nassau St.

SHEDDEL OR

HOOK SWINGING

ring routine of observances. This is a religion of *action*, and not a class of sentiments lying concealed and dormant in the soul. Every town and village has its sacred edifice, within which is an image of the patron deity whose worship claims the attention of one or more of the priesthood. It is proverbial among the Hindoos that a "*man should not live where there is no temple.*" The erection of these consecrated buildings, and their endowment with a suitable revenue, is one of the most honorable and meritorious ways in which the rich can expend their wealth. Where private munificence fails, the object is attained at public expense. The temples at Benares, Juggernaut, Madura, Guserat, Ramperam, Seringham, &c., are presided over by thousands of priests, with other attendants in like proportion. In addition to these massive and extensive religious establishments, edifices smaller, but durable, are seen in places remote from all human habitations—on the banks of rivers—in the middle of streams—on the summit of lofty mountains—and beneath the wide-spread banyan. Connected with these are annual and more frequent festivals, which collect their thousands and tens of thousands from places near and far remote. Three classes of persons are in attendance upon every temple of any note, and whose presence is essential to a complete performance of all its ceremonial—the *Brahmins* or priests, who alone have the knowledge and authority to conduct the minute and tedious ritual—the *dancing women*, who in public chant the praises of the deity, but are in private the courtezans of the Brahmins—and the *musicians*, with tomtom, horn, and cymbal. The traveller cannot remain long in a place without learning something of the religion of the people. If he be near a temple, the sound of the *bell* tells him that the Brahmin is within the sanctuary, engaged in sacred duties demanded by his deity—his sleep is disturbed by harshly sonorous instruments, indicating the progress of some ceremony of religious worship—and as he leaves the village, he meets a company bearing offerings of plantains, rice, and flowers, as expressions of gratitude to the presiding divinity of the neighborhood. When the appointed day is at hand, preparations are made for the annual *car drawing*, while thousands are seen flocking to the festive spot. During the year the car has stood near the temple, and sheltered from the weather by a thatched roof. This is removed—necessary repairs are made—four long and heavy cables are brought out and attached to the cumbrous vehicle—garlands of flowers and tinselled ornaments are so suspended from the frame-work as to attract much notice and admiration. As evening approaches, the image is brought from its sacred enclosure and placed upon the vehicle, where also stand several priests paying it due attention and reverence, while the streets are thronged with persons of both sexes and all ages anxiously waiting the appointed hour. The time having arrived, the cables are seized by thousands of zealous hands, while to the sound of music, accompanied by shouts of enthusiastic zeal, the massive and gaudy structure is drawn through the principal streets and returned to its place of abode, there to remain during another twelvemonth. When the excursion is on the water, a raft is made, upon which is erected a canopy light and gorgeous. With great pomp the image is removed from his temple abode, borne on a decorated palanquin to the water-side, while the huge rope is carried ashore, which is seized by the vast concourse of worshippers, who draw the craft once and again around the tank to the sound of music, and with joyful acclamations. These both occur at night, and their attractiveness is much increased by the lamps and flambeaux, which may be numbered by thousands. The number of Hindoo festivals, including the monthly observances of the sun's passing from one side of the zodiac to another, is *one hundred and forty-five.* Of these ten are monthly, and twenty-five are anniversaries. Were these observances to go no farther than giving the image a drive or sail for a midnight airing, or in assembling at the temple and celebrating with music and recitation their favored deity, or making costly presents to the Brahmins, or forming clay images of Gunputtee, or spending the night in festivity and games of chance in honor of Lukshumee, or illuminating temple and street in honor of Siva ;—it can be alone said that they are puerile, childish, and that they consume a large amount of time which might be far more profitably spent otherwise. But it is not so. The most popular religious observances are positively harmful, being destructive to morals, or domestic peace and personal comfort. The character of the goddess Kaléé has been alluded to in the preceding chapter, and it was suggested, as a natural inference, that the worship required by such a being must be sanguinary and woful. Such we find to be the case. Soon after reaching Madras I had an opportunity of witnessing, for the first time, the much-famed *Sheddel*, or hook-swinging festival. I was residing upon the sea shore near the spot where the cruel festivity was to occur. At mid-day the multitude began to assemble, and before five o'clock the crowd could not have been less than five thousand persons of both sexes, and all ages and conditions of life. A beam about forty feet in height had been erected, across the top of which was placed a transverse pole of smaller size, to each end of which was tied a rope, the end of one of which trailed upon the ground ; while to the shorter one was attached two iron hooks, strong, pounded smooth, and sharp-pointed. The devotees who were to exhibit their devotion to their faith, were retained in an adjoining temple until the fitting hour arrived. One of them was then led out, preceded by Brahmins and musicians and friends. He approached the upright pole—lay upon his face while the hooks were thrust under the flesh on either side of the vertebræ, just below the shoulder blade, and then, the other ropes being well manned, he was hoisted up in mid-air, and swung round and round to the number of ten to thirty times, according as strength allowed or the vow made necessary. Twenty or more went through this ceremony that afternoon, many of whom, by way of manifesting their indifference of pain, scattered flowers and fruit, beat a tomtom, and smoked a cigar. Being sceptical as to the statement that the hook went into the flesh, and was supported by it alone, unaided by any exterior bandage, I went near enough to convince myself that such was the fact, and that no deception was practiced. The muscles are strong, and accidents from falling seldom occur.

On another occasion I walked out at evening, with my esteemed friend and colleague, Rev. Mr. Hutchings, to witness the ceremonial of *passing through the fire.* A plat of ground, several hundred yards in circumference, had been marked out, the soil removed, to the depth of several inches, and the surface covered with a kind of fuel, which, when ignited, emits an intense heat. Thousands were on the spot when we arrived, and, though the crowd gave way for us, the heat alone compelled us to keep at a considerable distance, and to cover our faces with our hands for the sake of protection and comfort. When the flame had subsided, and naught was left but burning coals, from ten to twenty persons, men and females, with no covering to their feet, and but a slight dress about their loins, walked deliberately from one side of this burning surface to another. One of the women carried her child with her, as she passed over, much to the admiration and astonishment of the gaping multitude, but more to our pity for the deluded votaries of such a system of faith and worship.

When the annual festival of drawing the car occurs at Madura, the multitude crowding the city during the week of its continuance, cannot usually be less than forty thousand strangers. Then may be seen devotees swinging between trees, with ropes attached to the shoulder and feet, above a fire enkindled on the ground below,—lying upon the earth with coals at the head, feet, and on either side—walking the streets with iron spikes thrust through the tongue and cheek—wearing a gridiron-shaped encumbrance upon the shoulder, the head being thrust through the grating—and like acts of superstitious and sanguinary devotion, especially to the goddess Kaléé.

Going to the Goomsoor country, lying in the northern part of the Madras Presidency, we find the people accustomed from time immemorial to flay alive innocent children, to avert the anger or secure the favor of the earth-goddess—she who rules the order of the seasons, sends the periodical rain, gives fecundity to the soil, and health or sickness to the people. I will not, need not, go farther into this fearful and deplorable detail.

"But how cruel the people must be—how inhuman!" says my reader. Not so, by nature. The Hindoos are characterized by mildness rather than ferocity. Their *religion* has made them what they are—a religion false in its teachings—dishonorable to that Holy and Merciful One whose will it professes to proclaim—destructive of personal happiness and domestic peace—and with no hope to its deluded votaries.

As to the effects of Hindooism upon the national character, the visible results of which it has been the producing cause, I could enlarge at much length, especially in the recording of facts which came under my personal observation while in that country. But my limits forbid this lengthened detail, and, besides, the topic is one with which the reader is familiar. I will therefore express my thoughts through the following paragraphs from the pen of the lamented Heber. I quote from his pages more readily on two accounts—his high position for learning and accurate observation, and his exceeding amiability, which lead him to view the Hindoos with a degree of charity and kindliness which stopped this side of, rather than exceeded the truth. These are the Bishop's words: But of all idolatries which I have ever read or heard of, the religion of the Hindoos, in which I had taken some pains to inform myself, really appears to me the worst, both in the degrading notions which it gives of the Deity; in the endless round of its burdensome ceremonies, which occupy the time and distract the thoughts, without either instructing or interesting its votaries; in the filthy acts of uncleanness and cruelty, not only permitted but enjoined, and inseparably interwoven with those ceremonies; in the system of castes—a system which tends, more than anything else the Devil has yet invented, to destroy the feelings of general benevolence, and to make nine-tenths of mankind the hopeless slaves of the remainder; and, in the total absence of any popular system of morals, or any single lesson which the people at large ever hear, to live virtuously and do good to each other. I do not say, indeed, that there are not some scattered lessons of this kind to be found in their ancient books; but those books are neither accessible to the people at large, nor are these last permitted to read them; and, in general, all the sins that a Soodra is taught to fear, are, killing a cow, offending a Brahmin, or neglecting one of the many frivolous rites by which their deities are supposed to be conciliated. Accordingly, though the general sobriety of the Hindoos (a virtue which they possess in common with most inhabitants of warm climates) affords a very great facility to the maintenance of public order and decorum, I really never have met with a race of men whose standard of morality is so low, who feel so little apparent shame on being detected in a falsehood, or so little interest in the sufferings of a neighbor, not being of their own caste or family; whose ordinary and familiar conversation is so licentious, or, in the wilder and more lawless districts, who shed blood with so little repugnance. The good qualities which there are among them, are, in no instance that I am aware of, connected with, or arising out of, their religion; since it is in no instance to good deeds or virtuous habits in life that the future rewards in which they believe are promised. Their bravery, their fidelity to their employers, their temperance, and, wherever they are found, their humanity and gentleness of disposition, appear to arise exclusively from a natural, happy temperament, from an honorable pride in their own renown and the renown of their ancestors, and from the goodness of God, who seems unwilling that His image should be entirely effaced, even in the midst of the grossest error.

# CHAPTER XXI.

## MEANS FOR ADVANCING CHRISTIANITY IN INDIA.

Harmony between these means—First Agency, *Preaching*, to Stated Congregations, in the Highways, at the Mission-House and at Tayats, with Trials of Body, Mind and Heart—Second Agency, *Bible and Tract Distribution*—Its Necessity and Success—Third Agency, *Education*, (1) Day Charity Schools, (2) Boarding Schools, (3) Literary Seminaries, (4) Theological Academies, and (5) English Schools—Concluding Remarks.

THAT system of Christian benevolence which passes under the name of the "*Foreign Missionary Enterprise*," has for its leading object the conversion of the unevangelized nations to the faith and worship of Jesus Christ. In the prosecution of this merciful scheme, a variety of means has been devised, each of which, though distinct in its mode of operation, unites with all the rest in promoting the desired result. In this respect, the system find its counterpart in the human frame—the head, the trunk, the limbs, have each their particular function in the physical economy, but all aim at one and the same object, and the "eye cannot say unto the hand, I have no need of thee, nor again the head to the feet, I have no need of you." In like manner, though a variety of means have been put in operation for bringing the Gospel to bear upon the minds and hearts of the heathen, they should be regarded not as antagonists and rivals, but as friends and allies, enrolled in a common cause, and leagued against a common foe. With these remarks, I ask the reader's attention to the three-fold agency now employed for bringing Scripture truth before the Hindoos.

*Preaching*, or the announcement, by the living voice, of the doctrines and duties of the Gospel, is the most efficient instrumentality as yet instituted for promoting the conversion of mankind to the religion of Christ. Missionaries allow no plans of benefiting the heathen to take the precedence of this *oral communication of divine truth.* There are, however, various ways of preaching, the employment of which must be regulated by the capabilities of the missionary, (especially his acquaintance with the native language,) and the circumstances in which he may be placed. The first of these is the *delivery of prepared discourses to stated congregations.* There are, connected with all mission stations in Southern India, churches or chapels, where the Gospel is preached, usually twice on the Sabbath, and once or oftener during the week. The Sabbath-morning audiences vary in size from one hundred and fifty to three hundred persons of both sexes. If these assemblies differ from those in Christian lands, in being smaller and more heterogeneous, the contrast is still greater in the style of address needful to arrest their attention, and carry conviction to the heart. Simplicity of arrangement and expression, parabolical or historical illustrations, and earnest appeals to the conscience, characterize the discourses of those who are most successful in gaining for the truth an attentive ear. Missionaries are in danger of rising superior to their simple-minded auditors, in the terms they employ, and in the construction of their sentences. Their style has often too much of the staidness and artificiality of Johnson, and too little of the simplicity of Addison and Swift. To obviate this serious evil, recourse is had to the practice of *ascertaining by a question*, (usually addressed to one or more of the older lads,) whether the argument used, and the illustration employed, convey the intended idea, and are appreciated and felt. I have heard it objected to that this catechetical mode detracts from the dignity of the pulpit; but I cannot but think that this objection indicates a mind more awake to an observance of the graces and elegancies of the pulpit, than a heart alive with zeal to do good.

Another department of preaching is that of *addressing mixed audiences* in the highways, the markets, and other places of public resort. Of all kinds of missionary labor, this makes the largest draughts upon the body, mind, and heart. The exertion of using the voice in the open air, and in a strange and foreign language, makes unusual calls upon the missionary's strength, while we cannot overlook his almost certain exposure to personal violence. The presence of a

Christian government renders this last-named a less formidable evil in India than in many other lands, especially those under Mahomedan rule, and yet, instances still occur, where the bitter enmity of the heathen to the truths of the Gospel displays itself in acts of outrage and violence upon whoever dares to become their public advocate.

The trials of *spirit* are scarcely less numerous than those of a physical nature. Two qualifications are indispensable in one who would proclaim the gospel successfully in the places of public concourse—*quickness of thought* and *command of temper.*

The objections urged against Christianity are of such a character, that a missionary would be not a little ashamed if conscious of an inability to return satisfactory replies ; and yet these may be presented in a form so novel, and urged with a manner so confident and earnest, that he is often quite at a loss what to say ; and the reader can well imagine the use that his opponent (if a shrewd and wily Brahmin) will make of his momentary hesitancy in turning against him the sneer and laugh of ridicule. "Do you believe the words of your Saviour ?" inquired a Brahmin, as a missionary was addressing an assembled audience. Upon hearing an affirmative reply, he continued, "Jesus said, 'if any man take away thy coat, let him have thy cloak also ;' you are well dressed and I half naked, pray give me your garments. He also said, 'Whosoever shall smite thee on thy right cheek, turn to him the other also ;' suppose I give you a blow on the face, will you act in obedience to this command?" Before the missionary had time to answer, there was general laughter and interruption. When a reply can be given something in the style of the question asked, the effect is often very good. As one of the first missionaries in Bengal was preaching in a street of Calcutta, a baboo passing by cast a contemptuous glance at him and said, "You, padres, are just like the hypocrites of whom your Jesus said, 'They love to pray standing in the synagogues and in the corners of the streets, that they may be seen of men.'" "Yes my friend," replied the missionary, "but with this difference, they did it that they might be praised, and we are scoffed at and despised for it."

A missionary in Bengal being asked by a philosophical Brahmin, "What do you preach here?" replied, "We teach the knowledge of the true God." "Who is he? I am God," said the Hindoo. "I thought," said the missionary afterwards, "that it would be an easy matter to confute him, but I soon discovered my mistake." "This is very extraordinary," said I, "are you then almighty?" "No," he replied, "if I had created the sun I should be almighty, but I have not." "How can you pretend to be God if you are not almighty?" "This question shows your ignorance," said he; "What do you see here?" pointing to the Ganges. "Water." "And what is in this vessel?" at the same time pouring out a little into a cup. "This is water likewise." "What is the difference between this water and that of the Ganges?" "There is none." "Oh, I see a great difference: that water carries ships, this does not. God is almighty; I am only a part of the god-head, and therefore I am not almighty; and yet I am God just as these drops in the cup are real water." "According to your representation God is divided into many thousand portions; one is in me, and another is in you." "Oh," said the Brahmin, "this remark is owing to your ignorance: how many suns do you see in the sky?" "Only one." "But if you fill a thousand vessels with water, what do you see in each?" "The image of the sun." "But if you see the image of the sun in so many vessels, does it prove that there are a thousand suns in the firmament? No! there is only one sun, but it is reflected a thousand times in the water. So likewise there is but one God, but his image and brightness are reflected in every human being." The missionary, instead of stopping to point out the falsity of the comparison, preferred trying to touch his conscience. "God," he continued, "is holy, are you holy?" "I am not; I am doing many things that are wrong, and that I know to be wrong." "How, then, can you say that you are God?" "Oh, I see," said the former, "that you need a little more intellect to be put into your head before you can argue with us. God is fire; fire is the purest element in the creation; but if you throw dirt upon it, a bad odor will arise; it is not the fault of the fire, but of that which is cast upon it. Thus God in me is perfectly pure, but He is surrounded by matter. He does not desire sin; He hates it; but it arises from matter." In this way the conversation continued long, but at the end the missionary found that he had made but little progress in convincing his opponent. Many a person who can fill a pulpit in America or England with respectability and credit, would undoubtedly break down if called to make an attempt among the Hindoos; and this not for want of mental strength or furniture, but from the peculiar manner in which objections are presented, and the confidence with which they are uttered. Readiness in apprehending the point of an opponent's arguments, and tact in returning a brief but satisfactory reply, are of far more value in such circumstances than depth of mind or extent of scientific acquirement. Quickness conquers where research loses the day.

Large calls are also made upon the *better feelings of the heart*, especially patience and forbearance. The missionary hears his motives impugned in a manner very painful to one of honorable purpose, and conscious of sincere integrity and benevolence. Said a missionary to a Hindoo: "What do you think is the reason why we leave our native country, come to your villages, establish schools, and expend so much in the education of your children?" One replied, "You expect by this good deed the more certainly to reach heaven," while another answered, "Oh, it is your nature, just as it is the nature of the jackal to prowl abroad at night stealing fowls and geese." How often have I been compelled to hear the name of the blessed Redeemer blasphemed, and his most gracious acts misconstrued and vilified in a manner tending to awaken feelings akin to those of the too zealous disciple when he said, "Shall we not call down fire from heaven and consume them!" But his thoughts and feelings, though bitter to agony, the missionary must not express, except in the language of pity and compassion; for to get his opponent irritated and vexed, is the Hindoo disputant's most earnest endeavor. This done, and he leaves the field with the triumphant exclamation, "The padre is angry—is angry, and the day is won!"

*Conversation with visitors at the mission house and at Zayats* comes under the general head of preaching. A missionary keeps open doors. His dwelling is a place of public resort, and he denies admittance to the person who calls to see him at the peril of withholding instruction and advice from one to whom he may be a guide to the heavenly world. *Zayats*, or small buildings in frequented parts of the city or village, where the missionary spends a part of each day in conversation with visitors, and in tract distribution, are less common in India than in Burmah, their place being supplied by the rooms in which the day schools are held.

The topic of preaching may be closed by the published opinion of the Rev. Mr. Buyers, of the Benares Mission. "It has been a sad mistake to suppose that inferior preaching talents may do for the missionary work. The contrary is the fact. Eloquence of a far higher and more varied order is required than that which will do in an English pulpit, where the preacher, from having to walk in a beaten track, may acquit himself, so far as ordinary ministrations are concerned, without professing any considerable oratorical powers. The fact that a man has to divest Christian doctrines of all technical words and phrases, and give it in new forms and combinations, is surely sufficient to show that preaching to the Heathen requires the exercise of no ordinary powers. He has not only to strike out a new and untrodden path, but has to arrange the whole tenor of his preaching so as to bring Christianity to bear on the extermination of systems of error quite new to himself, and to modes of speaking in which he has been educated. To speak well and efficiently with such difficulties in the way, he must be a man of ready eloquence, as well as a philosophical linguist, capable of moulding and bending figures of speech required for conveying to the minds of his hearers new trains of thought and doctrines unheard of before; and all at the spur of the moment, and amid acute and watchful adversaries, who will be glad to take advantage of every weak point, and turn it against him."

## II.

The *preparation and distribution of the sacred Scriptures and religious tracts and books* is the second agency for propagating Christianity in India. The occasions are many in which an oral communication of divine truth is impossible. Ignorance of the native language, the prejudices of the people, and a variety of other obstacles, may prevent personal instruction; and were there no other agency than that of the living voice, many of the people must remain in ignorance of Him who is "the way, the truth, and the life." But the various organizations formed for preparing and publishing Bibles and religious tracts come in to supply this desideratum; and such has been their practical utility, that they have long been deemed an essential part of the great system of foreign missionary effort. All the considerations that render them a means of usefulness in Christian lands, are greatly magnified in importance when carried to a Pagan country. Connected with each of the larger missionary stations is a printing establishment, from which the shelves of the missionaries are supplied with these silent, but eloquent and effective teachers of revealed truth, which can go into towns and villages to which the living preacher is denied an entrance, removing prejudices and preparing the way for his future instructions, or deepening impressions that his previous visits have already made.

Did my limits allow, I might detain the reader with a narrative of facts illustrative of the position, that while the oral communication of divine truth is worthy of the first place in the interest and effort of the Church, this of Bible and tract distribution cannot be neglected without serious harm to the cause of truth. To the friends of the American Bible and Tract Societies, I say with all earnestness, Sustain with undiminished, and, if possible, enlarged liberality, the foreign departments of your blessed institutions. You cannot give beyond the extent of profitable appropriation, and the character of your directing agents abroad is a proof that a judicious and honest use will be made of the funds committed to their care.

## III.

The third and last of the agencies in use for advancing the Gospel throughout India, is *Education.* There are five distinct classes of institutions which have for their object the inculcating of Bible doctrine and precept. Of these the first is that of

### *Day Charity Schools.*

There is no lack in India of primary schools for the instruction of the young. Cities and towns are full of them. You can scarcely pass the length of any street without seeing the verandah of one or more houses filled with youth from the ages of five to twelve, who are being instructed in the elements of Hindoo literature and science, especially in reading, arithmetic, and ethical proverbs selected from the writings of their sages. The teachers are of course all heathen, and the instruction they impart tends directly and by design to form their pupils to the opinions and practices of idolatry. To rescue one of these institutions from such an influence, and, while it remains the same in the place of its location, with the same master at its head, the same youth in attendance, to remove the heathen textbooks and place the Bible in their stead, is a most desirable object to secure. It is purifying the fountain, that its varied streams may be healthful and invigorating rather than deadly and noisome. Exception is taken to the system, by some, on the ground that it leads to the employment of heathen masters, who will, it is urged, use all possible means to neutralize the benefit that might be derived from the study of the revealed volume. In reply to this objection, which is not without weight, it is urged that Christian teachers cannot be obtained in sufficient numbers to meet the exigencies of the case; and that if they could be found and sent to the villages, the heathen master would not yield his post to a stranger; and the consequence would be a Christian school set up in opposition to the heathen, with the advantage to the latter of having the first occupancy of the place, and the prejudices of the parents in favor of that which strengthens the power of their own religion. In military tactics it is deemed more desirable to seize the enemy's fort and turn the guns against its former occupants, than to erect a new battery over against the old one.

But that the reader may see clearly the nature and amount of Christian instruction imparted in these institutions, I will state, with all brevity, the course of instruction pursued in the schools of which I had the charge while a resident of Madras and, formerly, of the city of Madura. Each school was divided into four classes, to each of which were allotted the following monthly studies:

1st class—A Scripture text for each day, the whole to be recited, seriatim, at the Sabbath morning service, and at the monthly examinations—two pages of a catechism of Christian doctrine and duty; the replies being given in the language of the Bible—ten pages of an elementary Church History—five stanzas of a Tamil dictionary in running rhyme.

2nd class—A daily text, as in the first class—two pages of a catechism of Scripture precepts—a chapter in a reading book, narrative and arithmetic.

3d class—One page of an elementary catechism—reading—spelling—and arithmetic.

4th class—Primary catechism and alphabet.

On the last day of the month all the scholars are assembled, and a careful examination takes place, in the presence of the native assistant, upon all the lessons pursued. This examination is conducted by the missionary, and that, too, with great strictness, as *payment, to the master, is graduated by the proficiency made by his pupils in each study.*

In addition to these lessons, the following requirements are made. *First*—Masters and monitors, and, at least, two-thirds of the pupils must be at religious services on Sabbath morning, and at the Sabbath school an hour previous. *Second*—All the pupils of the 1st and 2nd classes meet at the house of the missionary an hour of each Tuesday morning, to read the Bible and receive instruction. *Third*—Masters and monitors assemble on Tuesday afternoon at the church, where one hour is devoted to the lessons of the month, and the second to a lecture. *Fourth*—The missionary visits each school at least twice a month, where he hears the youth read, and then addresses them and the audiences that are naturally attracted to the spot. *Fifth*—The native assistant, bearing the name of superintendent, visits one of the schools daily, to see that masters and scholars are in their places, and to preach and distribute Bibles and tracts.

From this view the reader will perceive that great indeed must be the effort required to neutralize all the benefits that, with the Divine blessing, must necessarily attend so great an amount of effort expended in their instruction. Immortal truth has gained a lodgment in the minds of a multitude of intelligent beings, and it cannot be dislodged by the most strenuous efforts of the emissaries of evil. It is by these schools more than by any other means, that an extensive change is taking place in the popular mind of India. Said an eminent missionary in Bengal, "Every youth who leaves our schools, does it with the law of Christ written upon his conscience, and a belief in the truth of Christ, deep-seated in his convictions; a remark, this, which will be responded to by Christian teachers, the country over.

The most serious objection urged against these primary schools is, that, though impressions favorable to Christianity may be, and often are, made upon the minds of the youth while they are in the school-room, there is a danger of their obliteration when he returns to his home, and mingles with his heathen relatives and friends. He there witnesses idolatrous ceremonies of the most imposing kind, and in them he is urged to take a part; and refuses at the peril of parental displeasure and punishment. The removal of this difficulty gave rise to

*Boarding Schools,*

The second class of educational institutions to which I would invite the reader's attention. Here the youth is removed quite away from his idolatrous connexions, with all their anti-Christian rites and ceremonies, language, and influence, and is brought under the direct and ever-urgent pressure of Gospel truth. From week to week, and month to month, he breathes a Christian atmosphere, with nothing to neutralize its healthful qualities, or diminish its power to invigorate and strengthen the better feelings of the heart. The youth are under the constant care and watchful eye of the missionary, and are forbidden to visit their heathen friends, except at distant intervals, and then but for a short period. One such institution is, when possible, established in connection with every missionary station; and they have proved themselves the nurseries of the Church.

The expense of sustaining them is of course greater than that of Day Schools. The latter can never be superseded by the former, for, even if there were a sufficiency of funds, very many parents would not allow the attendance of their children at a Boarding School, who would permit them to become members of a Day School.

In a mission where there are several Boarding

Schools for boys, there is one that takes the precedence of all the rest, and is termed

*The Seminary.*

A selection is made from among the most hopeful of the youth in the boarding schools, and these are placed under the instruction of a missionary who is qualified to carry them into the higher branches of learning. One of the oldest of these institutions is at Batticotta, Ceylon. It has been in operation for thirty years, during most of the time under Messrs. Poor and Hoisington; and, so far as literary and scientific advantages are concerned, is second to no other in India. The one in Madura under Mr. Tracy is of more recent establishment, but is in a prosperous state. They are in many respects like our colleges, though on a less extensive scale, especially as to the number of teachers. They need no fuller mention, as all the advantages that belong to boarding schools pertain to these in an eminent degree.

*Theological Academies.*

The remark has been made by an eminent missionary, and may be received with little or no allowance, that "the grand desideratum in the present system of India missions, is the want of a really superior and thoroughly efficient native agency—a race of native laborers endowed with the graces of God's Spirit, in happy and harmonious conjunction with the highest qualifications which the united wisdom, learning, and piety of the Christian Church can bestow."

Institutions of a kind calculated to prepare a class of men thus qualified, are being established in various parts of Southern India. One of this character has existed for several years at Bangalore, and is under the able superintendence and instruction of my valued friend, the Rev. Mr. Crisp of the London Missionary Society. There is no institution specially devoted to the object of preparing young men for the ministry in connection with either branch of the American Mission in Southern India, their place being in part supplied by lectures and theological reading in the Seminary.

There is throughout India an extensive and increasing desire to acquire the English language. To meet this prevalent wish, another class of institutions has of late years come into very general establishment, popularly styled,

*English Schools.*

Missionaries finding the desire so urgent to acquire the language of the West, and seeing that many would decline attending upon their instructions at any other time or place, have availed themselves of it, and have established these schools, in which no less of Christianity is taught than in boarding schools; while that instruction is afforded which will prepare the pupils for offices under government. While in the city of Madura, I had under my charge, in addition to a circle of day schools and a boarding school for girls, an English school. It contained more than one hundred youth, one half of whom were Brahmins.

I have thus brought to the reader's notice three distinct methods of extending the Gospel in India—*preaching* from the pulpit, in the highways, and at the mission-house and Zayat—*distribution of Bibles and tracts*, personally and through the medium of native assistants—and *education* in day and boarding schools, seminaries, theological institutions, and English schools. Here is an array of means calculated to effect wonders for the spiritual regeneration of that erring land. And so they will, if there be power in truth and reality in the Divine promises. The enemy may be subtle and malignant, the fortress strong and high-walled, but the beleaguering army have justice and heaven on their side, and they will prevail! It needs but that the friends of Christian truth allow no retrograde movement in either of these five-fold respects, but that each besieger be kept supplied with the necessary means of attack at every weak and assailable point; and though there may be much delay, long trial of patience and faith, with occasions when further effort seems fruitless and vain, yet not more certainly did the proud wall of Jericho fall before the armies of Israel, than the ramparts of Hindooism shall be levelled to the ground, and Christ shall rule throughout that idolatrous and now wretched land.

## CHAPTER XXII.

### LIGHTS AND SHADES OF MISSIONS IN INDIA.

Quotations from the Abbé Du Bois, with Remarks in Opposition—Considerations favorable to the Cause of Christian Truth in India—(1) Change in Governmental Policy; (2) Disconnection of Government from Hindoo Festivals and Superstitious Ceremonies; (3) Improved Character of Foreign Residents; (4) Posture of the Native Mind towards the Religion of Christ; (5) The existence in India of a Christian Church with many thousand Members; (6) The array of Organized Means for Propagating the Truth; and (7) The Practical Interest of all Christendom in the Prospects of the Hindoos—Certain Offsets to these Encouragements—Summing up of the whole subject.

Early in the present century the Abbé Du Bois, an eminent missionary of the Papal Church, returned from India to Europe, and communicated to his countrymen the following mature opinion: "The experience I have gained through a familiar intercourse with the Hindoos of all castes for twenty-five years, has made me thoroughly acquainted with the *insuperable obstacles* that Christianity will ever have to encounter there; and it is my decided opinion that the people of that land are lying under an everlasting anathema, have forever rendered themselves unworthy of the Divine favor, have been utterly forsaken by God, and given over forever to a reprobate mind on account of the peculiar wickedness of their worship, so that there is no possibility of converting them to any sect of Christianity." The reader may be assured that I am no convert to the Abbé's disheartening conclusion. I was in India less than one half of the time that missionary was, but while there I travelled much—acquainted myself by personal observation with the means mentioned in the previous chapter for promoting the advancement of Christian truth—observed the results as thus far attained—conversed with English officers, civil and military, who had long resided in the country, and visited its most distant provinces—heard the opinions of the learned Brahmins and other intelligent natives—and would record it as an opinion, deliberately formed, that there are considerations which, if contemplated with due and impartial attention, must convince the most hesitating observer that if there be much in the present state of Christianity in India to cause depression and sorrow, there is *far more* to awaken devout gratitude and joyful hope.

The *first* of several considerations which I would submit to the reader's attention, respects the *change which has taken place in the views and action of the British Government*. Says an English writer: "Never, in its introduction to a country, has the missionary enterprize met with greater difficulties than in India. As though it were not enough that we had fifteen thousand miles of ocean to traverse, and then contend with an insalubrious climate and a strange language; or that the heathen in their attachment to caste and other superstitions, or that our own countrymen in their infidelity and prejudice against the Gospel, or that the powers of darkness and spiritual wickedness in high places were against us; the *government*, in its policy and in its laws, were in direct hostility to our entrance into the field. It was impossible to go in a ship from Britain, bound to any of our Indian Presidencies. Dr. Bogue, Mr. Ewing, and other noble-minded and benevolent men, were interdicted from leaving our native country at all. Those who were not put under the ban, and whose zeal and intrepidity led them to brave every obstacle, had to find their way to Holland or to America, that from thence they might embark, and, peradventure, be smuggled like contraband goods upon the shores of Hindoostan. The Baptist missionaries Carey and Thomas, on their arrival at Calcutta, were not suffered to remain on British ground, and were obliged to take refuge in Serampore, a Danish settlement. Messrs. Judson, Newell, and Hall, from America, whose names are embalmed in the memory of the churches, were driven from Christian protection, and were exposed to a long night of trial, privation, and suffering." But a policy so baseless in its assumed necessity—so selfish, inconsistent, and wicked—could not stand the scrutinizing gaze and eloquent denunciation of the worthy in England. When the charter of the East India Company was to be renewed in the year 1813, William Wilberforce, the friend of man and justice, appeared as the advocate of liberty and truth; and by the power of unanswerable arguments, established facts, and manly eloquence, caused the introduction of that clause in virtue of which missionaries were permitted to enter the country at any point—to range throughout the length and breadth of the empire, propagating the Gospel in whatever ways were not inconsistent with the peace of the country and the majesty of Government. This change of policy has been progressing to the present time; so that if these questions were addressed to the Councils of Bengal, Madras, and Bombay—"Have the efforts of foreign missionaries contributed to the stability of the English Government and to the happiness of the people? and ought their longer continuance to be sanctioned and encouraged?"—who can doubt that the reply would be an earnest and emphatic *affirmative.* Not only are Christian teachers of all nations and creeds allowed full liberty to travel, speak, and act as they please, but each of the branches of government has afforded assistance, by pecuniary donations, and otherwise, to institutions in which Christianity is faithfully taught, and Hindooism boldly assailed,—while the highest functionaries preside at examinations of missionary seminaries, and aid in furthering efforts to evangelize the people. This is an encouraging feature of the subject, and we should be sadly wanting in becoming feelings, if we withheld the voice of grateful praise to Him who has the hearts of rulers in His hand, constraining them, as in this case, to extend to His cause their protecting and fostering care.

The past and present position of the British Government respecting the *public parades of Hindoo worship, the pilgrim tax, and the property of temples and pagodas*, is a second feature to be illustrated. Until lately, the Hindoos have not only been protected in the performance of their religious ceremonies, but open and most important encouragement has been afforded by their *Christian* rulers. The principal temples at the various great places of resort were taken under the paternal care of Government, and European officials had the entire direction of pecuniary receipts and disbursements. At the place of concourse fences were erected to prevent intruders, and those without a pass, from descending to the sacred stream, or from entering into the holy edifice, none could obtain admission without a government ticket paid for according to the rank of the applicant, and all means were used to render the festival profitable as possible to the public treasury. This was the case at Juggernaut, Gaya, and Allahabad in the north, and Trinomale, Conjeveram and Seringham on the south. On certain occasions the English regiment was called out, who, by their splendid equipage, music, and salutes, gave eclat to the idolatrous festivity. At other times, an officer of government, with much parade, presented to the officiating Brahmins a costly *shawl* with which to decorate the image. Surprise has been well expressed that the Indian government could induce a large body of educated English gentlemen so far to forget themselves as to perform the contemptible part of puppets in the procession of such images as Vishnu and other Hindoo deities. But so it was, and not till within a few years were the folly and wickedness of such a course made to be generally seen and felt. The agitation of the subject began with a few Christian officers, who were led to consider the relation they sustained to their heathen neighbors, and the meaning of the injunction "avoid even the appearance of evil." A consideration of the responsibility hereby involved, compelled them to the conclusion that they could not, as conscientious men, lend the sanction of their presence to the exalting of a senseless image into an equality with the "High and Holy One who inhabiteth eternity." "If," was their language to those who gave them their appointments, "*if the alternative be attendance at Heathen festivals or resignation of our commissions, duty to God requires the latter, and we are ready to meet the issue.*" Government being at that time wholly indisposed to yield the point, several resignations were sent in, among which was that of Sir Peregrine Maitland, commander-in-chief of the Madras Presidency, who withdrew from an honorable post, yielding an income of £15,000 per year, rather than give the weight of his influence to a system so glaringly unchristian and dishonorable to his Redeemer as this. Such instances of decision and self-sacrifice, with crowded petitions from all parts of the country, excited inquiry in England, and led to the agitation of the subject there, until after long debates in the Court of Directors, and pauses, which the Hon. Mr. Poynder allowed to be but brief, the resolution was passed directing a discontinuance of all such attendance and salutes as were made matter of just complaint on the part of the Christian officers and soldiers of the Indian army. Long delays occurred in carrying into full effect the will of the Directors, especially throughout the Madras Presidency. But it has, finally, to a large extent been accomplished. If governmental officers attend upon public festivals it is but to prevent a disturbance of public tranquillity. The pilgrim tax is no longer, or to but a trifling extent, collected, and the Brahmins are left, in most cases, to look after their own pecuniary affairs, excepting in cases where the government is the appointed and irreleasible guardian.

The days of ignorance and indifference upon this subject have gone by never to return; and the sentiment has taken a strong hold upon the public mind of England, that it is inconsistent and foolish to send to India bishops, chaplains, and missionaries—vain to establish schools and circulate Bibles—so long as a public sanction is given to the system which these means were designed to overthrow; while to send over the land pilgrim-hunters, to applaud the fame and sanctity of the shrines, and thus stimulate the ignorant multitude on to the gate of superstition, that the public revenue may be benefited by the iniquitous traffic, is, in the extreme, unchristian, wicked and cruel. All these are signs of the times favorable to the advancement of truth and goodness in that benighted and sin-enslaved land.

The *past and present character of European residents* presents a point worthy of attention. The Hon. Mr. Shore, an eminent Bengal Judge, in his published "Notes on Indian Affairs," uses this strong language: "The habits of the English in this country, till within the last twenty years, were, as far as religion is concerned, far below those of the heathen by whom they were surrounded. These at least paid attention to their own forms and ceremonies, but the English appear to have considered themselves at liberty to throw aside all consideration upon the subject. They lived 'without God in the world,' as if there were neither a heaven nor a hell." An old merchant said to the missionary Schwartz, "Do all Englishmen speak like you?" The reply was, "All Europeans are not true Christians, but there are many who believe and practice the faith I commend and preach." "You astonish me," said the native, "for from what we daily observe, we cannot but think the Europeans to be, with few exceptions, self-interested, incontinent, proud, full of contempt against us Hindoos, and even against their own religion." But how gratifying the change which has occurred and is still in progress. Many Europeans who now go to India, either carry their piety with them *without leaving it at the Cape of Good Hope;* or if, unhappily, they reach its shores without this needful blessing, they secure it through an attendance upon the Christian sanctuaries which are scattered throughout the country. In the days of Henry Martyn, the *chaplains* of the East India Company were, as a body, "blind leaders of the blind," "hirelings who cared not for the sheep;" but now, it were difficult to find in Christendom more conscientious and faithful ministers of divine truth than are to be met with in India. For an officer or soldier of the Indian army, or for a civilian of any age and rank to act the Christian, is no longer a reproach and disgrace, but rather a passport to respectability and public favor. The bearing of all this upon the advancement of Christianity in that land, is both negatively and positively beneficial: *negatively*, for one argument against our faith is thus wrested from the Hindoo priesthood, viz., that it exerts no salutary influence upon its disciples; and *positively*, for the teachers of the Gospel now enjoy the sympathy, influence, and pecuniary contributions of their fellow-believers. Let a few facts illustrate this last point. In the year 1844 a leading citizen of Madras offered the sum of $25,000 for the establishment of a Christian Institution in opposition to the Government University, which excluded the Bible, on condition that the public would subscribe a like sum. At the head of the list was placed the name of the Governor of Madras, the Marquis of Tweedale, who subscribed $5,000, followed by a long array of names from all classes in society, until, after the lapse of a few months, the whole sum was raised. When the missionaries of the Church of Scotland joined their seceding brethren, their friends in the Madras Presidency rallied at once to their aid, and have met their entire expenses, with the purchase of premises and buildings, to the sum of not less than $50,000. The two neat and commodious chapels of the American Mission at Madras, were erected without any drafts upon the Home Treasury, and mainly through the efforts of my worthy friend and colleague, the Rev. Mr. Winslow. Some branches of missionary operations in India are carried on wholly through contributions from the foreign residents. Some officers expend a large part of their incomes in the publication and distribution of tracts, and sustaining schools: others give a salary to a Christian catechist, who visits their family, reads to the servants, and instructs them in the doctrines and duties of Christianity. Without wishing to conceal the fact that there is very much of irreligion still remaining among the foreigners of India —much that is immoral, and vicious, and destructive —yet with all that need be subtracted of irreligion and vice, there remains much, very much, in the state and prospects of Anglo-Indian society there which calls for devout gratitude and joyful hope.

The *popular sentiment is evidently, though it may be slowly, turning against Hindooism, and in favor of Christianity.* There are traditions and prophecies current among the people, and recorded in the sacred books of the land, that the time is coming when the Brahminical religion is to be supplanted by one from the western world. The tenth avatar of Vishnu, a man on a white horse, is supposed by some to typify that advent. Be that as it may, the belief in that occurrence is common the country over. Multitudes are at the present hour thoroughly convinced that Christianity has truth upon its side, and are deterred from acting up to their convictions only because they cannot make up their minds to bear the sacrifices which such a profession must involve. These persons, like the "Ruler of the Jews" visit the missionary "by night," state their convictions and those of their friends, and inquire of him what they shall do. "We know," say they, "that we are in the wrong. You are the true worshippers, and we trust that our children will be of your faith; but how can we change now?" One of this class, a wealthy Brahmin of Benares, but a few years ago called upon a missionary, bringing with him his youthful son. "This child," he said, "I now give to you, and with him here are rupees 10,000 ($5,000) for his support. Take him, bring him up a Christian. I am too old to alter my faith, but I desire my child to be a follower of Christ." While this is a peculiar case in respect to the pecuniary donation, yet instances of a like kind are of increasingly frequent occurrence.

The people are changing their opinions and conduct towards their priests. In former times to regard a Brahmin with other than feelings of reverential awe, was deemed one of the highest of crimes. No matter what their character and principles—what the number of their lies, adulteries, and other vicious acts—they were regarded as the best and holiest of men. Their smile was better than the approbation of heaven—their anathema worse than the prospect of hell. But now, although the Brahmins still occupy the first place in Hindoo society—though to them, as priests, are entrusted duties of great importance and solemnity—they by no means enjoy the high honors and special prerogatives with which they were once favored. Their crimes are spoken of with the greatest freedom, and their threatenings command but little attention, and less alarm. If upon any part of the antique structure of Hindooism there be inscribed with special truth "*Ichabod*," it is upon the institution of the Brahminical priesthood!

The strength or weakness of religious zeal in any country may be with much correctness judged of by the condition of its *edifices for worship.* Apply this rule to the present condition of India, and it suggests much to encourage for Christianity. But few new temples are erected, while the old ones are fast going to ruins. A coat of paint and whitewash is annually allowed to temples of peculiar sanctity and resort, while the majority are left to the decaying power of time. There is the absence of that spirit of zeal and self-sacrifice for their faith which will compel parents and guardians to keep their children at home, or expend an amount for their education rather than send them to a missionary institution, where there is every prospect of having their faith in Hindooism shaken, and in Christianity confirmed. Instances have occurred in which the conversion of one or more pupils has led to a withdrawal of all the other scholars; but the missionary has but to wait a little and there will be a general return of the absentees. Mass meetings have been held at Calcutta and other places, in which speeches have been made of a character most denunciatory of the Bible and its teachers, and pledges formed of crushing the whole system. But most signal failure has always been the result. Of the moneys pledged not one per cent. is paid, and the resolutions have turned out to be "vox et preterea nihil." These things are noticed by intelligent Hindoos, and many of them speak out publicly and boldly. A letter addressed not long since by a native of Calcutta to the "Dhurma Subha," an association formed for the protection of Hindooism, contained sentences like these: "Oh, holy men, boast no more that you are Hindoos! Do you think that your people will remain faithful to the religion of their fathers? Give up all such vain hopes. The Padres are wandering in bands through the lanes and streets of Calcutta in order to destroy the Hindoo religion, and greedy boys, like hungry fishes, are caught by the hook of their sorceries. Many youth have given up their family caste and religion, and have been initiated into the mysteries of the Bible. Last week another boy *lifted his wing and flew to the tree of the love of Jesus Christ!* We cannot find fault with the missionaries, for it is the glory of their religion that they have crossed seven oceans and thirteen seas* to come into this country, and are now expending immense sums in education of the people. Our religion, having no means of

* A proverbial expression.

defending itself, is *dying and going to its last home.*" Such a state of things as now described is altogether new to India, and indicates a change of feeling most encouraging to the heart of those who desire the downfall of that ancient but destructive superstition.

The *existence in India of a Christian church composed of converted Hindoos* is another consideration which casts a cheering light upon the cause of truth in that land. It is no longer problematical whether the natives of Hindostan are susceptible of impression by the arguments and motives of the Gospel. The possibility of their evangelization is settled by the fact that Hindooism and Mohamedanism have yielded converts to Christianity. The Brahmin and Soodra have been cleansed by a holier ablution than by the waters of the Ganges; and sitting down at the table of the Lord, have eaten of one bread and drank of one cup in remembrance of Jesus. One of the north of India missionaries states the number of Protestant Christians in the Bengal Presidency and northwest provinces to exceed twelve thousand. The Secretary of the Church Missionary Society (Rev. Mr. Tucker) estimates the native Christians of Southern India at fifty thousand. It is difficult to gain an estimate altogether correct and faultless, and still more difficult to ascertain how large the proportion of those who "have a name to live." But making all lawful and required deductions, *many thousands* will remain as evidence, not to be gainsaid, that the Most High has not disinherited his children there, unworthy though they have rendered themselves of the Divine favor. Among the natives of India there are jewels which will shine brightly and forever in the Redeemer's crown of glory. That country is yet to form part of that universal empire of which the Lord Jesus is Saviour and King.

To these considerations may be added the interest expressed, by all Christian denominations, in the spiritual prospects of the Hindoos, the comparatively large number of missionaries sent among them, the invariable success of their efforts whenever carried on with perseverance and zeal, the extensive circulation of Bibles and Tracts, and other agencies, which, if space allowed, I would gladly illustrate.

I am not ignorant of the fact, nor would I attempt its concealment, that this subject has *shades*, as well as *lights*. The Hindoo, with his volumes of revealed truth, his multitude of propitiatory sacrifices, his festival days and deities, numerous and imposing, and his millions of fellow-believers, can hardly be made to believe that all are deceived, and the whole system a falsehood and deception. Then comes in the system of *caste*, with its terrific denunciations against all who dare to abjure the national faith, and attach themselves to the creed of strangers and foreigners. Upon this follows the certainty that persecution, in some of its hydra forms, will follow the act of baptism. To all which may be added a literature, extensive and antiquated, to which the Hindoo triumphantly appeals, with the question, How can we, who live in the *iron age* of learning, disbelieve and discard that creed which in the golden age was deemed divine in origin, and supreme in excellence?" These things operate as barriers to the progress of truth, and it is on account of these that the present missionary corps is so much like a "beleaguering army, that has as yet been skirmishing around the walls of a mighty fortress, who have just succeeded in taking a few stragglers as prisoners, and have begun to open some of their batteries, to breach the walls, but who well know that many more arduous struggles must be endured, and that many a hero must fall before the enemy's citadel is taken!

But when we consider that the Government of India gives the most ample protection to missionaries of all denominations, in the peaceable prosecution of their holy object—that a disunion is fast being effected between governmental patronage and the national religion, the latter being left to stand or fall on its own merits—that a most extensive and happy change has taken place in the character and consequent influence of European residents, civil, military, and ecclesiastical—that the impression is wide-spread and deep, among all intelligent and thoughtful Hindoos, that their system cannot endure a close contact with Christianity—that the Christian Church has obtained a footing in that land, and attached to itself scarcely less than 50,000 nominal disciples—that the whole array of evangelizing agencies, as Schools, the Press, Bibles and Tract Circulation, and Preaching, in its many forms, is in operation—that the whole of Christendom, without regard to creed or nation, is manifesting a deep and practical interest in the welfare of the Hindoos, and sending thither teachers of their faith—when these facts come before us, they tend to dissipate the dark clouds of discouragement and depression. "The walls of Jerusalem, compactly built together, did not fall at once, under the battering-rams of the Romans. Blow succeeded blow, before any important impression was made. But at length the huge stones were loosed and shaken, and, in spite of the desperate courage and skill of the defenders, the inner wall was reached; it toppled to its foundation, and a breach was opened into the heart of the city." So with Hindooism—it has been besieged, and an undermining process is going on, which, with the Divine blessing, will go on, until it shall be known but on the pages of history. While, therefore, it cannot be denied that the "night" of error and superstition still broods over that land, we may say, without the aid of prophetic vision, "*The morning cometh.*"

# CHAPTER XXIII.

## CHRISTIAN MISSIONS IN INDIA.

The interest felt by Christendom in India—St. Thomas—Roman Catholic Missions—Society for Propagating the Gospel—Danish Missionary Society—English Baptist Missionary Society—London Missionary Society—Scottish Missionary Society—Church Missionary Society—Free Church of Scotland Missions—American Board of Commissioners for Foreign Missions—American Baptist Missionary Society—Presbyterian Foreign Missionary Society—Free Will Baptist Missions—Evangelical Lutheran Missions—Concluding Remarks.

THE interest felt by the whole of Christendom in the spiritual position and prospects of the Hindoos, is a fact full of hope to that benighted and unhappy people. A nation that has, from any cause, lost the earnest sympathy of the Christian Church, and is debarred wholly or in part from a place in her prayers and evangelizing endeavors, is in a very deplorable and hapless state. Such is not the case with India. I know of no part of the vast Christian community which is not engaged directly and earnestly in bettering the condition of that idolatrous country. The late Bishop Heber favored the opinion that St. Thomas preached the Gospel in India, and was martyred at a place named Meilapoor, near the city of Madras. In that village is a small rocky knoll with a Roman Catholic church upon it, which, in honor of this apostle and early martyr, is called St. Thomé. As early as the fourteenth century, the Church of Rome sent forth her emissaries to that land; and with such zeal and earnestness were their efforts prosecuted under Robert de Nobili, Francis Xavier, with other Ecclesiastics, Carmelites, Capuchins, Augustinians and Jesuits, that in connection with that communion alone are not less than six hundred thousand natives. Most of these are the descendants of families converted, centuries back, to the creed of Rome, the conversions from heathenism to that faith being at the present time very few.

I would request the reader's attention, during the remainder of this chapter, to a rapid view of *Protestant Missions* as they have been and still are conducted in that country. The various organizations will be named in the order of their relative age.

I.

The "SOCIETY FOR THE PROPAGATION OF THE GOSPEL IN FOREIGN PARTS," was chartered by King William III., June 16, 1701. Its India stations are Vepery, (an environ of Madras,) Tanjore, Trichinopoly, Vellore, Cuddalore and Tinnevelly, with Bishop's College at Calcutta.

II.

The "DANISH MISSIONARY SOCIETY," was established

in 1705, by Frederick IV. of Denmark, and had for its primary object to make known the Gospel of Christ among the Hindoos on the Coromandel coast. The missionarles who have enjoyed the patronage of this Sooiety have been men eminent for talents and piety. The venerable names of Ziegenbalg, Plutscho, Grundler, Schubse, Schwartz, Gerické, Jonické, Kohloff, Rottler, Cammæren and others, their colleagues, will be honored so long as faith, zeal, and self-sacrifice are esteemed among men.

## III.

The "English Baptist Missionary Society" was the product of a volume from the pen of Rev. Andrew Fuller, entitled "*The Gospel of Christ worthy of all acceptation*," and a discourse from Mr. (afterwards Dr.) Carey, from Isaiah, liv. 2, 3, and having as its topic this important sentiment, "*Expect* great things from God; *attempt* great things for God." On the 2d of October, 1792, in the humble village of Kittering, this noble institution of Christian benevolence had its beginning in a series of resolutions adopted by Ryland, Fuller, Sutcliff, Pearce, and men of kindred aims and hopes. On the 13th of June, of the same year, Revds. John Thomas and William Carey, sailed for the East Indies. My readers are too familiar with the names of Carey, Marshman, Ward, Yates, Pearce, their place of abode—the world-renowned *Serampore*—and their great success in Bible translations, to require any farther details in regard to their operations. Besides

Serampore this Society have stations at Calcutta, Cutwa, Digah, and Monghyr, at each of which is a Christian church, with schools, and systematic Bible and Tract distribution.

IV.

The "LONDON MISSIONARY SOCIETY" was established in 1795, and consisted, at its formation, of Christians of several denominations, though now conducted almost entirely on the plan of discipline adopted by the body of independent Dissenters. This most useful organization had its origin in the zeal enkindled within the heart of Dr. Bogue, Rev. Mr. Steven, and a few others, by letters received from Carey and Thomas—a remarkable instance of the diffusive benefit of Christian benevolence. In addition to successful establishments in the South Sea Islands and South Africa, this Society has stations at Benares, Burhampore, Chinsurah, Kidderpore, Surat, Madras, Vizagapatam, Cuddapah, Chittoor, Belgaum, Bellary, Bungalore, and Travancore. From the year 1798, when the Rev. Mr. Forsyth was sent to Calcutta, to the present hour, this Institution has been doing much for the natives and Eurasians of India.

V.

The "SCOTTISH MISSIONARY SOCIETY" was formed at Edinburgh in February, 1796, and though limited in its sphere of operations has had a useful career. Its missions in the East Indies are at Bankote, sixty miles south from Bombay, Sevendroog and Bombay.

## VI.

In the year 1801 was instituted the "CHURCH MISSIONARY SOCIETY," of a kindred spirit and aim with that of the London Society; but conducted solely on the principles of the Church of England. It is understood to be the organ of the Low Church as the Gospel Propagation Society is of the High Church party of that religious denomination. In addition to Africa and Australia, this Society has many devoted and successful agents in Northern India, at Burdwan, Buxar, Benares, Chunar, Delhi, Agra, Surruckpore, and Meerut; and in Southern India at Madras, Tinnevelly, and Travancore. The Rev. Mr. Rhenius, one of the most eminent of India missionaries, the translator of the New Testament Scriptures, author of various tracts and Christian treatises, was long connected with this Society.

## VII.

When the disruption took place in the Established Church of Scotland, the seceders, calling themselves the "FREE CHURCH OF SCOTLAND," attracted to themselves the entire corps of Scottish missionaries in India. Among them was the Rev. Dr. Duff of Calcutta, the Rev. Dr. Wilson of Bombay, and the less eminent, though not less zealous and indefatigable and successful servants of God, the Rev. Messrs. Anderson, Braidwood, and Johnson of Madras. Instruction of the young rather than preaching to adults has characterized the efforts of these missionaries, and with their zeal and unwearied self-devotion they cannot fail to succeed.

VIII.

To these may be added the "GERMAN MISSIONARY SOCIETY," having stations in the southern districts and on the western coast, with others of little note, though useful, in their way.

The American Churches are represented in India by *five* societies, of which the first in age is that of the "AMERICAN BOARD OF COMMISSIONERS FOR FOREIGN MISSIONS." This board met for the first time at Farmington, Conn., September 5th, 1810. The present centre of its extensive operations is Boston, Mass., its presiding officer Hon. Theodore Frelinghuysen, LL.D., its secretaries Rufus Anderson, D.D., Rev. Selah B. Treat, and Swan L. Pomroy, D.D., assisted by a Prudential Committee. The large place which India has has held in the evangelistic efforts of this Society will appear from the following table, which contains the names of all persons, ministerial, lay, and assistants, who have been sent under its direction to the Mahrattas, in and around Bombay, to Jaffna in Northern Ceylon, to Madura and Madras on the continent.

1812.

| | |
|---|---|
| Reverend Samuel, and Mrs. Harriet A. Newell, | *Bombay.* |
| " " " Nott, | " |
| " Gordon Hall, | " |

1815.

| | |
|---|---|
| Reverend Horatio, and Mrs. R. F. Bardwell, | *Bombay.* |

| | | | |
|---|---|---|---|
| Reverend Daniel, | and Mrs. Susan Poor, | | *Ceylon.* |
| " James, | " Sarah Richards, | | " |
| " Benjamin C. | " Sarah M. Meigs, | | " |
| " Edward Warren, | | | " |

1817.

| | | |
|---|---|---|
| Reverend John, | and Mrs. Elizabeth Nichols, | *Bombay* |
| " Allen, | " Mary L. Graves, | " |
| Miss Philomela Thurston, | | " |

1819.

| | | |
|---|---|---|
| Reverend Miron, | and Mrs. Harriet L. Winslow, | *Ceylon.* |
| " Levi, | " Mary C. Spaulding. | " |
| " Henry, | " Lydia N. Woodward, | " |
| " John (M.D.), | " Harriet W. Scudder, | " |

1820.

Mr. James Garret, *Ceylon.*

1823.

Reverend Edmund, and Mrs. C. E. Frost, *Bombay.*

1827.

| | | |
|---|---|---|
| Reverend David O., | and Mrs. M. W. Allen, | *Bombay.* |
| " Cyrus, | " Miss A. F. Stone, | " |
| Miss Cynthia Farrar, | | " |

1830.

| | | |
|---|---|---|
| Reverend William, | and Mrs. Elizabeth H. Hervey, | *Bombay.* |
| " William, | " Nancy W. Ramsey, | " |
| " Hollis, | " C. H. Read, | " |

1832.

| | | |
|---|---|---|
| Reverend George W., | and Mrs. F. W. Boggs. | *Bombay.* |
| Mr. William C., | " Mary L. Sampson, | " |

1833.

| | | |
|---|---|---|
| Reverend George H., | and Mrs. Mary R. Apthorp, | *Ceylon.* |
| " Henry R., | " Nancy L. Hoisington, | " |
| " Samuel. | " Elizabeth C. Hutchings, | " |

| | | |
|---|---|---|
| Reverend William, and | Mrs. Lucy B. Todd, | *Ceylon.* |
| " Eastman S., | " Lucy B. Miner, | " |
| Nathan (M.D.), | " Harriet W. Ward, | " |
| Reverend James R., | " Margaret E. Eckard, | " |

1834.

| | | |
|---|---|---|
| Reverend Sendol B., and | Mrs. Maria L. Munger, | *Bombay.* |
| " Alanson C., | " Frances A. Hall, | *Ceylon.* |
| Mr. Amos A., | " A. W. Abbott, | *Bombay.* |
| " George W., | " E. B. Hubbard, | " |
| Miss Orpah Graves, | | " |
| " Abigail H. Kimball, | | " |

1835.

| | | |
|---|---|---|
| Reverend John M. S., and | Mrs. Harriet J. Perry, | *Ceylon.* |
| " John J., | " Mary H. Lawrence, | " |
| " Robert O., | " Mary B. Dwight, | " |
| Mrs. Catherine W. Winslow, | | *Madras.* |

1837.

| | | |
|---|---|---|
| Reverend Henry, and | Mrs. C. H. Cherry, | *Madura.* |
| " Edward, | " E. K. Cope, | " |
| " Nathaniel L., | " Julia A. J. Crane, | " |
| " Clarendon F., | " S. B. Muzzy, | " |
| " William, | " E. F. Tracy, | " |
| " Ferd. De W. | " Jane Ward, | " |
| | | And afterwards at *Madras* |
| John (M.D.), and | Mrs. Mary S. Steele, | *Madura* |
| And Miss Steele, since 1840, at | | *Jaffna.* |

1839.

| | | |
|---|---|---|
| Reverend Ebenezer, and | Mrs. Nancy G. Burgess, | *Bombay.* |
| " Ozro, | " Jane H. French, | " |
| " Robert W., | " Hannah D. Hume, | " |
| Mr. Phineas R., | " Abigail M. Hunt, | *Madras.* |
| Miss Eliza Agnew, | | *Ceylon.* |
| " Sarah F. Brown, | | " |
| " Jane E. Lathrop, | | " |

1841.

| | | | | |
|---|---|---|---|---|
| Reverend | Samuel G., | and Mrs. | Anna C. Whittlesey, | *Ceylon.* |
| " | Robert, | " | Martha E. Wyman, | " |
| " | J. C., | " | Mary S. Smith, | " |

1844.

| | | | | |
|---|---|---|---|---|
| Reverend | Horace S., | and Mrs. | Martha E. Taylor, | *Madura.* |
| " | Henry M., | " | Fanny L. Scudder, | *Madras.* |

1846.

| | | | | |
|---|---|---|---|---|
| Reverend | James, | and Mrs. | Elizabeth C. Herrick, | *Madura.* |
| " | Edward, | " | Nancy A. Webb, | " |
| " | John, | " | Jane B. Rendall, | " |
| " | George W., | " | Rebecca N. M'Millan, | " |
| " | A. H., | " | Elizabeth S. Fletcher, | " |
| " | Wm. W. | " | Susan R. Howland, | " |
| " | Royal G., | " | Eliza J. Wilder, | *Ahmednugger* |
| " | Samuel G., | " | Abby W. Fairbank, | " |
| " | A. H., | " | Martha R. Hazen, | " |
| " | John E., | " | Charlotte M. Chandler, | *Madura* |
| " | George, | " | Ann J. Ford, | " |
| " | Wm. W. | " | Catherine E. Scudder, | *Ceylon.* |
| " | Eurotas P. Hastings, | | | " |
| Dr. | Samuel F. Green, | | | " |

1847.

| | | | | |
|---|---|---|---|---|
| Reverend | George Bowen, | | | *Bombay.* |
| " | William, | and Mrs. | Lucy M. Wood, | " |

1848.

| | | | | |
|---|---|---|---|---|
| Reverend | John W., | and Mrs. | Harriet L. Dallas, | *Madras.* |
| Dr. | Charles S., | " | Henrietta M. Shelton, | *Madura.* |
| Reverend | Joseph T., | " | Elizabeth A. Noyes, | *Ceylon.* |
| " | Cyrus T., | " | Susan L. Mills. | " |
| " | Thomas S., | " | Martha Burwell, | " |

Of these one hundred and fifty persons, forty are deceased, eighty-five still connected with the mission, while the rest are in their native country, invalided, or as pastors. Of the company leaving in 1815, the Rev. Messrs. Meigs and Poor are still toiling on with zeal and hopefulness. Of the reinforcement sent in 1819, Rev. Messrs. Winslow and Scudder have resided at Madras, since 1835, being the honored founders of the American Madras Mission; and Rev. Mr. and Mrs. Spaulding still have the efficient and successful charge of the Female Boarding School at Oodooville, Jaffna, assisted by Miss Agnew. By a singular concurrence of reverse events, of the twenty-four who went to India during the years 1830, '32 and '33, but one person is on the field—Mr. Miner, at Jaffna.

Would the reader make himself more fully acquainted with the past history and present condition of the various missionary stations of this Board in India, he will do well to read, among other works, The *Christian Brahmin*, by Rev. Hollis Read, and published in 1836, a work replete with much information, both respecting the interesting convert Babajee, and the Hindoos generally; "*Journal of a Missionary Tour in India*, by Rev. Wm. Ramsay, published in the same year, an admirable description of missionary itineracy; "*Memoirs of Mrs. Winslow*," which none of my readers ought to omit reading; "*Ten Years in Ceylon and Southern India*, containing much respecting the theory of Hindooism not to be found in any other American work; "*Conquest of India by the Church*, by Rev. S. B. Munger, which, with the admirable appeals from the Rev. D. Scudder, cannot be read without awakening emotions of detestation for that false faith, pity for its enslaved votaries, and an earnest desire that the Truth may set them free.

The "American Baptist Board of Foreign Missions" was called into existence by an important change which took place in the theological views of the Rev. Messrs. Judson and Rice, during their voyage to India, as Missionaries of the American Board. The organization took place at Philadelphia, on the 18th of May, 1814. Its present centre is Boston, its President the Hon. George N. Briggs, with Solomon Peck, D.D., and Rev. Edward Bright, as Secretaries.

Until the year 1835, the operations of this Board were restricted to the Burmese and Chinese empires—but in that year, the Rev. S. S. and Mrs. Day were sent on a mission to the natives of Southern India, speaking the Teloogoo language. After residing for a time at Madras, they removed to Nelloor, a large sea-board town, about a hundred miles north from the metropôlis. In 1840 they were joined by the Rev. Mr. and Mrs. Van Husen; and they labored patiently, and with some degree of encouragement until 1845, when ill health compelled Mr. Van H. to relinquish his labors, and return to America, where he now is, a hopeless invalid. Mr. Day soon followed, but his health being sufficiently restored, he reëmbarked in 1848, accompanied by Rev. Mr. and Mrs. Jewett,—and all are now applying themselves with unwearied diligence and zeal, to the people of that idolatrous town. May God bless them more and more.

The "BOARD OF FOREIGN MISSIONS OF THE PRESBYTERIAN CHURCH IN THE UNITED STATES," was instituted June 7th, 1837, having been preceded by the "*Western Foreign Missionary Society*," which held its first annual meeting in the city of Pittsburg, May 9th, 1833. The present locality of the board is New York city, its President Archibald Alexander, D.D., its Secretaries, Walter Lowrie, Esq., and Rev. John C. Lowrie, and its missionaries, past and present, in India are as follows:

1833.

| | |
|---|---|
| Reverend John C., and Mrs. Lowrie, | *Lodiana.* |
| " William, " Reed, | " |

This company have all *deceased* except Mr. Lowrie, who is associated with his honored father in the Secretaryship of the Society.

1834.

| | |
|---|---|
| Reverend James, and Mrs. Wilson, | *Agra.* |
| " John, " Newton, | *Lahore.* |
| Miss Julia A. Davis (since Mrs. Goadby), | *Orissa.* |

1835.

| | |
|---|---|
| Reverend James, and Mrs. M'Ewan, | *Allahabad.* |
| " James R., " Campbell, | *Saharunpoor.* |
| " Jesse M., " Jamieson, | *Amballa.* |
| " William S., " Rogers, | *Lodiana.* |
| " Joseph, " Porter, | " |

1836.

| | |
|---|---|
| Reverend H., and Mrs. Morrison, | *Amballa.* |
| " Henry R., " Wilson, | *Futtehgurh.* |
| Mr. James, and Mrs. Craig, | *Saharunpoor.* |
| Mr. Rees, " Morris, | *Lodiana.* |
| Reverend Joseph, " Caldwell, | *Saharunpoor* |

1838.

| | |
|---|---|
| Reverend Joseph, and Mrs. Warren, | *Allahabad.* |
| " John E., " Freeman, | " |
| " James L. " Scott, | " |

1840.

| | |
|---|---|
| Reverend John C., and Mrs. Rankin, | *Agra.* |
| " William H. " M'Auley, | *Furrukhabad.* |
| " Joseph, " Owen, | *Allahabad.* |
| Miss Jane Vanderveer, | " |

1841.

| | |
|---|---|
| Reverend John, and Mrs. Wray, | *Allahabad.* |
| " Levi, " Janvier, | *Lodiana.* |

1842.

| | |
|---|---|
| Willis Green M.D., | *Lodiana.* |

1843.

| | |
|---|---|
| Reverend John J., and Mrs. Walsh, | *Mynpuric.* |

1846.

| | |
|---|---|
| Reverend Adolph, and Mrs. Randolph, | *Lodiana.* |
| " David " Irving, | *Futtehgurh.* |
| " Augustus H. Seeley, | *Furrukhabad.* |
| " Robert M. Munnis, | *Allahabad.* |

1847.

| | |
|---|---|
| Reverend A. Alexander, and Mrs. Hodge, | *Allahabad.* |
| " Charles W. Forman, | *Lahore.* |

1848.

| | |
|---|---|
| Reverend Julius F. Ullman, | *Futtehgurh.* |
| " John S., and Mrs. Woodside, | *Saharunpoor.* |

1850.

| | | | |
|---|---|---|---|
| Reverend | Horatio W., and Mrs. | Shaw, | *Allahabad.* |
| " | Lawrence G., " | Hay, | " |
| " | Robert S., " | Fullerton. | *Futtehgurh.* |
| " | D. Elliot, " | Campbell, | *Furrukhabad.* |
| " | James H. Orbison, | | *Lodiana.* |

These stations it will be observed, are all in the extreme North, near the base of the Himalayah Mountains, and reached by the way of Calcutta and the Ganges. For an interesting account of the rise and progress of that efficient mission, with a description of the vicissitudes and perils attending a trip up the sacred stream, the reader is referred to a volume from the pen of my worthy friend the Rev. Mr. Lowrie, the pioneer to that country, and at present an executive officer in the Society, with which he has been connected since its foundation.

The "FREE WILL BAPTIST FOREIGN MISSIONARY SOCIETY" was organized in the year 1833, the zeal which called it into being being enkindled by the "Macedonian call" of the Rev. Mr. Sutton, a missionary among the people of Orissa in South Bengal. Mr. S. visited this country, and upon his return to India in the year 1835, was accompanied by the Rev. Messrs. Noyes and Phillips, with their wives. In the year 1839, Mr. Otis R. and Miss Batchelder, and Miss Hannah W. Cummings, were sent to that interesting but needy field.

The Evangelical Lutherans have commenced missionary operations at Guntoor, having as their efficient and devoted agents the Rev. Messrs. Hyer and Gunn and Mrs. Gunn. Much encouragement has attended their efforts thus far.

With this large array of means in operation, the reader is expecting to hear of results proportionally abundant and gratifying. In forming a judgment upon this subject we must not overlook the obstacles with which the Christian missionary has to contend in the language, the system of caste, a false philosophy, an antiquated and venerated theology, together with the dense population, so far exceeding in proportionate numbers the few who are sent for their instruction. The whole missionary corps of India, able-bodied and ripe for action, cannot exceed one hundred and fifty at the farthest—the population is about *one hundred and fifty millions*, and speaking twenty different languages. When I tell my reader that the whole number of converts to Christianity, excluding the members of the Church of Rome, cannot exceed ten thousand, let him not be surprised and disheartened, but rather be thankful that against such fearful odds such results have been gained. England requires two hundred thousand well-disciplined troops to subjugate to her dominion the flesh and blood of India. And now, because some few scores of soldiers of the cross have not taken from Satan and all his principalities and powers, in these his high places of abomination and sin, this his most loyal province, and are not now with the millions of its redeemed people, shouting high and jubilant songs of conquest, there are, forsooth, those who begin to wonder at the protraction of the fight, and to despond of conquest. Reader, let me entreat you not to be of that number. India belongs to truth and goodness, though for a time in the power of error and sin; and the time is coming when the Almighty will assert His rights and reclaim His dominion. In His name, and by His direction, measures are in progress which tend to this blessed consummation. Far be it from the writer's wish that one who peruses his pages close his mind to facts however discouraging and sad; but let him look also at the encouragements—let him read the previous list and see if he does not find the name of a son, daughter, brother, sister, or other beloved friend, from whose tombstone there comes an appeal that India be cared for—with faith, and prayer, and self-sacrifice. If, after all this, any are disposed still to despond, let them remember Calvary, and say: "From the cross came the crown, out of the grave came heaven, through the gibbet's shame came the Church's glory." As it was in Judea, so is it in India. Though there be night the "morning cometh." This must be our motto, to warm our zeal and nerve our arm, to cheer our despondency and strengthen our faith—"FAINT YET PURSUING."

# CHAPTER XXIV.

## GLOSSARY:

### OR, VOCABULARY OF WORDS AND TERMS IN COMMON USE BY WRITERS ON INDIA, ARRANGED IN ALPHABETICAL ORDER.

### A.

ADAWLET—A court of justice, civil or criminal.
AMEER—A nobleman, a prince.
AMEEN—A guardian, arbitrator.
AMILDAR—A collector, or ruler.
ANNA—A silver coin about three cents in value.
ANNICUT—A dam.
AVATAR—An incarnation.
ACBAR—A native newspaper.
AUMEER—A collector of revenue.
AYAH— A nurse-maid.

### B.

BABOO—Title of a Hindoo gentleman.
BAGEE—Name of a grain.
BANG—Hemp, an intoxicating mixture made from hemp.
BANGY—A stick carried across the shoulders with slings at both ends for burdens, heavy mail bag.
BANYAN—A shopkeeper.
BATTA—Allowance to troops in the field.
BAZAR—Market, grocery store.
BEASTIE—One who carries water in a skin.

Beebee—Lady.
Begum—A lady of rank, a princess.
Brinjarry—Carriers of rice.
Bungalow—A thatched cottage.
Bandy—A gig or cart, (usually drawn by oxen.)
Bangle—A bracelet.
Begah—Land measure.
Boolee—A large well.
Boosa—Camel's food.
Budgerow—A large cabined boat used on the Ganges.
Bundur—A harbor.

## C.

Carcoon—The register of the collections under a Zimindar.
Catamaran—A water craft used on the Bay of Bengal.
Cawny—A ground measure equal to 1 1-4 acres.
Cazee—A Mohamedan judge.
Chokedar—A watchman.
Choultry—A building for public purposes.
Chunam—Lime, whitewash.
Circar—A district, a superintendent.
Compound—An enclosure, a front yard.
Conicopilly—An accountant.
Cooly—A laborer, porter, hire.
Coss—A measure, averaging two miles.
Crore—Ten millions.
Cumbly—A blanket.
Cutchery—A town hall, a court.
Cutwal—The chief officer of the police in a town.
Chattah—Umbrella.
Chowny—A whisp for driving off flies.

## D.

Dacoit—An attack made by robbers.
Dawk—Post for letters or bearers.
Dewan—Minister, steward.
Dirzee—The household tailor.
Doab—A tract of country between two rivers.
Dobash—An interpreter.

DOOLY—A light description of palankeen made of canvas.
DANDEE—A boatman, (applied to those on the Ganges.)
DUFFADAR—Officer, equivalent to lieutenant.
DURBAR—A court where a levee is held.
DURMAN—A gate keeper.

## F.

FAKEER—A Mohamedan devotee, *literally a beggar*.
FOUJDAR—The military governor of a town or district.

## G.

GANJA—Hemp, an intoxicating mixture used for drinking and smoking.
GHEE—Clarified butter.
GHURNY—An Indian hour, twenty-four minutes
GOBRUN—The porch tower of a pagoda, a gate.
GODOWN—Warehouse, storeroom.
GOMASTER—Agent.
GOOROO—Spiritual guide.
GHAUT—A landing place, a pass of a mountain, or a range of hills.
GRAM—A kind of grain.
GRIFFIN—Descriptive title of a foreigner during his first year in India.

## H.

HACKERY—A native bullock carriage.
HAREM—A woman's apartments.
HAVILDAR—Equivalent to sergeant.
HIRCARRAH—A courier, a messenger.
HOOKA—A pipe.
HOWDAH—A seat on an elephant.

## J.

JAGHIRE—Land granted in the way of pension.
JEMIDAR—An officer in the army.
JUNGLE—A thicket, land covered with brushwood.

## K.

Khan—A prince or lord.
Khas—A noble, private.
Khelant—A robe of honor.
Kist—A tax.
Khitmutgar—A footman.

## L.

Lack—A hundred thousand.
Lascar—A native porter.
Lubbie—A descendant of Arab settlers on the Coromandel Coast.

## M.

Mamoul—Custom, usage.
Mantra—A charm, a spell.
Maund—Name of a weight, about 25 lbs.
Maher-rajah—Great, king.
Mofutssil—The country in opposition to town.
Moollah—A learned man, answering to the word doctor.
Munsy—A judge.
Musnud—A throne.

## N.

Nabob—A governor of a district, deputy.
Naick—A chief.
Nizam—Administrator, governor.
Nullah—A streamlet, watercourse.
Nunjah—Dry cultivation.
Nuzzee—A gift.

## P.

Paddy—Rice in the husk.
Pagoda—A Hindoo idol temple, also name of a coin.
Palankeen—A litter or sedan.

Parcherry—A pariah village.
Peon—A footman, a constable.
Pariah—A stranger, an outcast.
Pergunnah—A subdivision of a Zulla.
Parwanal—A pass, permit, or warrant.
Peishwa—A leader, foreman.
Pice—A small copper coin, one-twelfth part of an arman.
Pettah—A native town near a fort
Phansegar—A thug, (which see.)
Polare—The headman of a village.
Poojah—Worship.
Pucca—Brick.
Punka—A large fan suspended from the ceiling.
Purana—Indian mythological poem.
Pundit—Learned man, title of a Brahmin lawyer.

## Q.

Qui-hi—Who waits? (Applied to Calcuttians.)

## R.

Rajah—Hindoo prince or king.
Ramazun—An epic poem describing the exploits of Rama.
Ranee—Hindoo princess or queen.
Rao—A prince.
Rupee—A silver coin whose value is about fifty cents.
Ryot—A tenant (of land,) subject.
Rutt—A car, chariot.

## S.

Sahib—Master, sir, lord.
Sanyassy—A Hindoo devotee.
Seer—A weight or measure equal to two lbs.
Sepoy—A native soldier.
Serishtadar—Title of a revenue officer.
Shastras—Hindoo sacred books and laws.
Shastry—An expounder of Hindoo law.
Shroff—A money changer, banker.

SIRDAR—A chief commander.
SUBADAR—Governor of a province, officer of highest rank in the native army.
SUDDER—Chief, Supreme.
SYRANG—Captain, overseer.
SOODRA—Fourth of the Hindoo castes.
SUWARREE—Retinue.

## T.

TASILDAR—A collector, tax gatherer.
TALOOK—A manor, division of land.
TANADAR—A station man, police officer.
TANK—An artificial pond, or small lake.
TANNA—A watchhouse.
TAPPAL—A post, for letters or bearers.
THAKOOR—A lord, chief.
THUG—A robber, cheat, applied in the western provinces to stragglers on the highway.
TATTEE—A mat made of cuscos grass.
TINDAL—A tent pitcher, captain of a coast vessel.
TOPE—A clump of trees.
TONJON—A chaise-like palanquin.
TUSSELDAR—A taxman.

## V.

VAKEEL—An ambassador, agent, lawyer.
VIZIER—A minister of state.
VEDAS—Hindoo scriptures.

## Y.

YOGI—Religious mendicants.

## Z.

ZENINDAR—A landholder.
ZILLAH—A district.
ZEMINDARY—A province.

FINIS.